CW00765812

Recourse to Force
State Action Against Threats and Ar

The nations that drafted the UN Charter in 1945 clearly were more concerned about peace than about justice. As a result, the Charter prohibits all use of force by states except in the event of an armed attack or when authorized by the Security Council.

This arrangement has only very imperfectly withstood the test of time and changing world conditions. It did not anticipate the Cold War which incapacitated the Security Council through the permanent members' frequent recourse to the veto. In requiring states not to use force in self-defense until after they had become the object of an actual armed attack, the Charter failed to address a growing phenomenon of clandestine subversion and of instantaneous nuclear threats. Perhaps most of all, the Charter failed to make allowance for the dramatic rise in public support for human rights.

Fortunately, although the Charter is very hard to amend, the drafters did agree that it should be interpreted flexibly by the United Nations' principal political institutions. In nearly sixty years, the text has undergone extensive interpretation through this practice. In this way the norms governing use of force in international affairs have been adapted to meet changing circumstances and new challenges. The book also relates these changes in law and practice to changing public values pertaining to the balance between maintaining peace and promoting justice.

THOMAS M. FRANCK is Murry and Ida Becker Professor of Law and Director, Center for International Studies at New York University School of Law.

Recourse to Force

State Action Against Threats and
Armed Attacks

THOMAS M. FRANCK

New York University School of Law

CAMBRIDGE
UNIVERSITY PRESS

CAMBRIDGE UNIVERSITY PRESS
Cambridge, New York, Melbourne, Madrid, Cape Town, Singapore, São Paulo, Delhi

Cambridge University Press
The Edinburgh Building, Cambridge CB2 8RU, UK

Published in the United States of America by Cambridge University Press, New York

www.cambridge.org
Information on this title: www.cambridge.org/9780521104203

First published 2002
Sixth printing 2005
This digitally printed version 2009

A catalogue record for this publication is available from the British Library

Library of Congress Cataloguing in Publication data

Franck, Thomas M.
Recourse to force : threats and armed attacks/Thomas M. Franck.
p. cm. – (Hersch Lauterpacht memorial lectures; 15)
Includes bibliographical references and index.
ISBN 0-521-82013-8 (hc.)
1. Aggression (International law) 2. Self-defense (International law) 3. Intervention
(International law) 4. United Nations–Armed Forces. I. Title. II. Series.
KZ6374.F73 2002
341.5′8–dc21 2002067079

ISBN 978-0-521-82013-4 hardback
ISBN 978-0-521-10420-3 paperback

Summmum ius summa iniuria
"Extreme justice is injustice"

> Legal maxim cited by Cicero in *De Officiis* I, 10, 33. The
> maxim, in slightly different form, is attributed to Terence
> [Publius Terentius Afer], *The Self-Tormentor*, 1.796 (*"Ius summum
> saepe summa est malitia"*).

Harriette and Norman Dorsen in gratitude for a lifetime of shared intuitions and values

Contents

Acknowledgments

This book has developed from a series of lectures given in November 2000 at Cambridge University's Lauterpacht Research Centre for International Law. Both that institution's founder, Professor Sir Elihu Lauterpacht, and its director, Professor James R. Crawford, served up invaluable insights together with fulsome hospitality. The Centre's faculty, fellows and students stimulated and prodded my thinking about the role of law in a world still so far short of the goals set by Judge Sir Hersch Lauterpacht.

I am also grateful for the continuing support of the Filomen D'Agostino Research Fund of New York University's School of Law, the US Institute of Peace and for the invaluable research assistance of John Chung, Benjamin Rosen, and Robert Dufresne.

It is difficult to account fully for the progenitors of a work that deals with very contemporary events. Almost every conversation, these past three years, has turned, one way or another, to this book's subject and I am fortunate, indeed, to have friends so richly and generously conversant with the law and literature. They will each recognize from what I have written, and perhaps even from what I have *not* written, how deeply I value their counsel.

Once again, my deepest appreciation is reserved for my career-long colleague Rochelle Fenchel.

1

The United Nations' capacity for adapting to radical changes of circumstance

The legacy of Sir Hersch Lauterpacht

When, in 1933, Judge Lauterpacht wrote *The Function of Law in the International Community*, he reasoned from first principles that the world's legal system must be grounded in an absolute rule: "There shall be no violence" by states. He described this as the "primordial duty of the law."[1]

At the same time, he concluded prophetically that the League of Nations' Covenant would fall far short of establishing that rule in law, let alone in fact. It was full of loopholes for aggressors and their appeasers. Loopholes drew his scorn. "It is impossible," he observed, "in the scheme of things devised to secure the reign of law, to provide machinery calculated to disregard the law..."[2]

Loopholes, as we shall see, are the subject of this study, which will argue that they can be bad, but that they also have an important role to play in saving law from itself.

After the Second World War, with Lauterpacht's participation, the Nuremberg tribunal was called upon to draw a much brighter line than hitherto against aggression. So, too, at Dumbarton Oaks and San Francisco, a UN Charter was written that makes absolute the obligation of states not to resort to force against each other and to resist collectively any breach of this prohibition.

New remedies, as we know from medicine, tend to produce unexpected side effects. Article 2(4) of the Charter seemingly cures the Covenant's normative ambiguities regarding states' "threat or use of force" against each other. It plugs the loopholes. But did it intend to

---

[1] Hersch Lauterpacht, *The Function of Law in the International Community* 64 (1933).
[2] Lauterpacht, *The Function of Law in the International Community* at 372–73.

prevent a state – one facing imminent and overwhelming attack – from striking first in anticipatory self-defense? Did it intend also to immunize against foreign intervention a state whose government is engaged in genocide against a part of its own population? Are there circumstances in which the prohibition on recourse to force in effect endorses that which itself is wholly unconscionable? Did the Charter try to plug too many loopholes? Has the pursuit of perfect justice unintentionally created conditions of grave injustice?

The use of force under the UN Charter system

On its face, the UN Charter, ratified by virtually every nation, is quite clear-eyed about its intent: to initiate a new global era in which *war* is forbidden as an instrument of state policy, but *collective security* becomes the norm. Collective security is to be achieved by use of international military police forces and lesser but forceful measures such as diplomatic and economic sanctions. Recourse to such measures is to be the exclusive prerogative of the United Nations, acting in concert.

This new way of ensuring peace and security was to be the prescribed cure for the disorders so evident in the first half of the twentieth century: passivity in the face of aggression – Manchuria, Ethiopia, Czechoslovakia – and the egregious pursuit through violence of narrowly perceived national interests.

The Charter text embodies these two radical new concepts: it absolutely prohibits war and prescribes collective action against those who initiate it. We are thereby ushered into the "post-war" era through Charter text: Articles 2(4), 42, and 43.

Article 2(4) essentially prohibits states from using force against one another. Instead, Articles 42 and 43 envisage the collective use of force at the behest of the Security Council upon its determination – Article 39 – that there exist what Article 2(4) forbids, a threat to the peace, breach of the peace, or act of aggression: one that must therefore be met by concerted police action. Article 42 sets the parameters for collective measures, including the deployment of military forces. Under Article 43, such forces are to be committed by member states to the service of the Security Council.

In the idealized world of the Charter, no state would ever again attack another: and if one did, its aggression would be met by a unified and overwhelming response made under the authority and control of the Security Council.

Even in 1945, however, there were doubts as to whether this idealized world order was as imminent as the post-San Francisco euphoria predicted. Thus, two articles of the Charter provide alternatives, just in case. Article 51 authorizes states to act alone or with their allies in self-defense against any military aggression ("armed attack") that the Security Council might have failed either to prevent or to repel. Article 106 makes further provision for "transitional security arrangements" by the five permanent Council members (Britain, China, France, Russia, and the US). These may "consult with one another" on "joint action," if the Security Council is disabled, "for the purpose of maintaining international peace and security." They are licensed to act in concert until such time as the Council can "begin the exercise of its responsibilities."

In this way, the Charter establishes a two-tiered system.

- The upper tier consists of a normative structure for an ideal world – one in which no state would initiate armed conflict, but in which any acts of aggression that did occur would be met by effective armed force deployed by the United Nations or, for a transitional period, by the Security Council's five permanent members.
- A lower tier is to operate whenever the United Nations is unable to respond collectively against aggression. Subject to certain conditions, states may invoke an older legal principle: the sovereign right of self-defense. Acting alone or with allies, the Charter authorizes members to use force to resist any armed attack by one state on another until UN collective measures come to the victim's rescue. But they may do so only after an actual armed attack.

Thus did the Charter visualize this bifurcated regime, one that postulates a common, absolute global response to aggression, but which also makes realistic allowance for state action during the potentially prolonged transition from contemporary realpolitik to an ideal future of UN-orchestrated collective security.

Both tiers, almost immediately, were seen to fail to address adequately four seismic developments that, even as the Charter was being signed, were beginning to transform the world.

One was the advent of the Cold War, which, because of the veto, froze the Security Council's ability to guarantee collective security under Articles 42 and 43 of the Charter and precluded operation of Article 106's interim Big Power protectorate.

Another was the ingenuity with which states effectively and dangerously substituted indirect aggression – the export of insurgency and covert meddling in civil wars – for the sort of traditional frontal military aggression the Charter system was designed to prohibit by Article 2(4) and to repress by Article 42.

The third development was the technological transformation of weaponry (nuclear, chemical, and biological) and of delivery systems (rocketry). These "improvements" tended to make obsolete the Charter's Article 51 provision for states' "inherent" right of self-defense. In an effort to prevent the right of self-defense being used, in Lauterpacht's words, "to provide machinery calculated to disregard the law in a manner binding on the party which is willing to abide by the law,"[3] Article 51 limits "self-defence" to situations where an "armed attack" has occurred. However, the acceleration and escalation of means for launching an attack soon confounded the bright line drawn by the law, effecting a *reductio ad absurdum* that, literally, seems to require a state to await an actual attack on itself before instituting countermeasures. Inevitably, states responded to the new dangers by claiming a right of "anticipatory self-defence." That claim, however, is not supported by the Charter's literal text. And "anticipatory self-defence," too, is vulnerable to *reductio ad absurdum*. If every state were free to determine for itself when to initiate the use of force in "anticipation" of an attack, there would be nothing left of Articles 2(4) and 51, or of Lauterpacht's "primordial duty" to eschew violence.

The fourth development was a rising global public consciousness of the importance of human freedom and the link between the repression of human rights and threats to the peace. This link should have been apparent from the history of Hitler's rise from domestic tyrant to global menace. But the text of the Charter puts human rights rather at its periphery while focusing on the prevention of aggression. That deliberate drafting choice reflected the concerns of some states that the cause of human rights might be used to justify intervention in their sovereign affairs. The drafters, of course, did not anticipate the imminent end of colonialism and communism, the rise of a democratic entitlement, and a tectonic shift in public values during the 1990s, each of which altered perceptions of sovereignty and its limits.

All four of these developments might have been (and to some extent were) foreseen, but the Charter's text is not facially responsive to the challenge of change. It, like other grand instruments written for the long term, has had to meet the threat of obsolescence with adaption.

---

[3] *Ibid.*

Clark and Sohn, already in 1958, presented an elegant blueprint for top-to-bottom overhaul.[4] Such radical revision, however, by dint of the Charter's Chapter XVIII, could have been accomplished only by an unachievable agreement among the deeply divided permanent members of the Security Council.

Nevertheless, change there has been: far more extensive and profound than is generally acknowledged. It has come about not by the formal process of amendment but by the practice of the United Nations' principal organs.

Adaptability of the Charter as a quasi-constitutional instrument

The UN Charter is a treaty, one to which almost every state adheres. This universality, alone, distinguishes it from the general run of international agreements. That the drafters of the Charter recognized its special quality is evidenced by Article 103, which purports to establish an unusual principle of treaty law:

In the event of a conflict between the obligations of the Members of the United Nations under the present Charter and their obligations under any other international agreement, their obligations under the present Charter shall prevail.

This legal primacy of the Charter over subsequent agreements can only be construed as a "quasi-constitutional" feature. Clearly, it illustrates that the drafters intended to create a special treaty different from all others.[5] This difference becomes relevant when we consider the instrument's capacity for adaption through the interpretative practice of its organs and members.

There were spirited debates at San Francisco in 1945 about the process by which the Charter would be interpreted. Some states argued that this ought to be the exclusive prerogative of the Organization's judiciary, the International Court of Justice (ICJ). Others preferred to leave each political organ free to interpret its own sphere of authority. In the event, the Charter was framed so as to allow for interpretation both by the political and the judicial organs.

---

[4] Granville Clark and Louis B. Sohn, *World Peace Through World Law* (1958).
[5] *See* Articles 58, 59 Vienna Convention on the Law of Treaties, May 23, 1969, 1152 U.N.T.S. 331 (1969); 8 I.L.M. 679 (1969). Entered into force 27 January 1980.

But it is the political organs that have done most of this interpretative work, especially but not solely with respect to the fraught boundary between the United Nations' jurisdiction and the jealously guarded sovereignty of its members. In the words of Professor, now Judge, Rosalyn Higgins: it "is...significant that at the San Francisco Conference the proposal to confer the point of preliminary determination [of jurisdiction] upon the International Court of Justice was rejected."[6] For example, two key questions regarding the interpretation of the Charter's important Article 2(7) – whether a matter is beyond the United Nations' jurisdiction because it is "essentially within the domestic jurisdiction" of states and whether, consequently, the United Nations is barred from taking a proposed action because to do so would violate the requirement not to "intervene" in such matters – usually are decided by the political organ in the course of dealing with a crisis. "[S]uffice it to say," Higgins has concluded, "that the political organs of the United Nations have clearly regarded themselves entitled to determine their own competence."[7] Moreover, these interpretations of the Charter are made in the relevant political organ not by a formal vote but as a merged, or even submerged, part of its "decisions on the matter at issue, and often...by implication."[8] While, under Article 96 of the Charter, the International Court *may* be asked to render an advisory opinion, Higgins stressed, judicial "consultation is not obligatory"[9] and resort to it has been infrequent, although not without significance.

What emerges from the vast legacy of recorded debates and decisions of the principal political organs is that they tend to treat the Charter not as a static formula, but as a constitutive instrument capable of organic growth. Borrowing a phrase coined by the Imperial Privy Council speaking of the Canadian constitution, the Charter is "a living tree."[10]

Ordinary treaties are not "living trees" but international contracts to be construed in strict accord with the black-letter text. Not so the Charter. The Charter also differs from most treaties not only in

---

[6] Rosalyn Higgins, *The Development of International Law Through the Political Organs of the United Nations* 66 (1963) and n. 27, discussing the failure of a Greek proposal to give sole *kompetenz-kompetenz* which secured 14–17 support, but not the necessary two-thirds majority needed to amend the draft.

[7] Higgins, *The Development of International Law Through the Political Organs of the United Nations* at 66–67.

[8] *Ibid.*

[9] Higgins, *The Development of International Law Through the Political Organs of the United Nations* at 67 and n. 34.

[10] *Edwards* v. *A.G. Canada* [1930] A.C. 124 at 136 (P.C.).

enumerating rights and duties but also in elaborating institutions to carry them into effect. Two political organs (the General Assembly and the Security Council) were given Charter-implementing powers: Chapters IV and V, respectively. An independent civil service, the Secretariat, headed by a Secretary-General, enjoys autonomous, Charter-based power to construe and apply the Charter and decisions of the political organs.[11] Although the International Court is authorized to interpret the Charter in adversarial proceedings between states or at the request of the principal political organs,[12] the extent to which the Charter establishes political and executory machinery for implementing its purposes, principles and norms distinguishes it from ordinary treaties and invests it with a potential for adaption through organic practice. In this, it is both unusual and quasi-constitutional.

Further, the Charter makes allowance for its interpretation through state practice. It reserves an ample sphere of autonomy for member states by giving each an equal vote in the General Assembly while guaranteeing members' "sovereign equality,"[13] prohibiting the United Nations from intervening "in matters which are essentially within the domestic jurisdiction of any state" (subject to one exception),[14] and preserving each state's "inherent right of individual or collective self-defence if an armed attack occurs..."[15] Taken together, these provisions ensure that the Charter will be subjected to continuous interpretation and adaption through the member states' individual and collective practice: their actions, voting, and rhetoric.

Each principal organ and the members thus continuously interpret the Charter and do so in accordance with the requisites of ever-changing circumstances. This necessarily means that the Charter text is always evolving. One important example pertains to Article 27(3), which contains the key "veto power." It provides:

Decisions of the Security Council on all [non-procedural] matters shall be made by an affirmative vote of nine members including the concurring votes of the permanent members...

In practice, for many years, each President of the Security Council (the post rotates monthly among Council members) has interpreted this provision to mean that an abstention by a permanent member is not counted as a veto. A strict-constructionist reading of Article 27(3)

---

[11] UN Charter, Articles 97–101.   [12] UN Charter, Chapter XIV.
[13] UN Charter, Article 18 and Article 2(1), respectively.
[14] UN Charter, Article 2(7).   [15] UN Charter, Article 51.

might have predicted otherwise. Still, in 319 instances,[16] very important decisions have been made in the face of – and without objection from – abstaining permanent members. It may be concluded that the treaty text of Article 27(3) now conveniently permits a permanent member to register discomfort with a proposed course of action by abstaining on a resolution authorizing it, while still permitting the resolution to pass and, by virtue of Article 25, to become binding on all members. The Court has given this interpretation-in-practice its blessing. In the 1971 Namibian advisory opinion, it found "abundant evidence" of members' acceptance of the principle that a voluntary abstention by a permanent member does not constitute a veto.[17] The

---

[16] While it is not always clear whether a Security Council Resolution decides a procedural matter for the purposes of article 27(2) of the UN Charter, it can be approximated that, as of 2001, the Security Council had adopted 319 resolutions on non-procedural matters in which at least one permanent member either abstained or did not participate in the vote. These resolutions include the following: S/RES/4 (1946); S/RES/17, 18, 19, 22, 23, 28, 30, 31, 32, 35, 36 (1947); S/RES/38, 39, 40, 41, 42, 46, 48, 49, 51, 52, 53, 54, 55, 61, 63, 64, 65, 66 (1948); S/RES/68, 69, 70, 71, 73, 74, 75, 76, 77, 78 (1949); S/RES/79, 80, 81, 82, 83, 84, 85, 86, 89 (1950); S/RES/91, 92, 93, 95, 96 (1951); S/RES/98 (1952); S/RES/101, 102, 103 (1953); S/RES/109, 110 (1955); S/RES/122, 123, 126 (1957); S/RES/128, 131, 134, 135, 138, 143, 146, 156, 157 (1960); S/RES/161, 162, 163, 164, 166, 167, 169 (1961); S/RES/171, 176 (1962); S/RES/179, 180, 181, 183 (1963); S/RES/188, 190, 191, 193, 199 (1964); S/RES/202, 205, 215, 216, 217, 218 (1965); S/RES/221, 232 (1966); S/RES/252, 255, 259 (1968); S/RES/264, 265, 268, 269, 271, 273, 275 (1969); S/RES/276, 280, 282, 283, 284, 285, 290 (1970); S/RES/294, 301, 302, 305, 307 (1971); S/RES/309, 310, 311, 312, 314, 315, 316, 317, 318, 319, 320, 321, 323, 324 (1972); S/RES/326, 327, 328, 330, 332, 333, 334, 338, 339 340, 341, 343, 344 (1973); S/RES/346, 347, 348, 349, 350, 355, 359, 360, 362, 363, 364 (1974); S/RES/368, 369, 370, 371, 376, 378, 381, 383 (1975); S/RES/387, 389, 390, 391, 393, 396, 397, 398, 401 (1976); S/RES/403, 408, 410, 415, 416, 420, 422 (1977); S/RES/423, 425, 426, 427, 429, 430, 431, 434, 435, 437, 438, 439, 441, 443 (1978); S/RES/444, 445, 446, 447, 448, 449, 450, 451, 452, 454, 456, 458, 459, 460, 461 (1979); S/RES/463, 467, 468, 469, 470, 471, 472, 474, 475, 476, 478, 481, 482, 483 (1980); S/RES/485, 486, 488, 493, 498 (1981); S/RES/501, 502, 511, 515, 517, 519, 523 (1982); S/RES/529, 536, 538, 539, 545 (1983); S/RES/546, 549, 550, 554, 555, 556 (1984); S/RES/561, 566, 569, 573, 575 (1985); S/RES/581, 587, 592 (1986); S/RES/601, 605 (1987); S/RES/608, 611, 623 (1988); S/RES/636, 641 (1989); S/RES/678 (1990); S/RES/686, 688 (1991); S/RES/748, 757, 770, 776, 777, 778, 781, 787, 792 (1992); S/RES/816, 820, 821, 825, 855, 883 (1993); S/RES/929, 940, 942, 944 946, 955, 964 (1994); S/RES/970, 975, 988, 998, 1003, 1021 (1995); S/RES/1054, 1058, 1067, 1070, 1073, 1077, 1082 (1996); S/RES/1101, 1114, 1129, 1134 (1997); S/RES/1160, 1180, 1199, 1203, 1207, 1212 (1998); S/RES/1239, 1244, 1249, 1277, 1280 (1999); S/RES/1290, 1305, 1322 (2000).

[17] *Legal Consequences for States of the Continuing Presence of South Africa in Namibia (South West Africa) notwithstanding Security Council Resolution 276 (1970), Advisory Opinion*, [1971] I.C.J. Rep. 16 at 22, para. 22.

long-term implications of that adaption have been immense. For example, the Council was able to authorize Operation Desert Storm against Iraq in November 1990 despite the abstention of China.[18] So, too, the 1999 resolution establishing the interim international administration for Kosovo was adopted by the Council despite China's abstention.[19]

There are many other instances of such adaption, effected by the practice of the principal organs. We shall be examining this practice insofar as it pertains to the use of force. What such an examination will demonstrate, aside from substantive changes in an applicable norm, is the system's capacity for change.

Of course, one must be parsimonious in advancing this thesis, lest, as Lauterpacht warned, the line between violation and adaption becomes hopelessly blurred. Nevertheless, the Charter cannot today be understood without regard for these changes. In particular, we will examine the effect of Charter adaption in two respects not contemplated by its authors:

1. Where collective force has been deployed or authorized *by the United Nations itself* to confront a *threat to the peace or breach of the peace* that has arisen not solely out of state-to-state aggression but, also, from events occurring solely or primarily within one state.
2. Where force has been deployed autonomously *by states* claiming to act in individual or collective *self-defense* not against an actual military attack by an aggressor state but either in anticipation of such an attack or in response to indirect aggression such as the harbouring of insurgents or terrorists; or in response to an act by a terrorist group that is not a state; or in an assertion of a right of *self-help* to end persistent and egregious violations of international law and human rights.

Before addressing in detail the Charter adaptions that may have occurred through institutional or state action, it is useful to consider the historical context of the salient Charter provisions and how they came to be shaped in the inceptive period, 1943–45.

War in the pre-Charter era

The League Covenant and the UN Charter together mark a radical departure in systemic response to violence among states. The Lauterpachtian first law of an international order – "there shall be no

---

[18] S/RES 678, of 29 November 1990.   [19] S/RES 1244, of 10 June 1999.

violence" – is a radical innovation in a legal system which had hitherto been careful to distinguish between legally permissible and impermissible wars and permissible and impermissible modes of conducting war.[20] Neither the *jus ad bellum* nor the *jus in bello* regarded recourse to violence as a wrong *per se*. Oppenheim, writing in 1906, castigated naive "fanatics of international peace" who "frequently consider war and law inconsistent … It is not difficult," he said, "to show the absurdity of this opinion."[21]

A dozen years later, viewed across the killing-grounds of the First World War, the "opinion" began to seem less "absurd." The first indications of the very modern idea that the use of force by a state against another could itself be violative of the legal order's very foundations is found in the Covenant of the League of Nations, which set forth some elementary provisions intended to limit the right of states to make war, and sought to impose a mandatory "cooling off period" on disputants.[22] While the Covenant did not precisely prohibit war, it did oblige states not to resort to force as long as a dispute was under consideration by the League's Council. However, once this process failed to produce a settlement the disputants remained free "to take such action as they shall consider necessary for the maintenance of right and justice."[23]

The Covenant also empowered the League Council to impose collective sanctions on states resorting to war in violation of its stated requirement to seek peaceful settlement[24] and obliged states to act individually or collectively through the Council to defend victims of aggression.[25] Thus, for the first time, the Lauterpachtian injunction – "there shall be no violence" – is both stated and given rudimentary tools of enforcement. Nevertheless, these injunctions were directed (in Articles 12 and 16) only against states' "resort to war" – a very narrow term of the draftsman's art invoking a formal declaration – even though earlier drafts of the Covenant had proposed a much wider ban on "resort to armed force."[26]

In the inter-war period, a series of multilateral treaties attempted to reinforce the new rule against war-making. In Article 2 of the Locarno Treaty, Germany, Belgium, and France undertook "in no case [to] attack or invade each other or to resort to war" and, more

---

[20] A history of these distinctions is found in Thomas M. Franck, *Fairness in International Law and Institutions* 245–83 (1995).

[21] Lassa Oppenheim, II *International Law* 55 (1906).

[22] F.S. Northedge, *The League of Nations* 2 (1986).

[23] League of Nations, Covenant, Article 15(7).

[24] League of Nations, Covenant, Article 16.

[25] League of Nations, Covenant, Article 10.

[26] Ian Brownlie, *International Law and the Use of Force by States* 60 (1963).

significantly, these nations, together with Britain and Italy, each undertook "immediately to come to the help" of a "Party against whom...a violation or breach has been directed as soon as [the guarantor] has been able to satisfy itself that this violation constitutes an unprovoked act of aggression..."[27] Adherence to the pact was terminated by Germany, however, in 1936.

Broader in membership and more durable was the 1928 Pact of Paris, the Kellogg–Briand Pact for the Renunciation of War,[28] which, by 1938, had sixty-three state parties.[29] They were committed, by Article 2, to the rule "that the settlement or solution of all disputes or conflicts of whatever nature or whatever origin they may be, which may arise among [the Parties] shall never be sought except by pacific means." Its preamble proclaims an outright renunciation of war as an instrument of policy.

This inter-war system, as we know to our cost, collapsed under the weight of Japan's invasion of Manchuria in 1931, Italy's conquest of Ethiopia in 1936, and Russia's attack on Finland in 1939. At the time of the bombardment of Pearl Harbor, Japan was still a party to the Kellogg Pact. Inevitably, this failed attempt at behavior-modification invited skepticism. Professor Arthur Nussbaum, in 1947, wrote that "even sober observers" had believed that they had seen "inaugurated a new era of international law, but history has not justified that belief."[30]

Whether, thereafter, the Covenant's successor, the UN Charter, has actually succeeded in inaugurating a new era remains to be seen; but its text, and the negotiations leading to its adoption at San Francisco, leave little doubt that this was the solemn intent of its framers.

The Charter's constraints on violence

The Charter's absolute prohibition on states' unilateral recourse to force, Article 2(4), is deliberately located in Chapter I, entitled "Purposes and Principles." The drafters considered these enumerated principles of transcendent importance, elucidating all other provisions of the Charter and indicating "the direction which the activities of the Organization are to take and the common ends of its members."[31]

---

[27] Treaty of Mutual Guarantee, done at Locarno, October 16, 1925, 54 L.N.T.S. 290, article 2, 4(3).
[28] 94 L.N.T.S. 57.   [29] 33 Am. J. Int'l L. Supp. 865 (1939).
[30] Arthur Nussbaum, *A Concise History of the Law of Nations* 251 (1947).
[31] Leland Goodrich and Edvard Hambro, *Charter of the United Nations: Commentary and Documents* 22 (2nd edn., 1949).

In its Dumbarton Oaks preparatory conference draft, the text of Article 2(4) was simply rendered as:

All members of the Organization shall refrain in their international relations from the threat or use of force in any manner inconsistent with the purposes of the Organization.[32]

A year later, at San Francisco, many of the states that had not been at Dumbarton Oaks insisted that this provision be strengthened by introducing a duty to respect the territorial integrity and political independence of states.[33] Australia offered an amendment that, after the prohibition on the use of force, added the words "against the territorial integrity or political independence of any member state..." This was adopted unanimously by the participants. Unintentionally, they thereby created an opening for some, later, to argue that the prohibition against force did not extend to "minor" or "temporary" invasions that stopped short of actually threatening the territorial integrity of the victim state or its independence. Such a reading of Article 2(4) is utterly incongruent, however, with the evident intent of the sponsors of this amendment.

Further wishing to strengthen Article 2(4)'s prohibition against the use of force by states, Mexico, at San Francisco, led a movement to add the following principle:

No State has the right to intervene, directly or indirectly, and whatever be the reason, in the domestic or foreign affairs of another.[34]

This did not succeed as an amendment to Article 2(4), although it did resurface, somewhat perversely, in Article 2(7) which deals with the use of force by the United Nations itself, rather than by individual states. The resultant Principle reads:

Nothing contained in the present Charter shall authorize the United Nations to intervene in matters which are essentially within the domestic jurisdiction of any state or shall require the Members to submit such matters to settlement under the present Charter...

---

[32] 1 U.N.C.I.O., Dumbarton Oaks Proposals, Doc. 1, G1, at 3.

[33] Australia, Bolivia, Brazil, Chile, Czechoslovakia, Ecuador, Ethiopia, Mexico, New Zealand, Panama, Peru, and Uruguay made proposals to this effect. See, for example, Opinion of the Department of Foreign Relations of Mexico concerning the Dumbarton Oaks Proposals for the Creation of a General International Organization, 3 U.N.C.I.O., Restr. Doc. 2, G/7(c), April 23, 1945, 65. (Hereafter: Mexico.)

[34] Mexico at 66.

This "domestic jurisdiction" provision of Article 2(7) echoes a similar formulation in the League Covenant. There, however, it had applied to interventions by states. In adding the prohibition to the Charter article pertaining to actions by the Organization, the Mexican government's expressed intent was hardly well-served. Its representative had made clear that his country:

would condemn any States acting on its [*sic*] own authority to intervene in the internal affairs of another State. It would not preclude action taken on behalf of the Community of States and with the mandate of a competent agency of the Community of States, in the event that conditions prevailing in a State's territory should be found to menace international peace and order.[35]

When the non-intervention clause landed in Article 2(7), its effect was mitigated by the drafters to *permit* intervention in matters essentially within a member's domestic jurisdiction whenever the Security Council, acting under Chapter VII, undertook an "enforcement action" against a state whose conduct is deemed to constitute a "threat to the peace" or "breach of the peace" requiring collective UN action in accordance with Article 39. The result, to say the least, is a murky text.

Its very elasticity, however, was seen to be beneficial by the US. Its representatives at San Francisco viewed Charter-drafting through the lens of US constitutional practice. John Foster Dulles argued passionately for breadth and simplicity. "The Organization in none of its branches or organs," he said, "should intervene in what was essentially the domestic life of the members." However, he added according to the minutes,

this principle was subject to evolution. The United States had had a long experience in dealing with a parallel problem, i.e., the relationship between the forty-eight states and the Federal Government. Today, the Federal Government of the United States exercised an authority undreamed of when the Constitution was formed, and the people of the United States were grateful for the simple conceptions contained in their Constitution. In a like manner... if the Charter contained simple and broad principles future generations would be thankful...[36]

---

[35] Mexico at 68.
[36] 6 U.N.C.I.O., Commission I, Committee I, Doc. 1019, I/1/42, June 16, 1945, 507 at 508.

In support, Britain's Lord Halifax, propounded a masterful tautology:

> When a situation threatened the peace it would cease to be essentially within the domestic jurisdiction and all powers would revert to the Security Council.[37]

Even Russia's Andrei Gromyko agreed that "there might be such an internal transformation in a state as to involve a danger to the maintenance of international peace and security [in which case] the Security Council should be free to take the necessary measures."[38] Arthur Evatt, the Australian Foreign Minister, pointedly asked US Secretary Stettinius "whether it was not proper for the Organization to interfere in the domestic concerns of any state in a case where that state might be persecuting its Jewish population, for example."[39]

In the final flurry of drafting, however, these sorts of difficult questions were scarcely recognized, let alone discussed.[40] Development of applicable rules was left to the case-by-case practice of the Council, which has used this latitude in fashioning its response to such crises as the military coup in Haiti, the collapse of civil governance in Somalia, the protection of besieged cities in the Bosnian civil war, and the sponsoring of terrorism and subordination of women by the Taliban authorities in Afghanistan. To understand the real meaning of Article 2(7), therefore, it is necessary to turn to these and other practical responses of the Organization, rather than rely solely on the drafting history or a parsing of the text.

Anticipated problems in banning violence: between the desiderata of perpetual peace and perfect justice

At San Francisco, proposals for renunciation of state-to-state violence and the substitution of collective security were widely welcomed in principle. At least some states understood, however, that political considerations might prevent the Council from using its new powers effectively

---

[37] Minutes of the Sixteenth Five-Power Informal Consultative Meeting on Proposed Amendments, San Francisco, June 6, 1945, 1 Foreign Relations of the United States, 1945, 1176 at 1187.

[38] Minutes of the Sixteenth Five-Power Informal Consultative Meeting on Proposed Amendments at 1186–87.

[39] Minutes of the Sixty-Third Meeting of the United States Delegation, San Francisco, June 4, 1945, 1 Foreign Relations of the United States, 1945, 1137 at 1142.

[40] Minutes of the Sixty-Fifth Meeting of the United States Delegation, San Francisco, June 6, 1945, 1 Foreign Relations of the United States, 1945, 1171 at 1173–76. Agreement on the text of Article 2(7) was recorded in the Minutes of the Sixteenth Five-Power Informal Consultative Meeting on Proposed Amendments, San Francisco, June 6, 1945, 1 Foreign Relations of the United States, 1945, 1176 at 1189.

and impartially. Once again, there were a few attempts to anticipate the problems that might arise and to develop applicable principles and processes. The Netherlands' representative, with the 1938 Munich partition of Czechoslovakia in mind, warned of future political temptations to buy peace at the cost of justice.

that price might well seem unreasonable to many; such a settlement could not be expected to command respect and therefore to endure, and if another and better settlement were not found, the prestige of the Security Council and of the organization generally, would suffer accordingly. In other words, it does not seem possible to leave everything to mere opportunism.[41]

He called, therefore, for inclusion in the Charter of "some standard of justice": a rather tall order. "The Netherlands Government," he conceded, "do not claim to have found the ultimate solution, but they have asked themselves whether a reference to those feelings of right and wrong, those moral principles which live in every human heart, would not be enough."[42]

But principles need to be linked to a credible process for applying them, he added. "It clearly could not be left to the Security Council to decide, for if that were done this Council would be allowed to sit in judgment on its own proposals. Nor could it, for practical reasons, be left to the Assembly, or to the arbitrary appreciation of individual member-states." Instead, he proposed

the appointment of an independent body of eminent men from a suitable number of different countries, men known for their integrity and their experience in international affairs, who should be readily available to pronounce upon decisions of the Security Council whenever an appeal to that effect were addressed to them, either by the Council or by a party to the case in question. This body, it should be emphasized, should pronounce upon the matter solely from the point of view of whether the Council's decision is in keeping with the moral principles ... and should render its decision within a set number of days so as to avoid all undue delay ...[43]

[41] Suggestions Presented by the Netherlands Government Concerning the Proposals for the Maintenance of Peace and Security Agreed on at the Four Powers Conference of Dumbarton Oaks as Published on October 9, 1944, 3 U.N.C.I.O., Doc. 2, G/7(j), January 1945, 312.

[42] Proposals for the Maintenance of Peace and Security Agreed at the Four Powers Conference of Dumbarton Oaks at 313. A similar appeal to accommodate the "supremacy of moral law as the guiding motive ... which governs relations between states" was made by Ecuador, 3 U.N.C.I.O. General, Doc. 2, G/7(p), May 1, 1945, 398.

[43] 3 U.N.C.I.O. General, Doc. 2, G/7(p), May 1, 1945 at 313.

Thus it becomes apparent that, even before the Charter was signed, ratified, and implemented, there was unease, at least in some quarters, that states were being asked to renounce recourse to violence in return for a community-based system of collective measures that would be geared primarily to averting threats to, or breaches of, the peace rather than to preserving justice and redressing injustice: a concept for which the Charter made little provision. Although the Netherlands stood no chance of succeeding with its proposal for a council of wise and independent elders to represent the cause of justice in the system's operation, the issue to which this solution was directed remains important and still essentially unresolved.

In practice, the problem of injustice in the operation of the Charter has turned out to be manifest less in unconscionable actions of the Council than in its inaction owing to the veto. Otherwise, however, time has not abated the problem. The very same paradoxical juxtaposition between the Charter's insistence on order (non-violence) and the common moral instinct (justice) was posed to the UN General Assembly by Secretary-General Kofi Annan in the Fall of 1999:

To those for whom the greatest threat to the future of the international order is the use of force in the absence of a Security Council mandate, one might ask, not in the context of Kosovo but in the context of Rwanda, if, in those dark days and hours leading up to the genocide, a coalition of States had been prepared to act in defence of the Tutsi population, but did not receive prompt Council authorization, should such a coalition have stood aside and allowed the horror to unfold?

To those for whom the Kosovo action heralded a new era when States and groups of States can take military action outside the established mechanisms for enforcing international law, one might ask: is there not a danger of such interventions undermining the imperfect, yet resilient, security system created after the Second World War, and of setting dangerous precedents for future interventions without a clear criterion to decide who might invoke these precedents and in what circumstances?[44]

Annan returned to this quandary in his report to the Millennium Assembly of the United Nations:[45]

Few would disagree that both the defence of humanity and the defense of sovereignty are principles that must be supported. Alas that does not tell us which principle should prevail when they are in conflict.

[44] 54 G.A.O.R., 4th Plen. Meeting, September 20, 1999, A/54/PV.4, at 2.
[45] We the peoples: the role of the United Nations in the twenty-first century, Report of the Secretary-General, A/54/2000, March 27, 2000, p. 35, para. 218.

What it may tell us, nevertheless, is that there cannot be an absolute priority either for the claim of sovereignty (in the name of peace) or of humanity (in the name of justice); that extreme peace – in the sense of an absolute priority – creates the conditions of war, while extreme justice similarly generates the conditions of injustice. If this is so, then the claims of sovereignty and humanity must, whenever possible, be reconciled and, when impossible, be weighed against one another in accordance with a widely agreed, situationally specific system of weights and measures.

The search for elusive criteria, principles, and procedures for making that assessment – the paradoxical juxtaposition between the institutional pursuit of order (non-violence) and the moral pull to justice – all these were anticipated by a few, the most prescient, participating governments at San Francisco. They perceived but did not resolve the paradox between prohibiting aggression, on the one hand, and doing justice, on the other. In the Second World War the world had learned the importance of organizing collective measures able to prevent a recurrence of events such as Hitler's attack on Poland. But the same era had also demonstrated the need to guard against the sacrifice of justice for peace, as in the craven Anglo-French surrender at Munich to Hitler's "humanitarian" demands on Czechoslovakia in the name of the Sudeten-Germans.

Is peace more precious than justice? Is peace, conscionable, or even possible, without justice? At San Francisco, the representative of Australia, in emphasizing the priority of principles of non-aggression and state sovereignty, added, "At the same time we recognize that in the course of time adjustments in the existing order may become necessary, not so much for the preservation of peace as for the attainment of international justice."[46] Indeed, some delegations pressed for greater parity in the Charter's guiding principles between order and justice. Britain, in its proposals at Dumbarton Oaks, had argued that "international peace must be ... not only kept by ... suppressing violence [but also] ... by guarding the right of man to seek his freedom, and by increase in the well-being of human society."[47] Norway proposed a new provision in Article 2:

All members of the Organization undertake to defend life, liberty, independence and religious freedom and to preserve human rights and justice.[48]

[46] 1 U.N.C.I.O., Plenary, Doc. 20, P/6, April 28, 1945, 174.
[47] Tentative Proposals by the United Kingdom for a General International Organization, July 22, 1944, 1 Foreign Relations of the United States, 1944, 670 at 671.
[48] 3 U.N.C.I.O., General, Amendments and Observations on the Dumbarton Oaks Proposals, Submitted by the Norwegian Delegation, May 3, 1945, Doc. 2, G/7(n)(1), May 4, 1945, 366.

France offered an amendment to the prohibition on interference in a state's domestic affairs (Article 2(7)) that, while not accepted at San Francisco, may increasingly seem to have been adopted in practice. It sought to legitimize international intervention when a state's "clear violation of essential liberties and of human rights constitutes in itself a threat capable of compromising peace."[49]

At San Francisco, evidently, the time had not yet come for such parity between the new system's commitment to the hard-won Lauterpachtian principle – "there shall be no violence" – and newer and as-yet dimly perceived principles of justice that, conceivably, might sometimes warrant recourse to collective or even state-to-state force. In 1945, Britain, despite its lofty rhetoric, joined the Soviet Union in opposing all drafts of the Charter that would have made illegal a state's violence against persons and subjected it to the same sanctions as violence perpetrated against another state. Sir Alexander Cadogan at Dumbarton Oaks opposed a proposed reference to human rights and fundamental freedoms in what became Article 1(3) of the Charter, saying that this might encourage the organization to engage in criticism of the internal affairs of member states. Ambassador Andrei Gromyko added that "the reference to human rights and basic freedom is not germane to the main task of an international security organization."[50] As a result of these objections,[51] it was agreed to eliminate a provision in the draft Charter which read:

2. It is the duty of each member of the Organization to see to it that conditions prevailing within its jurisdiction do not endanger international peace and security and, to this end, to respect the human rights and fundamental freedoms of all its people and to govern in accordance with the principles of humanity and justice. *Subject to the performance of this duty* the Organization should refrain from intervention in the internal affairs of any of its members [emphasis added].[52]

Had this been adopted, a government's non-performance of "this duty" would have suspended the Organization's obligation to "refrain

---

[49] 12 U.N.C.I.O., Commission III, Committee 2, Doc. 207, III/2/A/3, May 10, 1945, 179 at 191.

[50] Memorandum by the Under Secretary of State (Stettinius) to the Secretary of State: Progress Report on Dumbarton Oaks Conversations – Eighteenth Day, September 9, 1944, 1 Foreign Relations of the United States, 1944, 789.

[51] Memorandum by the Under Secretary of State (Stettinius) to the Secretary of State, 1 Foreign Relations of the United States, 1944, 824 at 825.

[52] Joint Formulation Group's draft of September 20, 1944. Memorandum by the Under Secretary of State (Stettinius) to the Secretary of State, September 20, 1944, 1 Foreign Relations of the United States, 1944, 828 at 829.

from intervention in the [state's] internal affairs." Although the provision was not incorporated in the Charter, the subsequent practice of the political organs could be seen as partially implementing its intent: for example, by imposing collective measures against the *apartheid* regime of South Africa and authorizing the use of armed force against the military junta of Haiti.

The drafters' vision

To study the *travaux* – the discursive and negotiating process by which the victors of the Second World War sought to imagine a peace in keeping with their lofty wartime aims – is to become aware of two overriding concerns. First, the nations, or a significant number of their negotiators, were well aware that the League had failed to prevent state violence by making too conditional states' commitment not to resort to – and collectively to resist – armed aggression. They aspired to a more definitive commitment to peace. Second, at least some of them also sensed that this lesson of the past, while underscoring the importance of firm collective guarantees against aggression, was an insufficient prescription for the future. To preserve peace, they knew, would also require an effective response to massive injustices of the kind perpetrated by Nazi and Fascist governments against their own and other populations.

These latter, justice-based concerns were not, finally, much addressed by the text adopted in 1945. Nevertheless, they did not dissipate and, subsequently, they have steadily increased their pull on institutional practice. Indeed, some observers claim that the modern emphasis on humanity and justice is being given such priority as to verge on injustice, as well as posing a threat to the peaceful order based on respect for state sovereignty. Succeeding chapters will examine the implications of this shifting balance between peace and justice and its effect on the law pertaining to recourse to force by the United Nations, regional and mutual-defense organizations, and individual states.

2

Use of force by the United Nations

The Charter and uses of force

Chapter 1 has provided a brief synopsis of the origins of a post-war Charter-based system pertaining to the use of force in international affairs. For the first time, international law fully and formally embraced the Lauterpachtian ground-norm: "there shall be no violence." Article 2(4) obliges all member states to "refrain...from the threat or use of force": not just to renounce war but all forms of interstate violence.

This dedication to non-violence by states is coupled in the Charter with an extensive commitment to collective measures against violators of the peace of nations. Article 39 authorizes the Security Council "to determine the existence of any threat to the peace, breach of the peace, or act of aggression," and empower it to "make recommendations, or decide what measures shall be taken...to maintain or restore international peace and security." Article 25 requires all members of the United Nations to join in implementing such decisions. Finally, Article 42 authorizes the Council, lesser measures having failed, to "take such action by air, sea, or land forces as may be necessary to maintain or restore international peace and security." To that end, Article 43 pledges all members "to make available to the Security Council, on its call and in accordance with a special agreement or agreements, armed forces, assistance, and facilities, including rights of passage, necessary for the purpose of maintaining international peace and security."

This, then, was to have been the ultimate triumph of the Lauterpachtian ground-norm: there was to be no more violence. States abjured not only the right to make formal war, but all recourse to military force. Failure to adhere to this new law was to be met by decision of the

Security Council acting, first as a jury to determine whether there had been a breach of the peace, by whom, and how serious it was, and then deciding what collective measures might appropriately be taken to put matters right. Although, at the time of the Dumbarton Oaks Conference, it had been agreed by the Big Powers not to attempt to define what would constitute a threat to international peace and security but to leave this question open to the Security Council's case-by-case implementation,[1] all states agreed to abide by such a determination and, if asked by the Council, to participate in implementing the prescribed remedy, using force collectively when necessary.

It was noted in chapter 1 that four new geopolitical developments simultaneously interfered with the implementing of this visionary new scheme. The first was the advent of the Cold War. The second was the growing resort to indirect aggression through states' support of surrogates in the civil wars of other states. The third was the scientific revolution in weaponry that logically supported the claim of "anticipatory self-defence." The fourth was the unexpected momentum, powered by public opinion, of concern for decolonization and human rights: the "justice" factor subordinated at San Francisco in 1945 by security concerns. All four of these developments combined to make unworkable a strictly literal interpretation of the Charter's collective security system. Instead, the member states, in applying the Charter, have interpreted it to accord with changing circumstances and social values.

Collective use of armed force: original intent

In return for states' agreeing to abjure autonomous recourse to violence, the Charter holds out the promise of an effective global gendarmerie to guard the peace. This is set out in Article 42, which authorizes the Security Council to "take such action by air, sea, or land forces as may be necessary to maintain or restore international peace and security." A Council decision to use force is made binding on all members by Article 25, which obliges them "to accept and carry out decisions of the Security Council..." These provisions are central to the Charter enterprise. Their drafting history helps illuminate the original intent behind the language.

---

[1] Memorandum by the Under Secretary of State (Stettinius) to the Secretary of State (Hull), September 1, 1944. 1 Foreign Relations of the United States, 1944, 761, 762.

In an early (1943) memorandum by Secretary of State Cordell Hull to President Roosevelt it was envisaged that "the four major powers will pledge themselves [to] ... maintain adequate forces and will be willing to use such forces as circumstances require to prevent or suppress all cases of aggression."[2] To this end, the memo said, all members must accept the obligation to "make such contribution to the facilities and means which the Council may require for the enforcement of its decisions or for the prevention or repression of aggression as may be agreed upon in advance or, in the absence of such agreement, as the Executive Council may deem appropriate."[3] From this it may be gathered that, in 1943, the US was beginning to think of a Council able to enforce its decisions by military forces that were either placed permanently at its disposal by prior agreements with individual states, or, alternatively, would be provided *ad hoc* for a particular instance of enforcement, in response to a call by the Council.

By 1945, however, the *ad hoc* alternative appears to have been largely set aside in favor of the more direct mode of implementing universal security envisaged by Article 43. This obliges all Members to enter into "special agreements" with the Council making permanently available "on its call ... armed forces, assistance and facilities ..." to carry out the mandate "of maintaining international peace and security."

The Dumbarton Oaks proposals (Chapter VIII, Section B, paragraphs 4 and 5) foreshadowed both Articles 42 and 43. Although at San Francisco there were extensive discussions about ancillary matters – whether non-military means should be exhausted before the Council resorted to force, whether the concurrence of the General Assembly should be required, about the non-applicability of the restriction on intervening in a member's domestic affairs, about the role of regional organizations in enforcement, and whether there should be a collective "duty" to deter aggression – the Dumbarton provisions which became Articles 42 and 43 were adopted with relatively little debate. The *ad hoc* approach to enforcing Council decisions, mooted by Hull in 1943, did not surface at San Francisco. This is ironic because, in fifty years of practice, the United Nations has relied for enforcement entirely on *ad hoc* arrangements.

What is especially remarkable is the lack of attention to whether Article 42 and Article 43 were interdependent: that is, whether the

---

[2] Memorandum by the Secretary of State to President Roosevelt, December 29, 1943. Arrangements for Exploratory Discussions on World Security Organization, 1 Foreign Relations of the United States, 1944, 614 at 615.

[3] Memorandum by the Secretary of State to President, Roosevelt, December 29, 1943 at 620.

Security Council would have the option to employ force even in the absence of the standing contingents that were to be put at its disposal by the members. The lack of disquisition on this issue is in marked contrast to the questioning approach taken by states at San Francisco with respect to many other of the draft provisions. States meticulously combed the text for frailties. They proposed all sorts of solutions to imaginatively anticipated problems. Surprisingly, however, once there was acceptance of the principle that collective military measures should be directed by the Security Council (Article 42), it seemed simply to be assumed that states would provide the means by committing their forces in accordance with Article 43. In the words of the Rapporteur of the Committee that adopted the draft text of Article 42, the "principle of enforcement measures of a military nature being thus established, the Committee proceeded to study the methods of applying these measures."[4] In the ensuing study, however, no "method" was considered other than that of states' entering into agreements with the Security Council to provide specified forces for service when needed. No one questioned whether such agreements would indeed be forthcoming and what to do if they were not.

Were the Charter a static instrument based solely on the expressed intent of the framers, the fact that no Article 43 agreements have ever been made would have put paid to the Charter's vaunted collective military security system. Instead, the adaptive capacity of the Charter has functioned dramatically and controversially to fill the vacuum created by Article 43's non-implementation. This is no small feat. The gradual emancipation of Article 42 as a free-standing authority for deploying collective force, ad hoc, has prevented the collapse of the Charter system in the absence of the standby militia envisioned by Article 43. In commending the Charter for Senate advice and consent, Secretary Hull had said: "The whole scheme of the Charter is based on this conception of collective force made available to the Organization for the maintenance of international peace and Security."[5] Had he been right, there would be no United Nations today. Fortunately, however, the practice of the Organization in its first fifty-five years demonstrates the capacity of "the whole scheme of the Charter" to adapt to fulfill the purposes of the

---

[4] Report of Mr. Paul-Boncour, Rapporteur, on Chapter VIII, Section B, 12 U.N.C.I.O., Doc. 881, III/3/46, June 10, 1945, 502 at 509.

[5] Report of the President on the Results of the San Francisco Conference, June 26, 1945, US Congress, Senate Committee Hearings, 79th Cong., vol. 767, 1945, 34 at 55. (Hereafter: Report of the President.)

Organization by other means in the face of unexpected obstacles and unanticipated challenges.

The practice: uncoupling Article 42 from Article 43

Faced with its failure to establish a police militia under Article 43, the Security Council has adapted by using, or authorizing states to use, *ad hoc* forces put together for the purpose of responding to a specific crisis, rather as Hull had proposed in 1943. Far from being paralyzed by the failure to realize the potential of Article 43, the system, in actual practice, has developed new ways to deploy force to secure peace and resist aggression.

The Korean War is the first example of the Security Council's authorizing *ad hoc* collective measures in the absence of Article 43 forces. On June 25, 1950, Secretary-General Trygve Lie reported the previous night's attack by North Korea on the South. Qualifying the situation as a threat to international peace, he called on the Security Council as the "competent organ" to act at once[6] by determining that the attack was a breach of the peace, calling for a cessation of hostilities, embargoing all "assistance to the North Korean authorities," and calling "upon all Members to render every assistance to the United Nations in the execution of this resolution."[7] This was precisely the response voted by the Council. Its resolution determined that there had been a "breach of the peace" and thereby invoked Article 39, the prerequisite for collective measures under the Charter's Chapter VII.[8]

Collective military measures – at least in the sense envisaged by Article 43 – being unavailable, Resolution 83 of June 27 (passed with only Yugoslavia opposed and with the Soviet Union absent) recommended instead "that the Members of the United Nations furnish such assistance to the Republic of Korea as may be necessary to repel the armed attack and to restore international peace and security in the area."[9] On July 7, with the Soviets still absent and three abstentions (Egypt, India, and Yugoslavia), the Council recommended that all members providing military assistance make such forces available to a unified military command headed by the US, authorized that command to use the United Nations

---

[6] S.C.O.R., 5th Sess., 473rd Meeting at 3. U.N. Doc. S/PV.473 (1950), 25 June 1950.

[7] S.C.O.R., 5th Sess., 473rd Meeting at 3. U.N. Doc. S/PV.473 (1950), 25 June 1950.

[8] S.C. Res. 82 (1950) of 25 June 1950.   [9] S.C. Res. 83 (1950) of 27 June 1950.

flag, and requested the US to report "as appropriate" to the Security Council.[10]

Since the Charter makes no provision for a UN military response except with Article 43 forces, the Council's authorization of action in its name by *ad hoc* national contingents – what has since become known as a "coalition of the willing" – represented a creative adaption of the text. The practice of Security Council authorization of action by such coalitions of the willing subsequently became a firmly established part of the UN collective security system. In this first experience, the UN force was constituted by ground forces volunteered by ten states, naval units from eight nations, and air units from five.[11]

While the Soviet boycott of the Council had facilitated this innovation, so had the presence in Seoul of the field representatives of the United Nations Commission on Korea. It was they who were able to report the facts immediately and credibly to the Secretary-General, enabling him, in turn, to communicate authoritatively that it was North Korea that had instigated the conflict.[12] They thereby refuted North Korean and Soviet-satellites' pretence that the North had responded only in self-defense against aggression by the South.[13]

In 1960, the Security Council authorized another coalition of the willing to respond to an appeal by the Government of the Republic of the Congo to restore order and facilitate the removal of Belgian troops from that newly-independent state (see below).[14] Six years later, the Council authorized the British navy to enforce UN sanctions against the break-away white-supremacist regime of Ian Smith in the self-governing Crown Colony of Rhodesia.[15]

Forty years after the Korean episode, the Security Council – still lacking an Article 43-based military capability of its own – once again authorized a massive coalition of the willing: this time to undertake operation "Desert Storm" after Iraq's invasion of Kuwait. As in the earlier instances, the Council, in accordance with Charter Article 39, began by determining that Iraq's actions constituted a breach of the peace[16] to which a collective military response was warranted.[17] That finding was made by a vote of 14–0 with only Yemen abstaining. The resolution as a whole, invoking Chapter VII and requesting member states to "use all necessary means" to reverse Iraqi aggression, passed with only Cuba

---

[10] S.C. Res. 84 (1950) of 7 July 1950.   [11] 1950 U.N.Y.B. 8.   [12] 1950 U.N.Y.B. 251.
[13] S.C.O.R., 473rd Meeting, n. 6 above, at 3.   [14] S.C. Res. 143 of 13 July 1960.
[15] S.C. Res. 221 of 9 April 1966. See further S. Res. 232 of 16 December 1966.
[16] S/RES 660 of 2 August 1990.   [17] S/RES 678 of 29 November 1990.

and Yemen opposed and with China abstaining but not claiming to have cast a veto.[18]

The drafters of the Charter, as we have seen, did not envisage such Council-mandated use of force in the absence of an Article 43-based military capability. There is no reason, however, why the Council's responses to aggression cannot be understood as a creative use of Article 42, severed from, and unencumbered by, the failed Article 43.[19] Although the negotiators at Dumbarton Oaks and San Francisco undoubtedly had inferred that Article 42 would operate only in reliance on forces pledged by members under Article 43, the Charter does not make this interdependence explicit. On the contrary, Article 42 fully authorizes the Council to "take such action by air, sea, or land forces as may be necessary to maintain or restore international peace and security. Such action may include demonstrations, blockade, and other operations by air, sea or land forces of Members of the United Nations." Textually, Article 42 can stand on its own feet and it now may be said to do so as a result of Council practice. This practice, moreover, while not anticipated by the drafters, does no violence to their architecture. Article 39 states:

---

[18] As noted in Chapter 1 above, this is a prime example of the Charter's adaption through consistent practice by the relevant political organ of the United Nations. Article 27(3) of the Charter, interpreted literally and in accordance with the intent of the drafters, provides that an abstention *does* constitute a veto, since a decision on substantive matters requires "the concurring votes of the permanent members."

[19] It has been argued that the Council's Resolution 678, authorizing "States co-operating with the Government of Kuwait" to use force to uphold the Security Council's demands for Iraqi withdrawal "and to restore international peace and security" was no more than an acknowledgment of Kuwait's right, under Article 51, to implement its "inherent right of individual or collective self-defence" against "an armed attack." This legal analysis, however, is wrong. For Kuwait to exercise its right of self-defense under Article 51, the Charter neither envisages nor requires authorization by the Security Council. Furthermore, the right of states to join with Kuwait in its collective defense had already been acknowledged by the Council Resolution 661 of 6 August 1990, which had affirmed "the inherent right of individual or collective self-defence, in response to the armed attack of Iraq against Kuwait in accordance with Article 51 of the Charter." Resolution 678, coming almost four months later, did something radically different: it *decided*, under Chapter VII's mandatory authority, "to allow Iraq one final opportunity, as a pause of goodwill," to get out of Kuwait, S/RES/678 of 29 November 1990, para. 1. It *authorized* the coalition of willing states to use force "*if Iraq failed to comply by January 15, 1991*" S/RES/678 of 29 November 1990, para. 2 (emphasis added). With its passage, the Council, without abrogating Kuwait's right of self-defense, superimposed upon it a collective measure involving the use of military force that was now authorized under Chapter VII and subject to the Council's parameters regarding objectives, means, and date of initiation.

The Security Council shall determine the existence of any threat to the peace, breach of the peace, or act of aggression and shall make recommendations, or decide what measures shall be taken in accordance with Articles 41 and 42, to maintain international peace and security.

Article 39 thus empowers the Council to "take measures" under Article 42 without reference to Article 43, thereby creating room for the Council to order – or, more probably, to call for – states' participation in collective security measures whether or not they have entered into special agreements with the Council under Article 43.

If the Council were to *order* states to use force, Article 25 would require all members to "agree and carry out" that decision. To date, however, all the resolutions authorizing *ad hoc* military forces have merely "called on" or "authorized" states to use force.[20] While participation in military action has thus been voluntary, the authority and objectives of *ad hoc* forces have usually been formulated in mandatory terms. For example, in resolution 678, the Security Council speaks of Iraq's "obligation" to "comply" with its demands to restore Kuwaiti sovereignty and authorizes the use of force "to implement" those demands.[21] Moreover, the war was concluded not by a treaty between the participants but by Security Council decision establishing the mandatory terms on which member states would "bring their military presence in Iraq to an end..."[22] These, obviously, are exercises of the Council's power to make binding decisions under Chapter VII, even if they are enforced by voluntary "coalitions of the willing."

There have been several subsequent occasions on which the Security Council has authorized the use of force by states in coalitions of the willing: national military contingents assembled *ad hoc* for a particular task. The Council has also authorized a single state or a regional organization to lead a specified military operation. Whatever their composition, however, these operations increasingly have filled the void created by the lapse of Article 43. Thus, on November 30, 1992, the Secretary-General informed the Council that "the situation in Somalia has deteriorated beyond the point at which it is susceptible to peace-keeping treatment."

---

[20] For example, S/RES/678 of 29 November 1990, para. 3, and S/RES/794 of 3 December 1992. Note, however, that when economic sanctions have been imposed by the Council, compliance has been mandatory for all Members. See, for example, S.C. Res. 232 of 16 December 1966 mandating trade sanctions against Southern Rhodesia and S.C. Res. 418 of 4 November 1977 imposing an arms embargo on South Africa.

[21] S/RES/678 of 29 November 1990, preamble and para. 1.

[22] S/RES/687 of 3 April 1991, para. 6.

Accordingly, he reported, "I am more than ever convinced of the need for *international military personnel* to be deployed in Somalia" (emphasis added). He concluded that "the Security Council now has no alternative but to decide to adopt more forceful measures to secure the humanitarian operations... It would therefore be necessary for the Security Council to make a determination under Article 39 of the Charter that a threat to the peace exists... The Council would also have to determine that non-military measures as referred to in Chapter VII were not capable of giving effect to the Council's decision."[23] Promptly, the Security Council made the requisite finding under Chapter VII and authorized the US, and any others "willing," to "use all necessary means" through an *ad hoc* Unified Task Force (UNITAF) to achieve the specified objectives.[24] This was decided unanimously, demonstrating the assent of all members to the principle of Council-authorized coalitions of the willing.

It is notable that the Council, in authorizing military intervention in Somalia, followed precisely the requisites of Article 42. It first determined that measures short of the use of armed force (Article 41) had failed to achieve the objective of restoring order and removing a threat to the peace (Article 39). This made the operation, although conducted by the designated member state, subject to terms of reference set out in the authorizing resolution.

These were not trivial operations. UNITAF engaged 37,000 (primarily American) forces. Its multinational successor, UNOSOM II, deploying 30,000 military personnel, was placed by the Council under the control of the UN Secretary-General and charged with enforcement powers and the task of creating peace, democracy and unity in that riven land.[25] All the more significant is it to note that both operations – engaging the United Nations in an essentially humanitarian intervention with *ad hoc* forces and doing so even in the absence either of a clearly *international* crisis or the consent of Somalia – should have received the unopposed consent of the members of the Security Council. Although few members of the Council thought it prudent to spell out general principles of Charter-interpretation underpinning this use of collective force – and, indeed, in Resolution 794 states took care to note the "unique character" of the crisis to which they were responding – the actions of the Council cannot but be seen as precedent-setting.

---

[23] Letter dated 29 November 1992, S/24868. [24] S/RES/794 of 3 December 1992.
[25] S/RES/814 of 26 March 1993, para. 6. The transfer from UNITAF to UNOSOM II was set for May 1, 1993.

Another example of the expansion of the practice of deploying coalitions of the willing is the Council's – again, expressly "exceptional" – authorization, in 1994, of a multinational force under "unified command and control" to "use all necessary means" to facilitate the ouster from Haiti of the military leadership that had overthrown its democratically elected government.[26] On this occasion the resolution was passed by 13–0 with Brazil and China abstaining. (China's abstention once again was not seen as a veto.) Yet another instance is the mandate given by the Security Council to another *ad hoc* force, UNPROFOR,[27] in the former Yugoslavia and the gradual extension of that military mandate to include the defense of Bosnian "safe areas."[28] When those safe areas and the UN personnel in them came under attack, the Security Council authorized air strikes by NATO against Serb heavy weapons.[29] This UN cooperation with NATO, the "double key" approach to air strikes, was later extended by the Council to UNPROFOR operations in Croatia.[30] These resolutions, too, were adopted with the unanimous assent of Council members and widespread approval from states outside the Council.[31] Despite *pro forma* protest from the Russian Federation,[32] the ensuing "bombs of August"[33] constituted the first effective military partnership between a regional military organization and the United Nations' own *ad hoc* multinational force,[34] one that ultimately led to the defeat of Serb forces and, in turn, to the Dayton peace negotiations.

Reflecting on the air and land campaign from the perspective of Washington, Richard Holbrooke, then Assistant Secretary of State with special responsibility for the Yugoslav situation, has written of both the

---

[26] S/RES/940 of 31 July 1994.   [27] S/RES/743 of 21 February 1992.

[28] S/RES/836 of 4 June 1993, paras. 5 and 9.

[29] S/RES/836 of 4 June 1993, para. 10: "Member States, acting nationally or through regional organizations or arrangements, may take, *under the authority of the Security Council* and subject to close coordination with the Secretary-General and UNPROFOR, all necessary measures, through the use of air power, in and around the safe areas in the Republic of Bosnia and Herzegovina, to support UNPROFOR in the performance of its mandate . . ." (emphasis added).

[30] S/RES/958 (1994) of 19 November 1994.   [31] 1994 U.N.Y.B., vol. 84, 514.

[32] Statement of the Russian Federation, S/1994/443 of 11 April 1994.

[33] The term is borrowed from the section on NATO's 1994 bombing campaign in Richard Holbrooke, *To End a War* 101–05 (1998).

[34] According to Holbrooke: "When it was all over and we could assess who had been most helpful, my Washington colleagues usually singled out Kofi Annan at the United Nations, and Willy Claes and General Joulwan at NATO." Holbrooke, *To End a War* at 103.

cumbersome and historic qualities of this cooperative effort[35] between the US, NATO, and the United Nations. Cumbersome or not, it marked yet another instance in the adaption of the Charter to give the United Nations a flexible role in situations demanding a military response to threats to the peace and acts of aggression, albeit one quite possibly constituted in a manner – and with an operational mandate – not envisaged by the drafters at San Francisco half a century earlier.

There are other, even more recent examples of coalitions of the willing or individual states being authorized by the Security Council to use force as necessary, usually but not always under Chapter VII. Thus, the Security Council in 1994 authorized France to use "all necessary means" for security and humanitarian ends during the civil turmoil in Rwanda[36] and in 1997 authorized Italy, with others, to deploy forces to prevent civil war in Albania[37] and created INTERFET under Australian leadership to establish security in East Timor.[38] In an effort to contain the civil war in Sierra Leone the Council, in 1999, created UNAMSIL, a force of 11,000 with authority, under Chapter VII, to use force "to afford protection to civilians under imminent threat of physical violence" as well as to "assist . . . the Sierra Leone law enforcement authorities in the discharge of their responsibilities."[39]

It may thus be concluded that the failure to implement Article 43 has not seriously hampered the United Nations in carrying out its mission to provide collective security. On the contrary, *ad hoc* coalitions of the willing, in various logistical configurations, or designated surrogates, have not merely filled the gap left by states' reluctance to make long-term standby troop commitments but have been deployed with mandates, including interventions in essentially domestic conflicts for primarily humanitarian purposes, that were never contemplated and probably would not have been approved at San Francisco. This does not, however, mean that the Organization has become a "rogue cop," operating without license. It was the intention of the founders at San Francisco to create a living institution, equipped with dynamic political, administrative, and

---

[35] "To attack Option Three targets, a much broader group that included Serb troop concentrations and equipment throughout Bosnia, we would need to return to both the NATO Council and the U.N. Security Council for permission." Holbrooke, *To End a War* at 146.

[36] Operation Turquoise, authorized by S/RES/929 of 22 June 1994.

[37] Operation Alba, authorized by S/RES/1101 of 28 March 1997 and S/RES/1114 of 19 June 1997.

[38] S/RES/1246 of 11 June 1999.

[39] S.C. Res. 1270 of 22 October 1999 and S/RES/1289 of 7 February 2000.

juridical organs, competent to interpret their own powers under a flexible constituent instrument in response to new challenges. The United Nations has fulfilled that mandate.

The role of the General Assembly: original intent

Another issue left largely uncontemplated and wholly unresolved at Dumbarton Oaks and at San Francisco was this: what would happen if a palpable threat to the peace were to arise but the Security Council (either for lack of a majority or by exercise of the veto) were unable to act? From before the Dumbarton Oaks conference to the time of national ratifications of the Charter, little systematic thought was devoted to the potential for stasis in the Council. Yet this soon became the principal challenge to the effectiveness of the Charter system.

At Dumbarton Oaks some consideration had been given to allotting a secondary role to the General Assembly for the maintenance of international peace and security, but this was rejected. The Big Powers agreed that any member state "may bring to the attention of the General Assembly any condition, situation, or dispute the continuation of which is likely to impair the security or general welfare of itself or of any other member of the organization, or lead to a breach of the peace." The Assembly was to defer to the Security Council, however, in any situation "which it deems of sufficient gravity to require immediate consideration" of "measures."[40] Briefly, thought was given to a plan to allow the Assembly "to consider questions relating to the maintenance of international peace and security" subject only to the caveat that it could not "on its own initiative...deal with any such matter which is being dealt with by the Council."[41] This, too, did not make the final draft. At San Francisco, New Zealand made a last-ditch effort to insert a provision requiring joint action by the Security Council and General Assembly in implementing enforcement measures, except in "extremely urgent cases."[42] That also failed. A few other attempts to strengthen the

---

[40] Plan for the Establishment of an International Organization for the Maintenance of International Peace and Security. Memorandum by the Secretary of State (Hull) to President Roosevelt, December 29, 1943, 1 Foreign Relations of the United States, 1944, 614 at 619.

[41] Memorandum by the Under Secretary of State (Stettinius) to the Secretary of State, August 31, 1944, 1 Foreign Relations of the United States, 1944, 755.

[42] San Francisco, May 10, 1945, 1 Foreign Relations of the United States, 1945, 657 at 662.

Assembly's role were unfavorably noted in Secretary of State Hull's report to Congress, which spoke of strenuous efforts on the part of smaller nations "to give the General Assembly an equal share with the Security Council in the maintenance of peace and security." If some participants had had their way, he observed, "the Security Council would have been limited by the constant supervision of the General Assembly in the consideration of methods and measures to maintain peace and security."[43] These ill-advised initiatives, Hull was glad to say, had been successfully resisted.

Summarizing the intended relationship between the two bodies, Hull told Congress:

Unlike the functions of the Security Council, which are primarily political and in case of need may be repressive in character, the functions of the General Assembly will be concerned with the promotion of constructive solutions of international problems in the widest range of human relationships, economic, social, cultural and humanitarian.[44]

This prognosis would seem to exclude the Assembly from all security issues. Nevertheless, its power, set out in Article 11(2) of the Charter, does permit the Assembly to make recommendations as to "questions relating to the maintenance of international peace and security" as long as it refrains from doing so while "the Security Council is exercising in respect of any dispute or situation the functions assigned to it in the... Charter."[45] This can be (and indeed has been) interpreted to grant it wider jurisdiction than is indicated by Hull's report to Congress. Nevertheless, the intent of the Big Powers in drafting the Charter seems closer to Hull's view, or to those expressed by China at Dumbarton Oaks:

Any question on which action is necessary should be referred to the Security Council by the General Assembly either before or after discussion. The General Assembly should not on its own initiative make recommendations on any matter relating to the maintenance of international peace and security which is being dealt with by the Security Council.[46]

This makes all the more remarkable the evolutionary growth of Assembly jurisdiction in matters requiring collective action, including the deployment of military forces. This adaption has occurred through

---

[43] *Report of the President,* n. 5 above, at 69.   [44] *Report of the President* at 71.
[45] UN Charter, Article 12(1).
[46] Proposals of China for the Establishment of a General International Organization, 1 Foreign Relations of the United States, 1944, 890 at 892.

two developments: the adoption of the "Uniting for Peace Resolution" and the invention of "Chapter 6 1/2."

Adapting General Assembly powers: "Uniting for Peace"

After being absent from the Security Council in June 1950 at the inception of North Korea's aggression, the Soviet Union resumed its participation in August. This presaged renewed deadlock in that organ. Accordingly, in October, at the beginning of the General Assembly's annual meeting, the US introduced an agenda item entitled "United Action for Peace."[47] It was debated in Committee from October 9–21 and in Plenary from November 1–3.

Secretary of State Dean Acheson proposed that the Assembly "organize itself to discharge its responsibility [for collective security] promptly and decisively if the Security Council is prevented from acting." Declaring that the Council's firm response to the Korean invasion in June had "marked a turning point in history for it showed the way to an enforceable rule of law among nations," Acheson urged that when the Council is "obstructed" by the veto this ought not to "leave the United Nations impotent..." because Charter Articles 10, 11, and 14 also gave the Assembly "authority and responsibility for matters affecting international peace."[48] Responding to those who thought the proposal distorted the drafters' allocation of functions, US Ambassador Benjamin Cohen reasoned that the Charter should be interpreted flexibly to allow new responses to unanticipated changes of circumstance. He cited US constitutional practice in allowing the making of "executive agreements" supplementing the formal treaty power, and the recognition of "implied powers" of Congress by the Supreme Court's decision in *McCulloch* v. *Maryland*.[49] Cohen touted these American constitutional precedents as creative examples for the United Nations to emulate in construing its own constitutive instrument.[50]

Whatever Assembly delegates may have made of these references to US constitutional practice, they endorsed the "Uniting for Peace"

[47] G.A.O.R., 5th Sess., Annexes, vol. 2, Item 68, U.N. Doc. A/1377 (1950).

[48] 23 Department of State Bull. 524–25 (1950). See also Dean Acheson, *Present at the Creation* 450 and 2 Foreign Relations of the United States, 1950, 335–37.

[49] 4 Wheat. 316 (1819).

[50] Benjamin V. Cohen, The United Nations, *Constitutional Developments, Growths, Possibilities* 18–19 (1961).

resolution by a resounding vote of 52–5 with only the Soviet bloc in opposition, and 2 abstentions (India and Argentina).[51] The resolution:

1. *Resolves* that if the Security Council, because of lack of unanimity of the permanent members, fails to exercise its primary responsibility for the maintenance of international peace and security in any case where there appears to be a threat to the peace, breach of the peace, or act of aggression, the General Assembly shall consider the matter immediately with a view to making appropriate recommendations to Members for collective measures, including in the case of a breach of the peace or act of aggression the use of armed force when necessary, to maintain or restore international peace and security. If not in session at the time, the General Assembly may meet in emergency special session within twenty-four hours of the request therefor. Such emergency special session shall be called if requested by the Security Council on the vote of any seven members or by a majority of the Members of the United Nations.

Soviet Ambassador Andrei Vyshinsky angrily opposed the new initiative. "Do you not propose therein," he asked, "that armed forces should be transferred to the control of the General Assembly?... do you not disregard Chapter VII of the Charter, where, beginning with Article 43, it is expressly stated that only the Military Staff Committee shall be responsible under the Security Council for the direction of armed forces, and that they may be used only by decision of the Security Council and not of the General Assembly...?" He concluded that "when the measures envisaged call for action in the sense of enforcement action, particularly by means of armed forces, the General Assembly can do nothing, since the Charter does not give it the right to act."[52] Turning to another US representative, he asked of him: "Is John Foster Dulles really so ignorant a person that he does not know all this?"[53]

In a better-tempered reply, Canadian Secretary of State for External Affairs, Lester B. Pearson conceded that "some honest doubts have been expressed about [the resolution's] constitutionality and... the sponsors... respect them. Nevertheless... [w]e believe that the General Assembly has the power to make recommendations on the subjects dealt with [in the Charter], although it would not have the power to make decisions which would automatically impose commitments or enforce obligations on the Members of the United Nations."[54]

[51] G.A. Res. 377(V). G.A.O.R., 5th Sess., 302nd Plen. Meeting, 3 November 1950, A/PV.302, 341 at 347.
[52] G.A.O.R., 5th Sess., 301st Plen. Meeting, 2 November 1950, A/PV.301 at 334.
[53] G.A.O.R., 5th Sess., 301st Plen. Meeting, 2 November 1950 at 328.
[54] G.A.O.R., 5th Sess., 302nd Plen. Meeting, 3 November 1950, A/PV.302 at 342.

Left unexamined in this explanation, however, is the difference between the effect of a General Assembly resolution on the entire membership – which could only be recommendatory – and its potential effect on parties affected by the recommended action, which might well be dispositive. For example, under "Uniting for Peace" may the Assembly be convened to resist an act of aggression or even to stop a government committing genocide against a minority of its population? Could the Assembly recommend that states deploy force against an aggressor or a genocidal government? Even if such a resolution by the Assembly were cast in purely recommendatory language – "calling upon" states asked to commit armed force – its purport would be more than a recommendation to those against whom force was to be deployed. While this was scarcely touched upon during the debate, both advocates and opponents of "Uniting for Peace" understood that its effect, in some unspecified instances, would be to empower the Assembly to deploy military force.[55]

The resolution had its first full-scale test in 1956,[56] during the Suez crisis. Israel having invaded the Sinai, and with Britain and France bombing Suez Canal cities in anticipation of an expeditionary landing, the US, on October 30, convened the Security Council demanding that it determine that there had been a breach of the peace and order Israeli forces back to the armistice lines established by the Council's cease-fire order of 11 August 1949.

With the UN Truce Supervisory Organization (UNTSO) already deployed in the area, the Secretary-General, as in the previous instance of North Korea's attack on the South, was in a position to report the facts. He rejected Israel's claim to be acting in self-defense against an Egyptian attack. The US then introduced a draft resolution[57] calling for withdrawal of Israeli forces and insisting that Britain and France not intervene. It received 7 votes in favor, with 2 opposed and 2 abstentions. The two negative votes having been cast by Britain and France, the resolution was vetoed.

Immediately, Yugoslavia, which had vigorously opposed "Uniting for Peace" in 1950, offered a resolution which, "taking into account" that

---

[55] UN Charter, article 18(2).

[56] A few states argued before the General Assembly in November 1950, after Chinese armed forces had entered the Korean conflict, that Assembly action in response to this event should be taken under the newly adopted "Uniting for Peace" procedures. 1950 U.N.Y.B. 245. This, however, did not become the basis for further Assembly initiatives on this item.

[57] U.N. Doc. S/3710 (1956).

the Council had been prevented "from exercising its primary responsibility for the maintenance of international peace and security" called for an emergency session of the General Assembly.[58] China, Cuba, Iran, Peru, the USSR and the US joined Yugoslavia in supporting this invocation of "Uniting for Peace," while France and the U.K. voted against, and Australia with Belgium abstained.[59] As the Yugoslav resolution was procedural, it was not subject to the veto. With that, the matter passed into the hands of the first emergency session of the General Assembly, which convened the next day and met from November 1–10.

The Assembly quickly adopted a resolution that "urged" a cease-fire.[60] As fighting continued, Canada submitted a resolution, adopted in the early morning of November 4, urgently requesting the Secretary-General to propose a plan for an international emergency force (UNEF) to secure and supervise a cease-fire.[61] Such a proposal, presented to the Assembly the same day[62] and taken up the next morning,[63] was adopted by 57–0 with 19 abstentions. It appointed a Chief of Staff – the Canadian Commander of the UNTSO mission, Major-General E.L.M. Burns[64] – and authorized recruitment of a military force "from member states other than the permanent members of the Security Council."[65] The same day the Secretary-General received Israel's unconditional agreement to a cease-fire, followed one day later by French and British acquiescence.

In his second and final report to the Assembly on the establishment of the new force, the Secretary-General emphasized that it had been authorized by, and would operate under, the "Uniting for Peace" resolution. He noted that it was being deployed with the consent of the countries concerned and would be stationed on Egyptian territory with that country's agreement[66] as "required under generally recognized international law."[67] He further noted that "there was an obvious difference between establishing the Force in order to secure the cessation of hostilities, with a withdrawal of forces, and establishing such a Force with a view to enforcing a withdrawal of forces." Asked by a member of the Assembly what would happen if Israel failed to comply with the resolution requiring

---

[58] S.C. Res. 119, S/3721 of 31 October 1956.   [59] 1956 U.N.Y.B. 34.

[60] G.A. Res. 997 (ES-I) of 2 November 1956.

[61] G.A. Res. 998 (ES-I) of 4 November 1956.

[62] U.N. Doc. A/3289, 4 November 1956. First report of the Secretary-General on plan for emergency international United Nations force.

[63] G.A. Res. 1000 (ES-I) of 5 November 1956.

[64] G.A. Res. 1000 (ES-I) of 5 November 1956, para. 2.

[65] G.A. Res. 1000 (ES-I) of 5 November 1956, para. 3.   [66] 1956 U.N. Yearbook 32.

[67] U.N. Doc. A/3302 and Add. 1–30 and Add. 4/Rev.1.

its withdrawal to the pre-existing armistice line, the Secretary-General replied that, "were that unfortunate situation to arise, he would consider it his duty to bring it at once to the attention of the General Assembly or the Security Council."[68]

This reply suggests that, while the Secretary-General did not consider UNEF to have been authorized to engage in military enforcement, he thought it potentially within the Assembly's power to strengthen that mandate. In the event, this proved unnecessary. On November 7, the Emergency Session approved "guiding principles" for UNEF by a persuasive vote of 64–0 with 12 abstentions.[69] Even the Soviet representative, although reporting that his Government still believed that the Assembly was creating a military force in violation of the Charter,[70] did not cast a negative vote. The moment, clearly, had been seized. The Organization, adapting to the circumstances of Cold War stasis in the Security Council, had found a new way to authorize, recruit, and deploy the military force necessary to allow it to fulfill its mission.[71]

Less than four years later, the Assembly once again stepped forward to authorize UN military action in the face of Security Council deadlock. The force deployed in the Congo (ONUC) by the Security Council in July 1960[72] had become mired in a dispute between the West and the Soviet Union. By September, Moscow began to demand the operation's termination. On September 17, the US invoked "Uniting for Peace" to convene another emergency session of the General Assembly,[73] which, by a large majority, voted new instructions for the Secretary-General to "assist the Central Government of the Congo in the restoration and maintenance of law and order throughout the territory of the Republic of the Congo and to safeguard its unity, territorial integrity and political

---

[68] G.A.O.R., 567th Plen. Meeting, 1st Emergency Special Session, 7 November 1956, 115, para. 134.

[69] G.A. Res. 1001 (ES-I) of 7 November 1956.

[70] G.A.O.R., 567th Plen. Meeting, 1st Emergency Special Session, 7 November 1956, 127, para. 292.

[71] Little observed during this episode, which focused on the General Assembly, was the legal implication of a move by the Soviets to have the Security Council, acting under Article 42, authorize states to defend Egypt against Britain, France, and Israel. Moscow, by this time, had apparently become reconciled to the use of such *ad hoc* forces by decision of the Council, unimpeded by the non-implementation of Article 43. U.N. Doc. S/3736, reproduced in S.C.O.R., 11th Sess., 755th Meeting, S/PV.755 (1956), at 42.

[72] S.C. Res. 143 of 13 July 1960.

[73] S.C. Res. 157 of 17 September 1960. The resolution passed by 8–2 (Poland and USSR), with France abstaining.

independence in the interests of international peace and security."[74] This became an important extension of ONUC's mandate, leading to military operations against the secessionist regime of Katanga province.[75] Only a year later was the Council again able to assume operational control over ONUC.[76]

Large expenses were incurred by the United Nations to maintain ONUC's 25,000 military and support personnel. France and Russia, however, refused to pay their share, arguing that ONUC operations authorized by the Assembly were *ultra vires* the Charter. To test the legality of that proposition, the Assembly asked the International Court for an advisory opinion[77] as to whether these expenditures constituted "expenses of the organization" that, under Article 17(2) of the Charter, must "be borne by the Members as apportioned..." Since Paris and Moscow were also refusing to pay their share of the cost of UNEF's Sinai operation, the Court was also asked to consider the legality of that earlier Assembly-authorized deployment.

In responding, the Court had to decide on the legality of the General Assembly's role in military operations – UNEF and ONUC – under "Uniting for Peace." The judges, by a majority of 9 to 5, confirmed the *vires* of both.

Article 24 of the Charter states:

In order to ensure prompt and effective action by the United Nations, its members confer on the Security Council primary responsibility for the maintenance of international peace and security...

The Court reasoned that, while the text was clear in giving the Council "primary" responsibility, that term itself implied a "secondary" responsibility which the Assembly could exercise when the Council was stymied by a veto. In the majority's view, the Assembly has the right "by means of recommendations...[to] organize peace-keeping operations" although only "at the request or with the consent, of the States concerned."[78]

In this opinion, the International Court both endorsed and shaped the "Uniting for Peace" Resolution, deeming it a lawful means by which the

---

[74] G.A. Res. 1474 (ES-IV) (1960). Adopted by 70–0 with 11 abstentions.

[75] U.N. Doc. S/5038; 9 UN Rev. 5 (February 1962).

[76] Res. S/5002 of 24 November 1961. Adopted by 9–0 with 2 abstentions (France and UK).

[77] G.A. Res. 1731 (XVI) of 20 December 1961.

[78] Certain Expenses of the United Nations, Advisory Opinion of 20 July 1962, 1962 I.C.J. 163 at 164.

Assembly could exercise at least some of the Organization's responsibility for maintaining international peace and security when the Security Council was unable to do so. What the opinion leaves undefined is the circumference of the category of "states concerned" whose consent must be obtained. Logically, if there appears a likelihood of conflict between states A and B, the Assembly, following upon consent by state B, could position a peacekeeping force on its territory even without the consent of state A as it would have no lawful cause to be "concerned" with that peaceable deployment.

Inventing "Chapter 6 1/2"

"Uniting for Peace" established a new procedure expanding General Assembly jurisdiction over peacekeeping operations. Concurrently, the United Nations began also to expand the kinds of such operations and their missions. Thus, the large UNEF military deployment in 1956 was a new venture both in scale and kind. "Blue helmets," lightly armed but in persuasive numbers, were deployed to observe a truce and to interpose themselves between hostile parties. They were not to engage in combat but, if attacked or hindered, were authorized to defend themselves and their mission. Thirty-eight peacekeeping operations[79] based on this innovative precedent were deployed during the United Nations' first fifty years.[80]

Most of these operations, unlike UNEF, have been authorized by the Security Council,[81] but the resolutions creating them usually do

---

[79] Yearbook of the United Nations, Special Edition, UN Fiftieth Anniversary, 1945–1995, at 32, figure 1.

[80] The first, the UN Truce Supervisory Organization (UNTSO) actually preceded UNEF. It was established in 1948 but was of a much smaller scale.

[81] In 1948, six years before UNEF, the Council authorized deployment of almost 600 UNTSO military observers to monitor the Arab–Israeli cease-fire. Resolutions S/773 of 22 May 1948 and S/801 of 29 May 1948. Their operations were placed under the supervision of an office of mediator created by the General Assembly. UNTSO thus was a "hybrid peacekeeping operation." Henry Wiseman, "The United Nations and International Peacekeeping: a Comparative Analysis," in *The United Nations and the Maintenance of International Peace and Security* 263 at 270, UNITAR, 1987. UNEF, however, as we have seen, was authorized solely by the General Assembly. G.A. Res. 1000 (ES-1) of 5 November 1956. The 1960 ONUC operation in the Congo was authorized by the Security Council (S.C. Res. 143 (1960)). The resolution was adopted by 8–0 (China, France, and Britain abstained), although, for a time in late 1960–61, jurisdiction passed to the General Assembly. G.A. Res. 1474 (ES-IV) of 20 September 1960; G.A. Res. 1599(XV) of 15 April 1961; G.A. Res. 1600(XV) of 15 April 1961; G.A. Res. 1601(XV) of 15 April 1961.

not invoke the Council's unique Chapter VII enforcement powers. Yet, neither do they quite fit the parameters of Chapter VI, which deals only with "negotiation, enquiry, mediation, conciliation, arbitration, judicial settlement, resort to regional agencies or arrangements..." (Article 33). Hence, the blue helmets are commonly said to be authorized by "Chapter 6 1/2." This is yet another illustration of the Charter's adaption in practice.

These UN peacekeeping operations have involved more than 700,000 military personnel and cost approximately 12 billion dollars.[82] The space occupied by the fictive Chapter 6 1/2 is fluid, being defined by practice rather than Charter text. A Chapter 6 1/2 operation may begin by the parties' acquiescence in deployment of a peacekeeping force. Over time, however, the operation may incur the hostility of one or several of the parties, requiring either its withdrawal (as in the instance of UNEF in the Sinai) or its difficult and risky transformation into a peace enforcement operation (as with ONUC in the Congo and UNPROFOR in the former Yugoslavia). This phenomenon of "mission-creep," most dramatically evident again during the work of UNPROFOR in Bosnia-Herzegovina during 1993–95, illustrates the ambiguity which may arise in conducting UN "blue helmet" military operations which, although initially not authorized or armed to engage in Chapter VII-based enforcement actions, are assigned new tasks that may involve them in combat operations.[83] Nevertheless, the concept has proven to be of immense utility, filling the wide lacuna between the use of collective force to resist aggression, on the one hand, and, on the other, recourse to pacific measures of persuasion such as hortatory resolutions or mediation.

Expanding the concept of threats to the peace, breaches of the peace, and acts of aggression

Of particular significance is the gradual expansion of UN military intervention to meet threats to peace arising not out of aggression by one state against another but from events occurring within one nation.

The US legal justification for the deployment of ONUC military force to vanquish the Katanga separatists in the Congo was explained in

---

[82] Estimate based on United Nations Peace-Keeping Operations, PS/DPI/Rev. 7, July 1994.

[83] Report of the Secretary-General pursuant to General Assembly resolution 53/35, the fall of Srebrenica A/54/549, 14 November 1999.

February 1963, by then Deputy Assistant Secretary of State Richard N. Gardner, as follows:

First, the Government of the Congo asked the United Nations to come in.

Second, the Security Council authorized the U.N. to go in with a mandate to maintain law and order – a mandate which was subsequently expanded into a mandate to prevent civil war, protect the Congo's territorial integrity, and remove the foreign mercenaries.

Third, the military actions of the U.N. Force were taken in pursuit of these mandates and in self-defense.

He added that "this was not an internal matter – there was a clear threat to international peace and security because of the actual involvement or potential involvement of outside powers."[84]

Despite this explanation, it is clear from the drafting history of the Charter's Articles 39, 42, 43, and 51 that the representatives at San Francisco had not intended to authorize a role for the United Nations in civil wars. Rather, Charter Articles 2(4) and 2(7) appear to forbid such intervention. In practice, however, the Congo was but the first of several UN military involvements in precisely those sorts of conflict: in Yemen, Iraq, the former Yugoslavia, Somalia, Haiti, and Sierra Leone. It is worth emphasizing in this connection that the Charter's prohibition on UN intervention in matters "essentially...domestic" is not, textually, suspended even when a government asks for help in suppressing a domestic insurgency. Indeed, a literal reading of Article 2(7) precludes a positive response to such a request. The practice, however, has been much more flexible, treating an "invitation" from the government of a state as suspending the obligation not to intervene: or, alternatively, construing civil conflict, at least when it exceeds certain levels of virulence, as no longer "primarily...domestic."

The Charter also makes no provision for UN intervention in cases of gross violations of human rights, destruction of democracy, the disintegration of effective governance, or mass starvation and environmental degradation. The literal Charter text would appear to preclude any international action unless such "domestic" crises begin to threaten international peace. That threshold, however, has been gradually lowered in the practice of the United Nations' principal organs. In 1999, UN Secretary-General Kofi Annan stated that gross violations of human

---

[84] Department of State Press Release No. 99, February 22, 1963; 48 Department of State Bull. 477 at 478–79 (1963).

rights and denials of democratic fundamentals can no longer be regarded as purely "domestic" matters. He boldly called on the United Nations to "forge unity behind the principle that massive and systematic violations of human rights – wherever they may take place – should not be allowed to stand" and that the "sovereign state, in its most basic sense, is being redefined by the forces of globalization and international cooperation."[85]

The Secretary-General's observation, far from being outré, is based solidly on practice. Both the General Assembly and the Security Council have invoked Chapter VII measures, in 1966 against the white minority regime in Rhodesia and in 1977 against its equivalent in South Africa, in an effort to end those governments' gross racism.[86] Chapter VII was also invoked in 1994 and military enforcement measures were authorized to reverse the military coup against the democratically elected government of Haiti.[87] In 1998, Chapter VII was again used to threaten the Federal Republic of Yugoslavia with collective measures if it continued to repress its Kosovar minority.[88] On September 28, 2001, the Security Council invoked Chapter VII to impose mandatory sanctions on terrorist groups, thereby extending the Council's enforcement powers to reach non-state actors.[89]

It is increasingly apparent that, in practice, both the Security Council and the General Assembly now regard themselves as entitled to act against oppressive and racist regimes, and, in situations of anarchy, to restore civil society, order, and legitimate governance where these have unraveled.[90] In some instances the United Nations has deployed military force (Congo, Somalia, Haiti, East Timor) or police (Namibia, Cambodia, Mozambique, Haiti) to neutralize or disarm factions or reintegrate them into a cohesive national army and otherwise to help recreate a civil society and establish democratic governance. In its decision in the *Tadic* appeal, the International Criminal Tribunal for the Former Yugoslavia, referring to evidence that "the practice of the Security

---

[85] Report of the Secretary-General on the Work of the Organization, G.A.O.R., 54th Sess., 4th Plen. Meeting, A/54/1, 20 September 1999.

[86] S. Res. 232 (1966) of 16 December 1966 (Rhodesia); S. Res. 418 of 4 November 1977 (South Africa).

[87] S/RES/940 (1994) of 31 July 1994.

[88] S/RES/1160 (1998) of 31 March 1998; S/RES/1199 (1998) of 23 September 1998; S/RES/1203 (1998) of 24 October 1998; S/RES/1244 (1999) of 10 June 1999.

[89] S/RES/1373 of 28 September 2001.

[90] S/RES 794 (1992) of 3 December 1992; S/RES 814 (1993) of 26 March 1993; S/RES 954 (1994) of 4 November 1994.

Council is rich with cases of civil war or internal strife which it classified as a 'threat to the peace' and dealt with under Chapter VII" concluded "that the 'threat to the peace' of Article 39 may include, as one of its species, internal armed conflicts."[91] This marks recognition of the role of practice in interpreting the Charter, sometimes in radical departure from original intent.

The gradual attrition, in UN practice, of states' monopoly over matters of "domestic jurisdiction" has occurred in tandem with an expansion of activities and conditions seen to constitute "threats to the peace." Aggravated instances of racism, colonial repression, massive violations of human rights, tactical starvation, genocide, the overthrow by military juntas of democratically elected governments, and the "harbouring of terrorists"[92] have all begun to be regarded as potentially constituting "threats to the peace" even if they are not instances of "aggression" in the traditional international legal sense.

This expansion of global jurisdiction has not happened at once and, like much legal reform, tends to occur in the guise of "legal fictions." We have noted Richard Gardner, on behalf of the US Government, defending ONUC's use of force to subdue Katanga secessionists in the Congolese civil war, by reference to the "potential involvement of outside powers" which threatened to turn "an internal matter" into "a clear threat to international peace and security."[93] In 1977, the Security Council, invoking Chapter VII, found that the racist policies of the Government of South Africa "are fraught with danger to international peace and security,"[94] thereby opening the way for its first exercise of enforcement powers against a member.[95] Later, the Secretary-General persuaded the Security Council to find a threat to the peace in the Somali civil war because of its "repercussions… on the entire region."[96] In agreeing to intervene with military force under Chapter VII, the Council carefully noted "the unique" and "extraordinary character" of that conflict without further defining it.[97] In determining in 1994 that the rule of the Haitian military junta constituted a threat to peace and security in the

---

[91] *Prosecutor* v. *Tadic*, IT-94-1-AR 72 (October 1995) para. 30.
[92] S/RES/1368 of 12 September 2001.   [93] See n. 84 above.
[94] S. Res. 418 of 4 November 1977.
[95] See Statement of the Secretary-General, S.C.O.R. (XXXII), 2046th Meeting, 4 November 1977.
[96] Letter dated 29 November 1992 from the Secretary-General addressed to the President of the Security Council, U.N. Doc. S/24868 of 30 November 1992.
[97] S/RES/794 of 3 December 1992.

region and authorizing military intervention by a coalition of the willing, the Council referred to "the desperate plight of Haitian refugees" as evidence of a threat to the peace.[98] This has rightly been called "unprecedented in authorizing the use of force to remove one regime and install another."[99] In 1998, the "flow of refugees into northern Albania, Bosnia and Herzegovina and other European countries" was cited by the Council as a justification for invoking Chapter VII in respect of the Kosovo crisis.[100] In reaction to the destruction of the New York World Trade Center, "international terrorism" was classified by the Council "as a threat to international peace and security"[101] and subjected to Chapter VII mandatory sanctions.[102]

These somewhat artificial "international" dimensions of what, in 1945, would have been seen as lamentable but primarily domestic tragedies or criminal matters subject to domestic police enforcement have not been advanced fraudulently or cynically. Rather, the meaning of "threat to the peace, breach of the peace and act of aggression" is gradually being redefined experientially and situationally. For the present, those doing this redefining understandably seek to contain it within familiar, or at least non-threatening, parameters. For example, an intervention to respond to the "inducing of massive flows of refugees" is as yet more acceptable to many governments than intervention to stop a government's slaughter of its own ethnic or political minorities, its subordination of women, or its failure to control calamitous domestic starvation and civil war.

Of course, unlike some governments, most *persons* might accept that the killing or dying of a population or its gross oppression in place deserves at least as much response as does large-scale population displacement across international borders. They might consider quite odd the recourse to anomalous fictions to obscure the gradual attrition of distinctions between what is "domestic" and "international." Nevertheless, the more remarkable fact is that the global system is responding, tentatively and flexibly, through *ad hoc* actions rather than by systematic implementation, to new facts and threats that are redefining the threshold of what is seen to constitute a threat to peace, requiring a powerful collective response.

---

[98] S/RES/940 of 31 July 1994.
[99] Simon Chesterman, *Just War or Just Peace* 151 (2001).
[100] S/RES/1199 of 23 September 1998.   [101] S/RES/1368 of 12 September 2001.
[102] S/RES/1373 of 28 September 2001.

3

The original parameters of self-defense

We have considered the Charter's primary thrust: the prohibition of aggression and enforcement of that ban by collective military measures taken in the name of the new Organization. Only as a secondary, fail-safe resort did the drafters permit members to deploy force in their individual, sovereign capacity, and then only in self-defense against an actual armed attack. Under pressure of changing circumstances, however, this exception to the general prohibition on nations' unilateral recourse to force has also undergone adaption and expansion through institutional practice.

Self-defense: the drafting history

A euphoric tone was set at the San Francisco Conference by the imminence of Allied victory over the Axis. Participants knew that this had been achieved primarily by the effort of the Big Powers. Presented with a draft prepared by those nations' leaders and diplomats, representatives of less-powerful states were little inclined to challenge its fundamentals. They appreciated that no organization for the preservation of peace could succeed unless the principal Powers were willing participants and they realized that such participation had a price.

On the other hand, lesser states had also sacrificed: some had been occupied as a result of failure of the League of Nations, others had voluntarily joined the Allied cause. All had suffered. Understandably, there was some doubt at San Francisco as to whether the new system would really afford better protection than had the Covenant.

Out of this disquiet came an effort, spearheaded by New Zealand, to change the draft from one basically dependent on the Security

45

Council's case-by-case political decisions to another more firmly rooted in a mandatory legal obligation to go to the aid of future victims. New Zealand's proposal would have attached to Article 2(4)'s general prohibition on state use of force a further obligation on "[a]ll members of the Organization ... collectively to resist every act of aggression against any member."[1]

Neither this proposal, nor a parallel version proposed by Norway, was adopted. As a result, the text seems to be clear enough: a mandatory, collective UN response to a threat to the peace or act of aggression must await – and depends on – a positive political decision by the Security Council, one requiring a voting majority[2] as well as unanimity among the permanent members. The adopted text thus imposes no *obligation* on states to respond through the United Nations in defense of a victim state unless the Security Council actually orders them to do so.

By thus making the Council so central to the process, the Charter in effect embedded the centrality of politics and, specifically, the achievement on a case-by-case basis of Big Power unanimity. The speed with which this requirement in practice came to obstruct the system astonished even the pessimists. Systemic weakness was both manifest in, and compounded by, the failure of states to implement Article 43 by committing troops to a standby force for the instant use of the Council against an aggressor. And, in practice, there has been no instance in which states have actually been *ordered* by the Council to respond militarily to defend a victim. To the extent we have had collective security, it has been both *ad hoc* and voluntary.

As we noted in chapter 2, the Council periodically has authorized armed expeditions by "coalitions of the willing." Although it has sometimes *ordered* states to comply with lesser measures, such as embargoes on military supplies, trade, or investment, the Council has only *called on* states to *volunteer* military deployment. This remained true even in the face of extreme provocations such as North Korea's attack on the South and Iraq's invasion of Kuwait. States were invited, but not required, to join the United Nations' military rescue of the victims. There being no legal obligation, most governments were perfectly free to decline the invitation and most did so, even when they agreed that there had been a "threat to the peace, breach of the peace, or act of aggression."

---

[1] 6 U.N.C.I.O., General, Commission I, Doc. 810, I/1/30, June 6, 1945, 342. (Hereafter: New Zealand.)

[2] In 1945, under article 27(3), this needed 7 of 12 votes. It now requires 9 of 15 votes.

The New Zealand representative at San Francisco understood the disappointment a weak form of collective security would engender. "It seemed," he said, "that if nations in the past had been prepared to guarantee security collectively there would have been no war. If it were left to an *ad hoc* decision to decide whether or not to take action, even after the Security Council had decided that an act of aggression had taken place, the door would be open to evasion, appeasement, weaseling and sacrifice... of small nations."[3] His proposed amendment, legally requiring all states to go to the defense of one attacked, actually generated surprisingly wide support, receiving 26 votes, with only 18 opposed. Nevertheless, the requisite majority for amendments at San Francisco being two-thirds, New Zealand's motion failed to carry.

Perhaps this did not really matter. Appeasement and evasion might well have happened anyway, through the attrition of common political will during the Cold War. But at San Francisco the notion of automatic collective responsibility – of all for all – was in the air, even if it failed to find resonance on the pages of the text being negotiated. Another manifestation of this took the form of a demand by some governments for the creation of a completely international police force. "Whatever its theoretical merits," Britain's Whitehall sniffed, "this postulates a greater advance in international cooperation than States are yet prepared to make, as it implies the existence of a world State. Practical questions of size, composition, maintenance, location and command would give rise to controversies on which international agreement would almost certainly be unobtainable. We conclude that the time has not yet come for the creation of such an international force."[4]

By the time the Allied nations gathered at San Francisco to review the draft, it had already become clear to most participants that the Charter would not establish a general normative obligation of all states to join

---

[3] New Zealand, n. 1 above, at 343. The New Zealand position was strongly supported by Peru.

[4] Tentative Proposals by the United Kingdom for a General International Organization, Memorandum A, July 22, 1944, 1 Foreign Relations of the United States, 1944, 670 at 686–87. The Soviet Union characterized the proposal for an "international police force" as "Utopian and unnecessary" although venturing, oddly, that an "international air police force might have value." The Ambassador in the Soviet Union (Harriman) to the Secretary of State, Moscow, July 24, 1944. 1 Foreign Relations of the United States, 1944, 696, 695. See also 1 Foreign Relations of the United States, 1944, Memorandum on an International Security Organization, by the Soviet Union, August 12, 1944, 706 at 711.

in providing every state with collective security, and that it also was far from certain that there would be a standing, or even a standby, military capability for enforcing peace. It followed that the defense of states against aggression could not be left to depend exclusively on the operation of the new global security system. At San Francisco, it became evident that there would have to be provision for states to look after their own self-defense.

The Big Powers, however, were reluctant to concede that collective security under their benevolent aegis might not actually work. The Dumbarton Oaks Proposals were notably silent regarding any residual right of national self-defense. France, the only member of the Big Five to have been vanquished by the Axis, was first to acknowledge the shortcomings of so heavy a reliance on Security Council measures against future aggressors. At San Francisco, its representative advanced a new text:

Should the Council not succeed in reaching a decision, the members of the organization reserve to themselves the right to act as they may consider necessary in the interest of peace, right and justice.[5]

This proposal, which recalls Article 15(7) of the League Covenant, was widely criticized as allowing states too broad discretion in deciding whether to resort to force. Even the terminology eventually agreed upon, preserving states' "inherent right of individual or collective self-defence if an armed attack occurs against a Member of the United Nations" (Article 51) was criticized by Archibald MacLeish, within the US delegation, as "too vague." He "recalled that Germany had entered Poland at the beginning of the present war on the pretext that Poland had attacked her."[6]

The new language did more than open the door to states' autonomous recourse to force. By adding the term "collective" to a provision that essentially licenses victims to defend themselves, it was also intended to accommodate regional or other mutual defense arrangements. One of these, in the Americas, was already in existence. Although essentially collateral to the Charter system, it was designed to do what the Charter does not: legally oblige member states to defend one another against

---

[5] Minutes of the Thirty-Seventh Meeting of the United States Delegation, San Francisco, May 12, 1945, 1 Foreign Relations of the United States, 1945, 674 at 679–80.

[6] Minutes of the Thirty-Sixth Meeting of the United States Delegation, San Francisco, May 11, 1945, 1 Foreign Relations of the United States, 1945, 663 at 665.

attack. Another, establishing the North Atlantic Treaty Organization (NATO), soon followed suit.[7]

Not everyone was happy with this language, which seemed to approve the members' supplementing UN collective security with these potentially free-standing mutual defense agreements. The British were "shocked" that Article 51 would authorize *collective* self-defense. Sir Anthony Eden was reported by the minutes of the US delegation as declaring it "a new thought that self-defence can operate outside of a nation's territorial limits."[8] Despite such misgivings, Article 51 was at last approved overwhelmingly. It represented a compromise with the Latin American champions of the first such regional (Western Hemisphere) defense pact, just then signed at Chapultepec.[9]

Article 51 is not quite a *carte blanche*. It extends the right of individual and collective self-defense only "until the Security Council has taken measures necessary to maintain international peace and security." Asked by US Senator John Connally whether this would not require states to stop defending themselves once the Council acted, John Foster Dulles assured him that "states were not obliged to discontinue their counter-measures taken in self-defence. In other words ... there was concurrent power" as between the Council and the states acting under Article 51.[10] That interpretation is not evident from the text, but it does correctly fore-see its actual implementation, notably during the crisis following Iraq's invasion of Kuwait,[11] and, again, after Al Qaeda's terrorist strike against Washington, DC and New York City. In both instances, the Security Council recognized the right of the attacked state to defend itself with the help of its allies and specifically reaffirmed that right after the Council began to order the taking of collective measures against the attackers.

[7] North Atlantic Treaty of April 4, 1949, T.I.A.S. No. 1964, 34 U.N.T.S. 243. This provides that, in the event of an attack against one party, every other party shall take "such action as it deems necessary, including the use of armed force ..." North Atlantic Treaty of April 4, 1949, articles 5, 11.

[8] Minutes of the Thirty-Sixth Meeting of the United States Delegation, n. 6 above, at 666.

[9] Act of Chapultepec, adopted March 3, 1945 by the Inter-American Conference on War and Peace. This became the progenitor of the Inter-American Treaty of Reciprocal Assistance (Rio Treaty) of September 2, 1947, 62 Stat. 1681, T.I.A.S. 1838, 21 U.N.T.S. 77 (1947). Entered into force December 3, 1948.

[10] Minutes of the Thirty-Sixth Meeting of the United States Delegation, n. 6 above, at 677.

[11] S/RES/678 of 29 November 1990, for example, authorizes "Member States" to use "all necessary means" to drive Iraq out of Kuwait, but also "reaffirms" S/RES/661 of 6 August 1990 which had confirmed Kuwait's authority to engage in individual and collective self-defense under article 51 of the Charter.

Nevertheless, Article 51 as drafted does not sanction continuation of the use of force by states in self-defense after the Council has taken measures. It is only by subsequent practice that the potential coexistence of collective measures with the continued measures in self-defense has become accepted practice.

The San Francisco Conference documents shed light on Article 51's other limitation on the right it accords states and regional organizations to act in self-defense. It was the US delegation which took the lead in inserting after the "inherent right of self defence" the important caveat that the right would arise only "if an armed attack occurs..." This limitation was challenged by Green Hackworth, the State Department's legal adviser, who thought it "greatly qualified the right of self-defence." Governor Harold Stassen, a leader of the American team, replied that "this was intentional and sound. We did not want exercised the right of self-defence before an armed attack had occurred."[12] When another member of the US delegation (Mr. Gates) "posed a question as to our freedom under this provision in case a fleet had started from abroad against an American republic but had not yet attacked" Stassen replied that "we could not under this provision attack the fleet but we could send a fleet of our own and be ready in case an attack came."[13]

This rather quaint exchange illustrates how little the advances in the technology of war had informed the thinking of the drafters, making it necessary thereafter for the Charter to adapt in practice. At San Francisco, however, it is beyond dispute that the negotiators deliberately closed the door on any claim of "anticipatory self-defence," a posture soon to become logically indefensible by the advent of a new age of nuclear warheads and long-range rocketry. In chapter 7 we will examine further the effect of that challenge on the way the Charter has been adapted in practice.

The decision to limit the right of self-defense to situations where there had been an "armed attack" also sadly failed to anticipate, let alone address, the imminent rise in surrogate warfare prompted by rogue states and international terrorists. This seems particularly myopic given the world's recent experience with the vicious surrogate warfare of the Spanish Civil War. Indeed, at Dumbarton Oaks, the Chinese sought to

[12] Minutes of the Forty-Eighth Meeting (Executive Session) of the United States Delegation, San Francisco, May 20, 1945, 1 Foreign Relations of the United States, 1945, 813 at 818.

[13] Minutes of the Thirty-Eighth Meeting of the United States Delegation, San Francisco, May 14, 1945, 1 Foreign Relations of the United States, 1945, 707 at 709.

deal with the problem by proposing a definition of aggression which, in addition to more traditional indicators, included the following acts:[14]

E. Provision [by a state] of support to armed groups, formed within [that state's] territory, which have invaded the territory of another state; or refusal, notwithstanding the request of the invaded state, to take in its own territory all the measures in its power to deprive such groups of all assistance or protection.
  [... and]
G. Provision [by a state] of arms and munitions, or financial or technical assistance to the nationals of another state, calculated to create civil commotion or to overthrow the government of such state.

No action was taken on the Chinese proposals, leaving it to future state practice to reshape states' "inherent right of self-defence" in response to the proliferation of the very acts anticipated in the Chinese proposal. This development will be considered in chapter 4.

Analyzing practice of collective self-defense

The drafting history shows that Article 51 was the result of intense negotiation and uneasy compromise. Its terms sought to elicit maximum support through minimal specificity. The Charter does not even begin to define its key terms: "inherent right," "self-defence" or "armed attack." All this was left, perforce, to interpretation: primarily by the United Nations' political organs and by the actual practices of members and regional groupings.

It is to this interaction between text and practice that we now turn. Although difficult to evaluate, it can provide evidence of the "live" meaning given to inert words by existential experience and transactional process. To evaluate the effect of these meaning-imbuing interactions one must turn to the records of the Security Council and the General Assembly. How is one to interpret this practice and its impact on the relevant norms of the system?

The practice of these organs consists of members' speaking and voting. Faced with one or more of their number seeking to justify resort to armed force, members register their response: positive, negative, or non-committal. In fifty-five years of practice, a pattern of justifications has emerged, sometimes explicitly spelled out, sometimes implicit in the

[14] Tentative Chinese Proposals for a General International Organization, August 23, 1944, 1 Foreign Relations of the United States, 1944, 718 at 725.

situation. Much of the rest of this study focuses on how the members, individually and collectively, in word, vote, and deed, have reacted to these patterns of state practice and explication, which, taken together, may constitute the best available evidence of what the Charter really means today.

Five kinds of justifications stand out, each based on a "creative" interpretation of Article 51:

1. The claim that a state may resort to armed self-defence in response to attacks by terrorists, insurgents or surrogates operating from another state;
2. The claim that self-defence may be exercised against the source of ideological subversion from abroad;
3. The claim that a state may act in self-defence to rescue or protect its citizens abroad.
4. The claim that a state may act in self-defence to anticipate and preempt an imminent armed attack;
5. The claim that the right of self-defence is available to abate an egregious, generally recognized, yet persistently unredressed wrong, including the claim to exercise a right of humanitarian intervention.

These five kinds of claims will be examined in ensuing chapters. In practice, some are now routinely vindicated, others not.

A preliminary question arises. In reviewing UN practice, how much weight should be given to conduct of its organs acting as the collective voice of the members and to the views of states, expressed in word or deed, as a guide to interpreting the text of the Charter? When states repeatedly claim that Article 51 permits use of force in situations at best figuratively or creatively analogous to an "armed attack" and such usage meets with active approval or passive acquiescence in UN political organs, may one conclude that the Charter text, over time and in response to new circumstances, has adapted to permit the claimed "right" to use force? When actions justified in this way are condemned in the debates and resolutions of principal UN organs, may one conclude that the claim has been rejected? Is the verbal behavior and voting of states in UN political organs to be taken as fraught with legal consequences or merely as another manifestation of opportunistic politics?

An examination of some of the leading instances may prompt some answers.

4

Self-defense against state-sponsored terrorists and infiltrators

In December 1965, the General Assembly, without opposition, declared that "subversion and all forms of indirect intervention constitute a violation of the Charter of the United Nations"[1] and can lead "to the creation of situations which threaten international peace and security."[2] By thus linking subversion and indirect intervention to a "threat to international peace and security" which the Charter text (Article 39) brackets with "aggression," the Assembly may be seen to accept that the victims of such intervention are entitled to be the beneficiaries of Chapter VII collective measures ordained by the Security Council. It could also be argued that a state whose "peace and security" has been threatened might justifiably resort to the same use of force in "individual or collective self-defence," as is permitted victims of armed attack by Article 51 of the Charter.

This modification of the strict literal text of Charter Articles 2(4) and 51 has been further expanded in the Assembly's 1974 Resolution, which stipulates:

The actions of a State in allowing its territory, which has been placed at the disposal of another State, to be used by that other State for perpetrating an act of aggression against a third State;

The sending by or on behalf of a State of armed bands, groups, irregulars or mercenaries, which carry out acts of armed force against another State of

---

[1] Declaration on the Inadmissibility of Intervention in the Domestic Affairs of States and the Protection of Their Independence and Sovereignty, A/RES/2131(XX) of 21 December 1966, preamble.

[2] A/RES/2131 (XX) of 21 December 1966, para. 4.

such gravity as to the acts listed above, or its substantial involvement therein...
shall... qualify as an act of aggression...[3]

This, in fact, seemed to be the principle implemented after the terrorist attack on the World Trade Center on September 11, 2001. On the next day, the Security Council condemned that action "as a threat to international peace and security" and, accordingly, "recognized the inherent right of individual or collective self-defence in accordance with the Charter." It called on states "to work together urgently to bring to justice the perpetrators, organizers and sponsors of these terrorist attacks" in order to hold accountable "those responsible for aiding, supporting or harbouring the perpetrators, organizers and sponsors of these acts..."[4] This clearly confirms the right of victim states to treat terrorism as an armed attack and those that facilitate or harbor terrorists as armed attackers against whom, subject to the UN Charter and international law, military force may be used in self-defense.

In this section we will examine the claim of a right to use force in "self-defence" against the territory of a state harboring and abetting insurgents or terrorists and failing to prevent their excursions into other states. Typically, in these circumstances, the state resorting to force asserts that it is acting in self-defense, taking lawful countermeasures against subversion and direct or indirect intervention or aggression. Although the International Law Commission has now spoken on countermeasures,[5] the legality of recourse to force, especially against indirect attacks, remains controversial. Article 50 of the Commission's text on State Responsibility provides that countermeasures "shall not affect...[t]he obligation to refrain from the threat or use of force as embodied in the Charter of the United Nations."[6] It does not, however, try to specify the content of that obligation which, in turn, is determined by reference to the Charter's text and, by extension, to case-by-case institutional practice affecting that text's interpretation. Evidently, much depends upon the text and

---

[3] S. Res. 3314, **XXIX** of 14 December 1974, articles 3(f) and (g).

[4] S/RES/1368 (2001) of 12 September 2001, preamble and paras. 1, 3.

[5] The articles on State Responsibility of the International Law Commission are very relevant but not dispositive in assessing the legality of a state's resort to force in such instances. *State Responsibility, General Principles*, Pt 1, A/CN.4/L.602/Rev. 1 and 2, 9 August 2001. While, for example, it is fairly clear that a state is responsible for the consequences of allowing its territory to be used by forces attacking another state, it is less clear whether the Draft, in such circumstances, permits "countermeasures." In effect, these provisions seem to constitute a *renvoi* back to the auto-interpretative practices of the U.N.'s principal political organs.

[6] *State Responsibility, General Principles*, Pt 1, A/CN.4/L.602/Rev. 1.

practice pertaining to the meaning of "armed attack" in Article 51. Equally evident is the fact that practice has expanded significantly the meaning of that concept.

Actual case-by-case invocations of an expansive claim to self-defense against the bases used by terrorists and infiltrators have met with various legal objections: that a specific countermeasure was disproportionate to the threat posed; that the territory from which a provocation was launched, through no fault of the government, could not be brought under its effective control; or that an attack was directed only at illegally occupied territory, thus giving rise to no right to take countermeasures. This is essentially – as is so often the case – a legal discourse about political acts. But it is a legal discourse in which political organs have a legitimate part that needs to be considered in any account of the law. An examination of some actual instances illustrates the norm-shaping dynamic going on behind the sound and fury of such Charter-invoking claims and counterclaims.

Israel–Egypt (1956)

On October 29, 1956, Israeli armed forces crossed the 1949 cease-fire line into the Sinai. They soon occupied most of that peninsula.[7] The Israeli Government, justifying its recourse to force, argued that Article 51 should be construed to sanction its pursuit of infiltrators and the eradicating of their bases in Egypt. When the US convened the Security Council to propose an "immediate cessation" of hostilities, Israel responded by claiming a right of self-defense against a decade of cross-border provocations by Palestinian *Fedayeen*.[8]

Initially, this line of argument failed to strike a responsive chord among members of the Security Council. While recognizing the evidence of *Fedayeen* infiltration, most deemed Israel's response disproportionate. China, Cuba, Iran, Peru, USSR, US and Yugoslavia joined in voting to require immediate Israeli withdrawal.[9] The resolution failed only owing to British and French vetoes.

The General Assembly, when convened under "Uniting for Peace" procedures, voted to call for withdrawal by a resounding 64 to 5 with 6

---

[7] Chapter 2 examined how these events propelled the General Assembly into a new peacekeeping role ("Chapter 6 1/2").

[8] S.C.O.R., 748th Meeting, 29 October 1956, at 11, para. 71.

[9] Draft Res. S/3710, 749th Meeting, 30 October 1956.

abstentions.[10] The resolution, however, also tacitly acknowledged a link between provocation and response by calling for an end to Palestinian "raids across the armistice lines into neighbouring territory..."[11] That linkage was re-enforced in the mandate of the UNEF force that the Assembly interposed between the belligerents. This authorized UNEF not only to "secure and supervise the cessation of hostilities..."[12] but also to prevent *Fedayeen* infiltration into Israel.[13] It may also be significant that the Assembly at no point condemned Israel for the countermeasures it had taken.

OAS–Dominican Republic (1960)

In 1960, a right to take action against transnational subversion was claimed by the Organization of American States (OAS). Venezuela, an OAS member, had complained that the Dominican Republic's Trujillo dictatorship had tried to assassinate Venezuela's President and to overthrow its government. The OAS condemned this "intervention and aggression" and ordered countermeasures against the offender until it "ceased to constitute a danger to the peace and security of the hemisphere."[14]

Trujillo's dictatorship had few admirers at the United Nations. Nevertheless, Moscow objected to the precedent set by the OAS taking such "enforcement" measures without obtaining the prior approval of the Security Council, in disregard of Charter Article 53. To cure this defect, the USSR proposed that the Council retroactively authorize the regional sanctions already in place.[15]

This may have seemed a Solomonic solution to Moscow, but it generated little support at the UN. Instead, the Council merely took note of the OAS action.[16] The debate, however, did demonstrate widespread

---

[10] Draft Res. S/3710, 749th Meeting, 30 October 1956, para. 1.

[11] Draft Res. S/3710, 749th Meeting, 30 October 1956, para. 2.

[12] G.A. Res. 998(ES-I), A/3276, 563rd Meeting, 4 November 1956.

[13] S.C. Res. 1125(XI) of 2 February 1957.   [14] 1960 U.N.Y.B. 164.

[15] S.C.O.R. (XV), 893rd Meeting, S/4481/Rev. 1 (1960), 8 September 1960, at 2–5, paras. 7–27.

[16] S/4491 of 9 September 1960. Despite this inconclusive disposition, the incident may also have had another kind of significance. The Soviet proposal had proceeded on the assumption that an "enforcement action" taken by the OAS without Security Council authorization could retroactively be legitimated by later Council acquiescence or approval, S.C.O.R. (XV), 893rd Meeting, 8 September 1960, at 4–5, paras. 18–25. This is relevant to the arguments heard almost forty years later (and discussed in

agreement with the proposition that the Dominican subversion of a foreign government, even though not involving an actual armed attack – in the words of the Soviet ambassador – should be seen to constitute "aggression."[17] It also put the Soviets on record as asserting that a failure of a regional organization to secure the needed prior authorization of the Security Council before engaging in an enforcement action could be cured by a subsequent (retroactive) Council grant of permission: a point to which this study reverts in chapter 9.

Israel–Lebanon (1982)

By 1967, the kinds of attacks launched by Palestinians from Sinai before 1956 had become an increasing feature of Israel's border with Lebanon.[18] Israel retaliated with air strikes[19] and, on June 6, 1982, a full-scale invasion that culminated in the occupation of Lebanese territory up to West Beirut. Defending this action at the Security Council, the Israeli ambassador asserted that the Palestine Liberation Organization (PLO) had "turned southern Lebanon into a staging-post for its murderous incursion..." creating "bloody massacres of women and children..." Lebanon, he argued, had "lost much of its sovereignty over its own territory to the terrorist PLO"[20] and had failed to discharge a legal "duty to prevent its territory from being used for terrorist attacks against other States..."[21] Lebanon replied "in the most unequivocal terms" that it could "in no way be held accountable in this context" since the bases from which the attacks originated were not under its control.[22]

---

chapter 9, below) that measures taken by the Economic Community of West African States (ECOWAS) in Liberia and Sierra Leone, and by NATO in Kosovo, even if technically illegal for lack of prior Security Council authorization, could be redeemed by retroactive *ex post facto* Council endorsement.

[17] S.C.O.R. (XV), 893rd Meeting, 8 September 1960, at 3, para. 14.

[18] S/12598, Letter dated 13 March 1978 from the representative of Israel to the Secretary-General. See also S/15194, Report of the Secretary-General on UNIFIL for 11 December 1981–3 June 1982, 10 June 1982, at 11, paras. 49–50. See also Christine Gray, *International Law and the Use of Force* 100 (2000).

[19] S/12600, Letter dated 15 March 1978 from the representative of Lebanon to the President of the Security Council. See also S. Res. 425 (1978), calling for Israel "immediately to cease its military action against Lebanese territorial integrity and withdraw forthwith its forces from all Lebanese territory..." (para. 2).

[20] S.C.O.R. (XXXVII), 2331st Meeting, 23 February 1982, at 5, paras. 46, 49.

[21] S/15132, Letter dated 27 May 1982 from the representative of Israel to the Secretary-General.

[22] S/15087, Letter dated 17 May 1982 from the representative of Lebanon to the President of the Security Council.

Ireland introduced a resolution into the Council that made no judgment as between these contentions but demanded "that Israel withdraw all its forces forthwith..." This was adopted unanimously.[23] "When is the Council galvanized into action?" the Israeli representative complained. "When Israel, after years of unparalleled restraint finally resorts to the exercise of its right of self-defence, the fundamental and inalienable right of any State, which is also recognized by the Charter..."[24] Recounting the numerous attacks from Lebanese safe havens, he asked, "how many Israelis have to be killed by the PLO terrorists for the Council to be persuaded that the limits of our endurance have been reached?"[25] Israel needed to protect its citizenry against groups that "have their head-quarters, training grounds and bases of operation in Lebanon... the... logistic centre and refuge for members of the terrorist internationale from all over the world."[26] The plea fell on stony ground. A Spanish resolution rejecting Israel's justification and demanding that "all hostilities... be stopped" within six hours, although vetoed by the US as "not sufficiently balanced,"[27] nevertheless received the affirmative votes of all other Council members.

By June 24, the Israeli forces had come close to the center of Beirut. France proposed the despatch of a UN force to interpose itself and to neutralize West Beirut.[28] In the Security Council this proposal was vetoed by the US.[29] By then, having reached its objectives, Israel proclaimed a unilateral cease-fire.[30]

Four days later, the General Assembly, convened in its seventh emergency session in accordance with the "Uniting for Peace" resolution, voted 127 to 2 (with only Israel and the United States opposed and no abstentions) to express alarm at "Israel's acts of aggression..." to reaffirm the fundamental principles of Lebanese "sovereignty, territorial integrity, unity and political independence," and to demand that "Israel withdraw all its military forces forthwith and unconditionally." It also condemned Israel "for its non-compliance..." with earlier Council

[23] S/RES 509 of 6 June 1982.
[24] S.C.O.R. (XXXVII), 2375th Meeting, 6 June 1982, at 4, para. 36.
[25] S.C.O.R. (XXXVII), 2375th Meeting, 5 June 1982, at 4, para. 38.
[26] S.C.O.R. (XXXVII), 2375th Meeting, 5 June 1982, at 5, para. 41.
[27] S.C.O.R. (XXXVII), 2377th Meeting, 8 June 1982, at 3, para. 23 (vote) and para. 27 (US explanation of vote).
[28] S/15255, 25 June 1982.
[29] S.C.O.R. (XXXVII), 2381st Meeting, 26 June 1982, at 2, para. 12.
[30] 1982 U.N.Y.B. 440.

resolutions.[31] A cease-fire in the Beirut area finally took effect on August 12,[32] whereupon a three-nation peacekeeping force (France, Italy, US) was deployed.

By mid-December, despite further military and diplomatic[33] skirmishes, the situation had partially stabilized. Unanimously, the General Assembly again called for restoration of "the exclusive authority of the Lebanese State throughout its territory up to the internationally recognized boundaries."[34] However, it also "took note" of the decision of the Lebanese Government to expel all PLO forces from its territory:[35] the Assembly's way of loosely linking its demand for the occupiers' withdrawal with removal of the provocations that had engendered Israeli countermeasures.

Not everyone accepts such linkage or any other justification for the Israeli invasion. Professor Christine Gray reports that

the mere fact that many states regarded Israel's occupation of the West Bank and Gaza, the Golan and (until 2000) areas of South Lebanon as illegal was enough for them to condemn Israel's use of force against cross-border attacks by irregulars. They say that Israel has no right to be in these territories and so no right to invoke self-defence against attacks on their forces in these territories or against attacks on Israel designed to secure its withdrawal from the territories it occupied illegally.[36]

Perhaps. It needs to be recalled, however, that the stated purpose of these PLO attacks was not merely to recapture "illegally occupied territory" but to eliminate the State of Israel. In that light, Israel's claim to be acting in self-defense precisely poses the question whether such a right arises against a state which harbors infiltrators and permits transborder subversion, yet has not itself participated in these armed attacks. The Assembly appears at least tacitly to have understood here, as it did with respect to the Sinai war of 1956, that the curbing of those using a neighboring state as a base for attacks on Israel was a necessary part of any process for ending Israeli occupation of the territory used to stage such attacks.

---

[31] G.A. Res. ES-7/5 of 26 June 1982.   [32] 1982 U.N.Y.B. 452.

[33] See S.C. Res. 516 of 1 August 1982; S.C. Res. 517 of 4 August 1982; S.C. Res. 518 of 12 August 1982.

[34] G.A. Res. 37/123E of 16 December 1982.

[35] These forces were evacuated to Tunis with the agreement of the parties.

[36] Gray, n. 18 above, at 102.

US–Nicaragua (1980–1986)

In the El Salvador civil war (1980–86), the US claimed the right to use force to support the Salvadoran government against insurgents being aided by neighboring Nicaragua. Washington argued that this support was lawful as an exercise of collective self-defense. The issue was canvassed before the Security Council, the General Assembly, and the International Court of Justice. In those forums, the US claimed the right to combat Nicaraguan intervention by supporting an insurgency against Nicaragua's Sandinista government – fighting fire with fire – as well as by direct retaliatory military action against Nicaraguan facilities.

Nicaragua first took its complaints against US "covert aggression" to the Security Council in March 1982.[37] While denying Managua's charges as "groundless,"[38] Washington's representative accused Nicaragua of supplying arms and training to the El Salvador insurgents[39] and warned that the US would "assist others to defend themselves under circumstances consistent with our legal and political obligations and with the Charter."[40] A resolution offered by Panama that would have appealed to member states to refrain from direct or indirect, overt or covert, use of force against any country of the region[41] was vetoed by the United States on the ground that it failed to note Nicaraguan intervention in the affairs of neighboring states.[42] Nevertheless, it received 12 votes in favor, with only the US opposed and Britain and Zaire abstaining.[43]

The following year, Nicaragua convened the Council to examine "a new aggressive escalation of acts by the American Administration, in the form of massive infiltration of military units and task forces of counter-revolutionaries..."[44] The United States countered by asserting that Nicaragua's Sandinistas had sought "to destabilize the Government of El Salvador" and that those efforts "are so clear that they cannot any longer be denied..."[45]

Nicaragua made further complaints to the Security Council on May 5, 1983. On May 19 the Council unanimously reaffirmed "the right

---

[37] S.C.O.R. (XXXVII), 2335th Meeting, 25 March 1982 at 3, para. 31.
[38] S.C.O.R. (XXXVII), 2347th Meeting, 2 April 1982 at 2, para. 6.
[39] S.C.O.R. (XXXVII), 2347th Meeting, 2 April 1982 at 2, para. 7.
[40] *Ibid.*   [41] S/14941.
[42] S.C.O.R. (XXXVII), 2347th Meeting, 2 April 1982, at 14–15, paras. 142–148.
[43] S.C.O.R. (XXXVII), 2347th Meeting, 2 April 1982, at 14, para. 140.
[44] S.C.O.R. (XXXVIII), 2420th Meeting, 23 March 1983, at 1, para. 4.
[45] S.C.O.R. (XXXVIII), 2420th Meeting, 23 March 1983, at 12, para. 99.

of Nicaragua and of all other countries in the area to live in peace and security, free from outside interference . . ."[46] In the ensuing five months, however, Managua continued to complain of armed attacks and on September 12 requested another Council meeting to consider the aerial and naval bombardment of its ports and airports by the CIA,[47] which, it said, amounted to a generalized "policy of war and aggression . . ."[48] In March 1984, it reported that American forces had mined Nicaraguan harbors.[49]

Reaction in the Council was vigorous. For the first time, France joined in condemning this "blockade in disguise"[50] and Britain's representative said that his government "deplores the mining of Nicaraguan waters."[51] A resolution condemning these acts received 13 favorable votes but was vetoed by the US (with the UK abstaining).[52] Washington again claimed that the text took insufficient account of the violations of sovereignty committed under Nicaraguan sponsorship against its neighbors.[53] Clearly, however, support in the United Nations for the US position, never strong, was eroding rapidly.

The erosion extended beyond the political organs. In June 1986, responding to a formal complaint by Nicaragua, the International Court of Justice delivered a judgment relating to some of the same issues.[54] By a decisive vote of 12 to 3 the Court rejected "the [US] justification of collective self-defence . . ." because, for that justification to succeed, the victim state must adduce credible evidence of an armed attack. It also held that Article 51 requires any state claiming to use force in collective self-defense to report its action to the Security Council and noted that the US had not done so. It also found no evidence that El Salvador had invited US help against Nicaragua under Charter Article 51.[55]

More generally, the US was found to have violated the Charter's prohibition on the unauthorized use of force by mining and attacking

---

[46] S/RES 530 (1983). S.C.O.R. (XXXVIII), 2437th Meeting, 19 May 1983, at 3, para. 28.

[47] S.C.O.R. (XXXVIII), 2477th Meeting, 13 September 1983, at 1–2, paras. 3–18.

[48] S.C.O.R. (XXXVIII), 2477th Meeting, 13 September 1983, at 4, para. 37.

[49] S.C.O.R. (XXXIX), 2525th Meeting, 30 March 1984, at 2, para. 8.

[50] S.C.O.R. (XXXIX), 2527th Meeting, 2 April 1984, at 1, para. 7.

[51] S.C.O.R. (XXXIX), 2529th Meeting, 4 April 1984, at 18, para. 169.

[52] S.C.O.R. (XXXIX), 2529th Meeting, 4 April 1984, at 26, para. 252.

[53] S.C.O.R. (XXXIX), 2529th Meeting, 4 April 1984, at 25–26, paras. 238–249.

[54] Case concerning Military and Paramilitary Activities in and against Nicaragua (*Nicaragua* v. *United States of America*), Merits, Judgment, I.C.J. Reports, 1986, p. 14.

[55] *Nicaragua*, at 102–105, paras. 193–199.

Nicaraguan ports,[56] by "organizing and encouraging the organization of irregular forces or armed bands" in Nicaragua and by these "participating in acts of civil strife..."[57] Moreover, the Court was unconvinced that any support Nicaragua was giving the Salvadoran insurgents had crossed Article 51's requisite threshold of an armed attack[58] or met the General Assembly's Definition of Aggression.[59] To qualify, the Court thought, the evidence would have had to show a pattern of deliberate despatch of irregular armed forces into El Salvador from Nicaragua. For these purposes, mere evidence of "assistance to rebels in the form of the provision of weapons or logistical support"[60] would not suffice. Given the facts, the US might have been within its rights in aiding the Salvadoran authorities to combat their domestic insurgency on Salvadoran territory, but not in striking back by fomenting, arming, and aiding a counter-insurgency in Nicaragua.[61]

The decision of the Court has been criticized for misreading the facts, as well as the scale, of Nicaraguan involvement in the Salvadoran civil war. Even stronger has been criticism of the majority's decision that a state defending itself against an externally supported infiltration may not carry the war back to its source in a harboring state until the level of external support crosses the threshold of a major transnational military commitment.

This criticism is evident in Judge Sir Robert Jennings' partial dissent:

This looks to me neither realistic nor just in the world where power struggles are in every continent carried on by destabilization, interference in civil strife, comfort, aid and encouragement to rebels and the like. The original scheme of the United Nations Charter, whereby force would be deployed by the United Nations itself, in accordance with the provisions of Chapter VII of the Charter, has never come into effect. Therefore, an essential element in the Charter design is totally missing. In this situation it seems dangerous to define unnecessarily strictly the conditions for lawful self-defence, so as to leave a large area where both a forcible response to force is forbidden, and yet the United Nations employment of force, which was intended to fill that gap, is absent.[62]

---

[56] *Nicaragua*, at 118, para. 227.
[57] *Nicaragua*, at 118, para. 228.
[58] *Nicaragua*, at 119–121, 127, paras. 230–234, 248–249.
[59] G.A. Res. 3314(**XXIX**) of 14 December 1974.
[60] *Nicaragua* v. *United States of America*, n. 54 above, at 103–104, para. 195.
[61] *Nicaragua* v. *United States of America*, at 126, para. 246.
[62] Jennings, *Nicaragua* v. *United States of America*, at 543–44.

According to Professor Gray, however, "the vast majority of states remain firmly attached to a narrow conception of self-defence"[63] and the Court's majority appears to have captured that view, at least in part. Nevertheless, a threshold appears to have been recognized, even if the majority of judges did not think it had been crossed by the Nicaraguan authorities. It will also become apparent that Judge Jennings', rather than the majority's, view was adopted by the Security Council in its decision following the Al Qaeda attack on the US from Afghanistan (see below, chapter 6).

Turkey–Iraq (1995)

In 1995, the Iraqi Government reported the invasion of its north-western territory by Turkish forces in pursuit of Kurdish-secessionist insurgents. It condemned these violations of Iraqi sovereignty[64] and decried the Turkish military's bombardment of villages as well as attacks on civilians and property.[65]

Turkey responded that its forces had already withdrawn[66] and justified its actions as a necessary response to frequent Kurdish use of Iraqi territory for damaging cross-border attacks. Since Iraq appeared unable to curb these activities, Ankara said, its forces were entitled to act in self-defense.[67] To this Iraq replied that it had been the illegal US and UK military intervention in Northern Iraq – some of it from bases in Turkey – that had destroyed Baghdad's capacity to prevent such activity in its border region.[68]

The following year, Iraq complained anew of Turkish aggression in messages to the Secretary-General and the Security Council.[69] Notably, these complaints did not lead to a meeting of, let alone action by, the Council or the Assembly. This may be attributed, in part, to lack of sympathy with the regime of Saddam Hussein. It may also be that the international system, at least in practice if not yet in theory, was growing more accepting of the (proportionate) use of force by a state against neighboring states that persist in providing safe havens for the cross-border incursions of irregular forces. Thus, in 1996, we see self-defense

---

[63] Gray, n. 18 above, at 119.   [64] 1995 U.N.Y.B. 494. S/1995/272, 7 April 1995.
[65] S/1995/540, 9 May 1995.   [66] S/1995/605, 24 July 1995.
[67] *Ibid.*, 1995 U.N.Y.B. 494.   [68] S/1995/272, 7 April 1995.
[69] S/1996/401; S/1996/762; S/1996/860; S/1996/1018. See 1996 U.N.Y.B. 236–37. For Turkey's response, see S/1995/605; 1996 U.N.Y.B. 237.

invoked again, this time by Iran as it pursued Kurdish armed bands ("organized terrorist mercenaries") into Iraq and launched aerial assaults against the military bases from which their attacks on Iran originated.[70]

The law of countermeasures against terrorism

There are other instances in which states have asserted a right of self-defense against insurgents, including the right to strike back at territory from which the attackers originate. In the 1990s, Senegal invaded Guinea–Bissau, Thailand conducted incursions into Burma, and Tajikistan pursued irregulars into Afghanistan.[71] These are no longer exceptional claims, and the international system now appears increasingly to acquiesce in this expanded reading of the right of self-defense under Charter Article 51.

Two historic UN General Assembly resolutions are relevant to, although scarcely determinative of, the legal problem implicit in every use of force against so-called "indirect aggression." The 1970 Declaration on Principles of International Law concerning Friendly Relations and Co-Operation among States in Accordance with the Charter of the United Nations,[72] adopted by consensus, contains the following:

Every state has the duty to refrain from organizing, instigating, assisting or participating in acts of civil strife or terrorist acts in another state or acquiescing in organized activities within its territory directed towards the commission of such acts, when the acts referred to in the present paragraph involve a threat or use of force.

While this principle is clearly applicable to at least some of the cases considered in this section, the Declaration is silent as to what constitutes a "permissible level of response" to a violation of its prohibition on aiding and abetting civil strife.

In 1974, again by consensus, the Assembly adopted a resolution[73] that includes the following as part of a definition of prohibited actions constituting aggression:

(f) The sending by or on behalf of a State of armed bands, groups, irregulars or mercenaries, which carry out acts of armed force against another State of

---

[70] S/25843 and S/1996/602, 29 July 1996. See also 1996 U.N.Y.B. 268–69.

[71] Gray, n. 18 above, at 103.   [72] G.A. Res. 2625(XXV) of 24 October 1970.

[73] G.A. Res. 3314(XXIX) of 14 December 1974.

such gravity as to amount to [the forms of direct aggression] listed above, or its substantial involvement therein.

The prohibition does not specify what "sending" means. Does it include "permitting," or "tolerating"? It also does not explain what, if any, rights accrue to a state which is a victim of violations. Even if an action by one state in supporting the enemies of another were found to fit within the definition of "aggression" against which the Council may take collective measures under Article 39, would that also satisfy the requirement of an "armed attack" established by Charter Article 51 as a precondition to a lawful armed response in self-defense by the victim and its allies? It seems logical, but not necessarily self-evident, that any action rising to the level of "aggression" – including indirect aggression – would also satisfy the criterion of an "armed attack" against which forceful measures of self-defense may be taken until the Council has invoked effective collective measures.

The ICJ majority, in the *Nicaragua* case, set a high threshold but seemed to envisage that, if there were sufficient evidence of a persistent, large-scale pattern of support for indirect aggression, that would indeed qualify the victim to resort to military force in self-defense under Article 51. In practice, too, there may be emerging in the political organs a greater tolerance for states that carry their wars with terrorists and insurgents across borders to strike at safe havens.

Here, as elsewhere in the discussion of controversial legal doctrines, much appears to depend on evidence of the facts and their context. Most likely to be an unacceptable response is a prolonged invasion of sovereign territory, accompanied by high civilian casualties, as exemplified by Israel's occupation of Southern Lebanon in 1982. This was regarded as disproportionate, even in response to demonstrable and serious provocations. On the other hand, Israel's 1956 strike against *Fedayeen* bases in the Sinai, and the Turkish and Iranian incursions into Kurdish havens in Iraq, seem to have been allowed to pass as proportionate and tolerable, in response to serious and well-documented provocations. So, too, Senegal's 1992 and 1995 incursions into Guinea–Bissau to strike at safe havens used as bases by opposition forces[74] and Tajiki operations against irregular forces operating against its territory from Afghanistan.[75]

---

[74] *Keesings Contemporary Archives*, 1992, 3928; *Keesings Contemporary Archives*, 1995, 40396.

[75] Communications regarding Tajikistan's military response to incursions of mujahedin from Afghanistan. 1993 U.N.Y.B. 383. S/26110 of 14 July 1993 (Russia); S/26091 of

In none of these instances did the UN political organs feel it necessary to censure the (brief) use of force by an aggrieved party. Similarly, no UN censure followed the 1998 US bombing of targets in the Sudan and Afghanistan, although some criticism did emanate from states in non-UN forums.[76] Reporting its action to the Security Council under Article 51, Washington said it was acting in self-defense against those responsible for the destruction of American embassies in Tanzania and Kenya and to deter further attacks. Indeed, a year later, the Security Council condemned the sheltering and training of terrorists by the Taliban of Afghanistan,[77] and in May 2000, Russian President Vladimir Putin warned the Taliban authorities of his intent to take "preventive measures if necessary"[78] to stop support for Islamic militants fighting in Chechnya and the former Soviet Republics of Central Asia.

Some of these matters clarified beyond reasonable disputation when irregulars hijacked US civil aircraft and flew them into the twin towers of the New York World Trade Center and the Pentagon, reportedly killing more than 5,000 civilians. US President George W. Bush immediately promised to attack Afghanistan if its authorities failed to close down terrorist camps and networks on its soil.[79] The UN Security Council quickly recognized a right of the US and its allies to use force in individual or collective self-defense against this threat to international peace and security, while also recognizing the culpability of those "harbouring the perpetrators, organizers and sponsors" of terrorist acts.[80]

The speed and focus of the Security Council's response reflects in part its physical proximity to the scene of the crime. Presumably, it is clarity of the facts, the evidence, and the context that count most in determining systemic reaction. While several resorts to force have been approved, or passed over in silence by the UN system, not every such action has been condoned. Thus, in September 2000, the Security Council specifically rejected the Rwandan authorities' claim to a right to attack Hutu insurgents operating out of neighboring territory. It expressed "unreserved

---

Footnote 75 (*cont.*)
13 July 1993 (Tajikistan); S/26145 of 22 July 1993 and S/26814 of 7 October 1993 (Afghanistan).
[76] But see, below, ch. 6 (p. 95).   [77] S/RES/1267 of 15 October 1999.
[78] *New York Times*, May 25, 2000, at A7.
[79] *New York Times*, September 21, 2001, at 1.
[80] S/RES/1368 (2001) of 12 September 2001, preamble and para. 3. See, further in confirmation, S/RES/1373 of 28 September 2001.

condemnation" of this "violation of the sovereignty and territorial integrity of the Democratic Republic of the Congo."[81]

There is discernible evolution, as well as occasional reaffirmation, in the way the international system has reacted to the various instances of the use of force against insurgents' and terrorists' safe havens. The incongruities only partly obscure a growing consistent pragmatism that is essentially fact-specific without being idiosyncratic. In each recent instance, UN organs seem to have eschewed narrowly dogmatic insistence on a traditional armed attack by a national army as the sole justification for an armed response in self-defense. Instead, they have focused on relevant evidence, weighing the seriousness of each claim of necessity[82] and the proportionality of each aggrieved party's countermeasures.

It is becoming clear that a victim-state may invoke Article 51 to take armed countermeasures in accordance with international law and UN practice against any territory harboring, supporting or tolerating activities that culminate in, or are likely to give rise to, insurgent infiltrations or terrorist attack. That much is becoming cognizable as applicable law. But who applies that law? Not alone, surely, the state from which insurgents and terrorists launch their attacks, nor any state claiming to be the victim of such an attack. Rather, the international system has a "quasi-jury," consisting of the United Nations' principal political organs – the Security Council and General Assembly – and its judicial organ (the ICJ). These, of course, in their appreciation of the facts are influenced by the global information network through which public

---

[81] *New York Times*, May 20, 2000, at A4; S/RES/1304 of 16 June 2000, para. 1.

[82] It is sometimes asserted that the relevant standard was set out almost a century and a half ago in a famous exchange between Britain and the U.S. The 1837 *Caroline* incident involved a pre-emptive attack by the British in Upper Canada against a ship in American waters used by American Feenian raiders to challenge British rule in Canada. In an exchange of correspondence to determine responsibility for damage done, the American Secretary of State observed that such action in self-defense could be legitimate only if taken in response to a "necessity" that is "instant, overwhelming, leaving no choice of means and no moment for deliberation" and that this response should involve "nothing unreasonable or excessive, since the act justified by the necessity of self-defence must be limited by that necessity and kept clearly within it." For Britain, Lord Ashburton accepted the correctness of that statement of the law. Wheaton, *Elements of International Law* (1866), Carnegie Endowment Classics of International Law (1936), p. 441 n., citing *Webster's Dip. and Off. Papers* 112–20. While the continued relevance of this test is challenged by some modern scholars in light of article 2(4) of the UN Charter (*see* Gray, n. 18 above, at 105–06), Jennings and Watts assert that the *Caroline* "aptly set out" the "basic elements" of the law. Jennings and Watts, *Oppenheim's International Law*, 9th edn., vol. I, pt. 1, p. 420 (1992). See also Malcolm Shaw, *International Law* 691–92 (3rd edn., 1991).

opinion is informed and manifested. To these "quasi-jurors" a state taking countermeasures in self-defense must demonstrate that it has identified correctly the place from which it was attacked, that the authorities in that place deliberately, knowingly or recklessly permitted the attack to occur, and that the victim's response is proportionate, carefully calibrated to minimize casualties among the innocent, and concomitant with regard for the independence and territorial integrity of the state against which action is taken.

5

Self-defense against ideological subversion

In chapter 4 we examined the legality of states' use of force to pursue transnational insurgents or terrorists to their bases in neighboring states. We saw instances in which this recourse to force was justified successfully as "self-defence" within the meaning of the Charter's Article 51. We turn now to a related justification: the claim of a state to use force in collective self-defense against another kind of indirect aggression, namely, the export of "ideological subversion." By this has been meant the sort of encouragement given by communist states to peoples' liberation movements and by Western states to democratic resistance behind the Iron Curtain. Although the phenomenon rarely implicated outright military subversion of a government, it had important geopolitical ramifications during the Cold War, when any overturning of a government aligned with either the USSR or the US was seen to have direct strategic consequences for the balance of power. In that confrontational era, each side claimed that any ideological realignment of one of their clients, even if brought about by purely domestic events, must have been inspired by, and thus was attributable to, the other side, therefore giving rise to the right to use force as appropriate countermeasure in "collective self-defence."

The response of states and international institutions to this justification has been entirely and resoundingly negative. However, the same justification is recently beginning to be heard again, this time in the theological–ideological conflict between forces of Islamic fundamentalism and more tolerant societies, including other more liberal Islamic states, secular India, and the Western societies in which religions have been disestablished. It is too early to judge whether the claim of a right to use force in self-defense against the export of militant theocratic ideology, or of liberal democracy and religious pluralism, will encounter greater acceptance in the practice of states and international organizations than did the Cold War claim to a right to use force against the export of ideological subversion.

Warsaw Pact–Hungary (1956)

In 1956, just as Israel was embarking on its invasion of Egypt (chapter 4, p. 55 above), Soviet forces marched into Hungary, ousting the newly established liberal regime of Prime Minister Imre Nagy, which had announced its intention to leave the Soviet-dominated Warsaw Pact Organization and to declare Hungary neutral in the Cold War.

At the United Nations, Soviet representatives argued that the Hungarian uprising had been instigated by the West and was led by agents of NATO. The Warsaw Pact claimed to be acting in self-defense against an indirect aggression conducted by the West through stealth, propaganda, and ideological subversion.

This charge was discussed by the Security Council between October 28 and November 4, 1956,[1] with the Soviet representative accusing France, the US and the UK of giving "encouragement to the armed rebellion which is being conducted by a reactionary underground movement against the legal government of Hungary"[2] and pointing to "multi-million dollar appropriations" by the US Congress "to encourage subversive activities against the legal Governments of the peoples' democracies" of Eastern Europe in order to "overthrow them and replace them by...reactionary regimes..."[3]

In response, the US introduced a resolution "deploring the use of Soviet military forces to suppress the efforts of the Hungarian people to reassert their rights" and calling on the USSR "to desist forthwith from...armed intervention..." in that nation's internal affairs.[4] Although vetoed by the Soviets, it received the affirmative votes of all other members of the Council except India, which abstained. This constituted an unqualified rejection of the expansive "self-defence" justification advanced by Moscow. The Belgian representative stated: "We are faced with a case of flagrant aggression..."[5] No member of the Council accepted the Soviet representative's explanation that "this situation

---

[1] S.C.O.R., 746th, 752nd–754th Meetings, 28 October–4 November 1956.
[2] S.C.O.R., 746th Meeting, 28 October 1956, at 3, para. 14.
[3] S.C.O.R., 746th Meeting, 28 October 1956, at 3, para. 15.
[4] S/3730 and Rev. 1, 4 November 1956.
[5] S.C.O.R. (XI), 754th Meeting, 4 November 1956, at 6, para. 34.

in Hungary has come about partly as a result of the participation of Western Powers, particularly the United States of America in subversive activities against the people's regime"[6] or that "a powerful centre for subversive activities against the Hungarian People's Republic is at present operating in Austria, a centre which has as its object the instigation of further disorders in Hungary."[7] No credence whatever was given to the Warsaw Pact nations' claim to be invoking treaty-provisions for mutual assistance against aggression.[8]

Over USSR objections, the Council voted by 10 votes to 1[9] to convene the Second Emergency Session of the General Assembly. There, by a vote of 48 to 11 with 16 abstentions,[10] a resolution was quickly adopted expressing "deep concern" at "the violent repression by the Soviet forces" and calling on Moscow "to withdraw...without any further delay."[11] Over the next weeks, as the facts became clearer, the majority arrayed against the Soviet Union increased until, on December 12, a majority of 55 to 8, with 13 abstentions, voted to "condemn" Soviet violation of the Charter "in depriving Hungary of its liberty and independence and the Hungarian people of the exercise of their fundamental rights" while calling on Moscow "to desist forthwith..."[12] A month later, a decision to create a Special Committee to "establish and maintain direct observation in Hungary and elsewhere, taking testimony, collecting evidence and receiving information" received 59 votes to 8, with 10 abstentions.[13]

It is instructive to compare this Assembly action to its handling of the concurrent Israeli invasion of Egypt, discussed in chapter 4. In the absence of an actual armed attack on either, the members seemed to reject equally Israeli and Soviet efforts to justify their recourse to force as instances of "self-defence." Nevertheless, it is notable that the Soviets were much more strongly censured in both Council and Assembly than was Israel. Ireland's Ambassador Boland spoke for a large majority when he said of Moscow that "among the Members of the United Nations which have in the past held themselves out as champions of the right of national self-determination is the Soviet Union...I know that for us in Ireland – and I venture to think that for the peoples of many other of

---

[6] S.C.O.R. (XI), 754th Meeting, 4 November 1956, at 8, para. 47.
[7] S.C.O.R. (XI), 754th Meeting, 4 November 1956, at 9, para. 48.
[8] S.C.O.R. (XI), 754th Meeting, 4 November 1956, at 10, para. 53.
[9] S/3733, 4 November 1956.   [10] 1956 U.N.Y.B. 85.
[11] G.A. Res. 1005 (ESII), 571st Meeting, 9 November 1956.
[12] G.A. Res. 1131 (XI), 12 December 1956.
[13] G.A. Res. 1132 (XI), 10 January 1957. 1957 U.N.Y.B. 89.

the smaller nations represented here – any future mention of national independence or anti-colonialism or the right of self-determination by any spokesman of the Soviet Union will always invoke in our minds a single name, ... the name of Hungary."[14]

The Israeli invasion of Egypt evoked far milder criticism. This may have been in part because the Israeli attack on Egypt did not inflict anything comparable to the 100,000 casualties caused by Soviet forces in Hungary. Mostly, however, governments seemed to hold Egypt at least partly responsible for *Fedayeen* attacks from its territory on Israel but to disbelieve Russia's claim that the Hungarian uprising had been instigated by the West. The difference in reaction seems to be attributable less to differences between the legal justifications proffered by Israel and the Soviets than to the difference in credibility of the facts adduced in justification of resort to force. Evidence of "ideological subversion" in the Hungarian instance evoked little response at the United Nations, whereas evidence of the infiltration of armed bands carried considerable verisimilitude. This contrast in reactions is evident not only in words spoken at the United Nations but also in action taken. The Assembly continued for years to ostracize and treat as illegitimate the government installed by Russian troops in Hungary.[15] Its far milder response to Israel's invasion of Egypt was to establish a buffer zone in the Sinai, patrolled by UN "blue helmets" authorized to supervise Israeli withdrawal but also to prevent further *Fedayeen* cross-border infiltration.

US–Dominican Republic (1965)

On April 28, 1965, the US invaded the Dominican Republic, where a right-wing junta had been overthrown by young leftist officers. At the Security Council meeting convened on May 1, the USSR accused Washington of flagrant aggression.[16] In reply, the US argued that "a group of well-known communists, many trained in Cuba, had taken control of what was initially a democratic movement" to overthrow the

---

[14] G.A.O.R. (ESII), 568th Plen. Meeting, 8 November 1956, at 28, para. 93.

[15] For several years after 1956, the Assembly voted to "reserve its position" on the legitimacy of credentials presented by diplomats claiming to represent Hungary as a symbolic form of disapproval. Report of the Credentials Committee, G.A.O.R. (XII), Annexes, vol. 1, item 3, A/3773 (1957); other Reports of Credentials Committees: A/4074 (1958); A/4346 (1959); A/4743 (1960); A/5055 (1961); A/5395 (1962). The practice continued until 1963.

[16] S.C.O.R. (XX), 1196th Meeting, 3 May 1965, at 3, para. 12.

junta[17] and that this group's principles were incompatible with the inter-American system. Any taking of power by communism *per se* was claimed to be tantamount to foreign military intervention.[18]

Russia was not alone in condemning this "sanctimonious hypocrisy,"[19] finding support from the Foreign Ministries of Chile, Colombia, Peru, Uruguay, and Venezuela.[20] Uruguay, in particular, expressed deep "displeasure"[21] at actions that went "beyond the body of norms existing in the inter-American system…"[22] France, too, accused Washington of initiating an "armed intervention the necessity of which is not apparent."[23] Although a Soviet resolution condemning the invasion and calling for immediate withdrawal of US forces was voted down, Washington failed to obtain the support of such traditional friends as France, Ivory Coast, Jordan, Malaysia, and Uruguay.[24] When, thereafter, the matter was debated in the General Assembly, the US action was condemned not only by members of the Soviet bloc but also by Ecuador,[25] Kenya,[26] and Mexico.[27]

It is apparent from the debate in the UN organs that most states rejected not only the US version of the facts – that is, the alleged causal link between Soviet–Cuban subversion and the Dominican uprising – but also the legal principle advanced in support of the intervention. No representative expressed any enthusiasm for an interpretation of Charter Article 51 justifying use of force to repulse the spread of a militant ideology as if it were analogous to an armed attack.

USSR–Czechoslovakia (1968)

In 1968, the Warsaw Pact's armed forces entered Czechoslovakia to end the "Prague Spring" of economic and political reform, replacing Alexander Dubček's liberalizing regime with Communist hard-liners. Foreign Minister Andrei Gromyko defended this by claiming a right of collective self-defense against anti-communists:

[17] 1965 U.N.Y.B. 141.
[18] *Ibid.* See Thomas M. Franck and Edward Weisband, *Word Politics: Verbal Strategy Among the Superpowers* 70–95 (1981).
[19] S.C.O.R. (XX), 1196th Meeting, 3 May 1965, at 3, para. 16.
[20] 1965 U.N.Y.B. 142. [21] S.C.O.R. (XX), 1198th Meeting, 4 May 1965, at 3, para. 8.
[22] S.C.O.R. (XX), 1198th Meeting, 4 May 1965, at 4, para. 15.
[23] S.C.O.R. (XX), 1198th Meeting, 4 May 1965, at 24, para. 112.
[24] 1965 U.N.Y.B. 147.
[25] G.A.O.R. (XX), 1340th Meeting, at 4, paras. 36–39 (1965).
[26] G.A.O.R. (XX), 1352nd Meeting, at 12, para. 113 (1965). [27] *Ibid.*

the socialist states cannot and will not allow a situation where the vital interests of socialism are infringed upon and encroachments are made on the inviolability of the boundaries of the socialist commonwealth...[28]

The invasion was justified as an act of self-defense of the socialist community:

Czechoslovakia became a focal point in the struggle between the forces of imperialist reaction and counter-revolution, on the one hand, and the forces of socialism on the other. A deadly threat arose to the socialist state. The anti-socialist forces sought to divert the Czechoslovak people from their socialist path, to restore a bourgeois order in that country and sever it from the socialist community. Things reached a point when five socialist states saw no alternative but to send troops to the assistance of the Czechoslovak people.[29]

This step was taken to protect "against the encroachment of domestic and foreign enemies..."[30]

In meetings of the Security Council on August 21, 1968, the USSR found no receptivity for that justification. Even socialist Yugoslavia insisted that Czechoslovakia had not been threatened by the West, and concluded that the Warsaw Pact forces thus were guilty of "aggression."[31] The representatives of the ousted Czech Government continued to deny categorically that it had either invited intervention or had received support from the West.[32] Their refutation was widely accepted.[33] A resolution to "condemn the armed intervention of the USSR and other

---

[28] G.A.O.R., A/PV. 1679, 3 October 1968, at 26, 30–31.

[29] *New Times*, 35, September 4, 1968, at 1.   [30] *Kommunist*, April 21, 1969, at 1.

[31] S/8765, Letter of 22 August 1968 from the representative of Yugoslavia to the President of the Security Council.

[32] S.C.O.R. (XXIII), 1441st Meeting, 21 August 1968, at 13, paras. 133–143.

[33] See statements by Canada, S.C.O.R. (XXIII), 1441st Meeting, 21 August 1968, at 18, paras. 169–172; France, S.C.O.R. (XXIII), 1441st Meeting, 21 August 1968, at 18–19, paras. 173–180; Denmark, S.C.O.R. (XXIII), 1441st Meeting, 21 August 1968, at 19, paras. 181–189; Ethiopia, S.C.O.R. (XXIII), 1442nd Meeting, 22 August 1968, at 1–2, paras. 4–9; UK, S.C.O.R. (XXIII), 1442nd Meeting, 22 August 1968, at 2–3, paras. 9–13; China, S.C.O.R. (XXIII), 1442nd Meeting, 22 August 1968, at 2–3, paras. 14–24; Paraguay, S.C.O.R. (XXIII), 1442nd Meeting, 22 August 1968, at 6–7, paras. 57–61; Brazil, S.C.O.R. (XXIII), 1442nd Meeting, 22 August 1968, at 7, paras. 63–68; India, S.C.O.R. (XXIII), 1443rd Meeting, 22 August 1968, at 26, paras. 251–256; Algeria, S.C.O.R. (XXIII), 1443rd Meeting, 22 August 1968, at 26–28, paras. 256–270. Even socialist leaders President Ceausescu of Romania and President Tito of Yugoslavia, rejected the justifications for their actions of Warsaw Pact nations. S.C.O.R. (XXIII), 1443rd Meeting, 22 August 1968, at 10, para. 95. See also the statement of the representative of Yugoslavia to the Security Council, S.C.O.R. (XXIII), 1445th Meeting, 24 August 1968, at 10–11, paras. 101–106.

members of the Warsaw Pact" and calling on them to "cease all... forms of intervention in Czechoslovakia's internal affairs,"[34] although vetoed by Moscow, received 10 affirmative votes.[35]

Conclusions

The practice makes clear that there has been no support for interpreting Article 51 to permit a right to use force in self-defense against states exporting ideologies through militant but non-military means. Russia failed to persuade any but its closest allies that either Hungary or Czechoslovakia had been under anything analogous to a military attack by NATO so as to justify forceful countermeasures. The US equally failed to demonstrate that the leftist ideology of an uprising in the Dominican Republic justified its military intervention. Neither Moscow nor Washington were successful in seeking to portray the specter of an alien ideology as a sort of "armed attack" in disguise.[36] In the practice of the principal UN organs two things appear to have been clarified in practice. One is that infiltration and subversion may rise to the level of an externally-based armed attack against which, if proven, proportionate military countermeasures are permitted by Charter Article 51. The other is that, for such countermeasures to be lawful, the provocation must be demonstrably grievous, military in nature, and to have originated in the state against which such defensive military action is taken in self-defense.[37]

Thus, during the Cold War, a fairly bright line may be said to have been drawn between, on the one hand, a state's export of revolution by direct or indirect military action, against which a measured military response in self-defense is permissible, and, on the other hand, a state's export of revolution by propaganda, cultural subversion, and other non-military assistance, against which an armed response has consistently been regarded as an impermissible distortion of Article 51. It remains to be seen, if we are entering a new era of intense global ideological conflict, whether that line will hold.

---

[34] S/8761, sponsored by Brazil, Canada, Denmark, France, Paraguay, Senegal, UK, and US.

[35] S.C.O.R. (XXIII), 1443rd Meeting, 22 August 1968, at 29, para. 284. Negative votes were cast by the Soviets and Hungary, with Algeria, India, and Pakistan abstaining.

[36] Franck and Weisband, n. 18 above, at 33–39, 70–95.

[37] See Vaughn Lowe, "The Principle of Non-Intervention: Use of Force," in Lowe and Warbrick (eds.), *The United Nations and the Principles of International Law* (1994); Christine Gray, *International Law and the Use of Force* 75 (2000).

6

Self-defense against attacks on citizens abroad

This chapter examines instances in which an expansive concept of "self-defence" has been advanced by a state to justify using force to protect citizens abroad, either by military rescue or by forcibly deterring those who threaten their safety.

Powerful states have long claimed a legal right to use military force ("gun-boat diplomacy") to this end. In the nineteenth-century case of *Durand* v. *Hollins*,[1] the US Circuit Court of Appeals said:

Under our system of government, the citizen abroad is as much entitled to protection as the citizen at home. The great object and duty of government is the protection of the lives, liberty and property of the people composing it, whether abroad or at home; and any government failing in the accomplishment of the object, or the performance of the duty, is not worth preserving.[2]

At issue in *Durand* was the President's constitutional authority, without obtaining a Congressional declaration of war, to order a naval bombardment of San Juan del Norte (Greytown), Nicaragua, as reprisal against those of its inhabitants who "had perpetrated acts of violence against the US nationals and their property."[3] Although in upholding this exercise of plenary power, the Court was declaring US, not international, law, it acted in recognition of what it claimed was the widespread state practice of "humanitarian intervention" and "citizen rescue."[4]

These practices, whatever their currency at that earlier time, have now become problematic. They are criticized as a subterfuge used by

[1] 4 Blatch. 451 (1860).   [2] 4 Blatch. 451 at 454.   [3] 4 Blatch. 451 at 452.
[4] See Sir Robert Jennings and Sir Arthur Watts, 1 *Oppenheim's International Law*, 440–44 (9th edn., 1992).

the strong to interfere in the domestic affairs of the weak. This criticism arises equally whether the intervention is, or is not, approved by the government of the place where it occurs. When undertaken with consent, "humanitarian intervention" incurs the suspicion that its real purpose is less to rescue endangered persons than to save unpopular regimes from their domestic critics.[5] When it occurs without consent, the intervenor is likely to be accused of undermining a regime it does not like.[6]

It is the latter, non-consensual interventions that have been most common in practice[7] and most controversial in modern law. Does the UN Charter – as interpreted in practice – now definitively prohibit the practice? Articles 2(4) and 2(7), in promulgating a seemingly ironclad prohibition, accurately reflects the raw Latin American anti-interventionist sensibilities of the 1940s. In the 1960s, as more former colonies joined the United Nations, they, too, for historic reasons, embraced the rule's theoretically absolute ban. Nevertheless, such interventions continue, usually justified by the intervening state as permissible under a flexible reading of Charter Article 51's right of "self-defence."[8] The actual practice of UN organs has tended to be more calibrated, manifesting a situational ethic rather than doctrinaire consistency either prohibiting or permitting all such actions. A few examples will illustrate this divergence of pragmatic practice from pure theory.

[5] For example, in 1964 US and Belgian forces at the Congolese Government's request embarked on an expedition to rescue their citizens in Stanleyville, which had been seized by rebels. The intended effect, however, was to return that region to the control of the embattled central government and to defeat the rebellion. See G. Abi-Saab, *The United Nations Operation in the Congo 1960–1964* (1978). See also French–Belgian interventions in Zaire in 1978, and French rescue interventions in Mauritania in 1977, Gabon and Rwanda in 1990, Chad in 1992, and the Central African Republic in 1996. See further the UK intervention in Sierra Leone in 2000.

[6] The US interventions in the Dominican Republic in 1965, Grenada in 1983, and Panama in 1989 (see below) were each undertaken in part to rescue American nationals but had the effect of ousting the government in place at the time. In the opinion of Professor Christine Gray, in "all these cases of US intervention the defence of nationals was used to mask the use of force to overthrow the government; the motive of the USA was to install a new government more ideologically appealing to it." Christine Gray, *International Law and the Use of Force* 65 (2000).

[7] In a 1945 study for the World Peace Foundation on World Policing and the Constitution, James Grafton Rogers identifies 149 US episodes similar to that at Greytown between 1798 and 1941. Cited in Edward Corwin, *The Constitution of the United States of America* 488 (1952).

[8] See discussion in Christine Gray, *International Law and the Use of Force* 108–10 (2000) and references cited therein.

Belgium–The Congo (1960, 1964)

Immediately after the Belgian Congo attained independence in July, 1960, its army (the *force publique*) mutinied, provoking widespread looting and raping. Much of this was directed against the 100,000 remaining residents of Belgian nationality. Without the permission of either the Congo or the United Nations, Brussels deployed its paratroopers to restore order.

On July 12 the Congo's President and Prime Minister jointly asked the United Nations for protection, accusing the Belgian "aggressors" of "machinations" in ill-disguised support of tribal secessionists who had taken control of mineral-rich Katanga province.[9] Although China, France, Italy, and the UK expressed reservations, the Security Council swiftly created a UN military and civilian mission (ONUC) to assist the Congo and called "upon the Government of Belgium to withdraw their troops…"[10] The Soviet Union and Poland unsuccessfully championed an even tougher resolution.[11]

Belgium argued that it had intervened solely in accordance with a right to protect its citizens abroad and that its troops would be withdrawn as soon as the United Nations could guarantee order and safety.[12] In making its case, Brussels' representatives did not so much fail to convince their peers of the applicable legal rules as fail to justify their action in the specific situational context. Most states, rightly or wrongly, suspected Brussels of ulterior motives extending beyond the rescue of their nationals to the protection of other interests.

Although security on the ground continued to deteriorate, the Council kept up pressure to have Belgium withdraw its forces "immediately…"[13] Belgian troops were seen to be inflicting excessive civilian casualties. Even after the withdrawal of the paratroopers in September 1960, UN debates and resolutions tended to focus on the role of freebooting foreign advisers and mercenaries in supporting Katanga's secession, which was believed primarily to suit Belgian mining interests.

The same dim view of intervention was again evident in November 1964, when the embattled central government of the Congo invited

---

[9] 1960 U.N.Y.B. 52. S/4382, Cable of 12 July 1960.
[10] S. Res. S/4387 of 13 July 1960. Adopted by 8–0 with 3 abstentions.
[11] S/4386 of 13 July 1960, to amend Tunisian draft resolution S/4383.
[12] 1960 U.N.Y.B. 52.
[13] S. Res. 4426 of 9 August 1960. Adopted by 9–0 with 2 abstentions. See also S. Res. 4405 of 22 July 1960.

foreign intervention against secessionists holding Belgian, Indian, Pakistani, French, and American civilians hostage in areas under their control. US planes, flying from British bases, transported 600 Belgian troops to the Stanleyville region, where they succeeded in evacuating 1,800 foreigners and 300 Congolese. Together with Congolese forces advancing on the ground they effectively subdued the rebels but also imposed heavy casualties. In the Security Council, both the US and Belgium described the operation as one of purely humanitarian rescue,[14] a justification supported by Western European and some African members[15] but rejected by the Eastern Europeans and other Africans. The intervention was seen by many third world governments as primarily entrenching and expanding the authority of an unpopular pro-Western regime in Kinshasa at the expense of its leftist domestic opposition.

Despite these criticisms, the debate in the Security Council generated altogether only two statements by representatives asserting the absolute inadmissibility *per se* of the use of force by a state to rescue its citizens.[16] Most critics focused solely on the specific context in which the intervention had occurred, doubting its humanitarian provenance.[17] Ultimately, the resolution passed by the Council, while calling once again for the withdrawal of foreign forces, made no judgment as to the legal or factual basis for their introduction.[18]

Turkey–Cyprus (1964)

The claim to use force in self-defense is also occasionally advanced by a government on behalf of persons who are not its citizens but on whose behalf an historic protective relationship is claimed to exist. Turkey has asserted such a right *vis-à-vis* Turkish-Cypriots, as has Israel *vis-à-vis* Jews of the diaspora (see pp. 82ff.).

[14] See Security Council meetings: S/6060, S/6062 (1964), and S/6063 (1964).

[15] See Letters of 24 and 26 November 1964 from Democratic Republic of the Congo, Belgium, United Kingdom, United States, and of 1 December 1964 by 22 African and Asian states. S/6060, S/6062, S/6063, S6067, S/6068, S/6069, S/6076, and add. 1–5. See also Letter of Prime Minister Maurice Tshombe of the Democratic Republic of the Congo to American Ambassador in Leopoldville dated 21 November 1964, in 12 Digest of International Law, 1963–73 (Marjorie Whiteman, ed.), p. 213.

[16] H. Weisberg, "The Congo Crisis 1964: A Case Study in Humanitarian Intervention," 12 Va. J. Int'l L. 261 (1972).

[17] For a discussion of the 1964 events see Sean A. Murphy, *Humanitarian Intervention* 92–94 (1996); A. Mark Weisburd, *Use of Force: The Practice of States Since World War II* 266–68 (1997).

[18] S.C. Res. 199 of 30 December 1964.

Cyprus became independent in 1960, under a complex constitutional formula which ensured its ethnic-Turkish minority a legislative veto over a broad array of governance issues. This arrangement, placing the onus on inter-communal cooperation, was guaranteed against unilateral abrogation in a treaty signed by Britain, Greece, and Turkey. It authorized the signatories to intervene collectively or singly to preserve those guarantees.[19]

The hoped-for cooperation between ethnic Greeks and Turks soon collapsed.[20] Late in 1963, the Cypriot government, headed by Archbishop Makarios, unilaterally decided to eliminate key constitutional provisions protecting Turkish-Cypriot interests. Turkey alleged that a serious campaign had begun, aimed at annihilating[21] its "compatriots."[22] When inter-communal fighting ensued, the Security Council, on March 4, 1964, voted unanimously to create and deploy a UN peacekeeping force (UNFICYP)[23] which, by June, had grown to 6,238 troops and 173 police contributed by nine states.[24] Even so, communal fighting continued sporadically. On August 8, Turkey attacked Greek-Cypriot targets by air, claiming to be acting to protect Turkish-Cypriots under the terms of the tripartite Treaty of Guarantee.[25]

With the Makarios Government denying that Turkish-Cypriots had been attacked[26] but with the newly established UN presence on the ground reporting otherwise, the Council ordered an immediate ceasefire.[27] It did not condemn the Turkish air-strikes, instead calling on all parties to cooperate with UNFICYP in restoring peace and security. In the ensuing Council debate it became clear that most members, while urging all parties to cease firing, did not consider the Turkish recourse to force of such illegality as to warrant censure. There appeared, instead, to be awareness of the provocative role played by the Makarios regime in upsetting the constitutional basis for peaceful (if deadlocked) coexistence between the two Cypriot communities. In the circumstances, the

---

[19] Treaty of Guarantee (Cyprus, Greece, Turkey, United Kingdom), August 16, 1960. U.N.T.S. vol. 382, No. 5475. Treaty Concerning the Establishment of the Republic of Cyprus (Cyprus, Turkey, United Kingdom), August 16, 1960. U.N.T.S. vol. 382, No. 5476.

[20] For a full discussion see Thomas Ehrlich, *Cyprus: 1958–1967* 37–38, 45–46 (1974).

[21] S/PV1085 of 27 December 1963, p. 10.

[22] S/PV1095 of 18 February 1964, p. 35.   [23] S. Res. 186 of 4 March 1964.

[24] 1964 U.N.Y.B. 156.   [25] S/PV1142 of 8 August 1963, at 9–15, paras. 59–85.

[26] S/PV1151 of 16 September 1974, at 15–17, paras. 62–70.

[27] S. Res. 193 of 9 August 1964. The vote was 9–0 with 2 abstentions (Czechoslovakia and USSR).

Council focused on seeking to end hostilities and bring about a military disengagement without apportioning blame.

US–Dominican Republic (1965)

Chapter 5 noted the UN system's strongly negative reaction to US President Johnson's attempt to justify US use of force in the Dominican Republic by reference to a right to prevent the incursion of an alien ideology into the Western Hemisphere. The system reacted almost as negatively to US efforts to justify the same operation as an exercise of its right to its citizens abroad. Once again, the emphasis was on the specific circumstances, rather than solely on the implementation of a legal principle.

During the Council debate, Ambassador Adlai Stevenson argued that "the purpose of the United States action...was to protect the lives of foreign nationals."[28] No other government accepted this as justification for the invasion. France did express some sympathy for the effort to ensure the safety of Americans, but joined the rest of the Council in demanding an end to the intervention.[29] Cuba asked: "what right can any country have...to land on the territory of another nation on the pretext of protecting the lives and property of its nationals? According to that criterion, there is no sovereignty or independence for any weak country..." Its representative pointed out that "not one United States citizen has lost his life..."[30] The Soviet ambassador said that the "miserable argument of 'protecting the lives of United States citizens' put forward as a motive for United States intervention...has deceived nobody."[31] He cited the history of other US interventions in Latin America "in Panama and Cuba, in Mexico and Nicaragua, in Haiti and Uruguay, in Chile and Brazil, in Honduras and Guatemala" and previously in the Dominican Republic itself.[32]

Even the representative of Jordan, a country normally sympathetic to US interests, insisted that the intervention "...was unjustified and contrary to the principles and provisions of the United Nations Charter." Such interventions "if condoned, would undermine the basic principles of the sovereignty and security of States."[33] As in the Congo, although

[28] S.C.O.R. (XX), 1212th Meeting, 19 May 1965, at 24, paras. 149–150.
[29] S.C.O.R. (XX), 1198th Meeting, 4 May 1965, at 24, para. 112.
[30] S.C.O.R. (XX), 1196th Meeting, 3 May 1965, at 26, para. 126.
[31] S.C.O.R. (XX), 1196th Meeting, 3 May 1965, at 41, para. 191.
[32] S.C.O.R. (XX), 1196th Meeting, 3 May 1965, at 42, para. 196.
[33] S.C.O.R. (XX), 1214th Meeting, 21 May 1965, at 21, para. 116.

the principle of armed rescue was not categorically rejected by the UN system, its application was found unacceptable in a context where the motives of the intervenor were widely suspect and where many states' representatives did not believe that evidence had demonstrated a genuine threat to the safety of those purportedly being rescued. While Cuba and a few other Latin American states did attack the doctrinal basis for a right of citizen rescue, most critics took a less absolute line, arguing, instead, that the specific facts of the case did not demonstrate the necessity for action in the circumstances.

Israel–Uganda (1976)

The right to resort to military action in self-defense of its citizens abroad, as well as of Jews of other nationalities, was claimed by Israel to justify its aerial assault on Entebbe, Uganda on the night of July 3–4, 1976. On June 27, pro-Palestinians hijacked an Air France airbus with more than 270 passengers flying from Israel to Paris. The French crew were ordered to take the flight to Libya and then on to Entebbe, where they were met by Uganda's President Idi Amin. According to survivors, the Ugandan military assisted in separating some 100 non-Jewish or non-Israeli passengers, who were allowed to leave. The rest were held as hostages. The demands of the hijackers included the release of fifty-three Palestinian prisoners being held in Israel, West Germany, France, Switzerland, and Kenya. In their rescue of the hostages, Israeli aerial commandos destroyed a part of Entebbe airport. A small number of hostages, Palestinians, and Ugandans died in the fighting.

In notifying the UN Secretary-General of the assault on July 4, the Israeli government pointed out that the terrorists had threatened to kill their hostages, that the President of Uganda had cooperated with the terrorists, that "the sand in the hour-glass was about to run out," and that it had acted solely in "[s]elf defence against the attacks of the terrorist organizations and the war against the terrorists within our own borders and abroad..."[34] The following day, Uganda responded with messages to the President of the Security Council and the Chairman of the Organization of African Unity (OAU), asserting that his country "has been attacked by Israel" and demanding "that Israel be condemned

---

[34] S/12123, Letter dated 4 July 1976 from the representative of Israel to the Secretary-General.

in the strongest possible terms for the aggression."[35] A resolution was introduced by Benin, Libya, and Tanzania that would have condemned "Israel's flagrant violation of Uganda's sovereignty and territorial integrity" and demanded payment of compensation for Ugandan lives and property.[36] Britain and the US introduced a competing resolution condemning hijacking and calling on nations "to prevent and punish all such terrorist acts" while reaffirming "the need to respect the sovereignty and territorial integrity of all States..."[37]

In the ensuing debate, Uganda proclaimed its innocence as an "honest broker" and reiterated its demands. This was supported by the Mauritanian representative, on behalf of the OAU. While conceding "that this action of the so-called Palestinians or pro-Palestinians has been disapproved of by everyone, and particularly by the Arab countries..."[38] he pointed to "the seriousness of the [Israeli] act itself, and particularly the dangerous precedent it constitutes."[39] He asked the Council to impose "unequivocal condemnation" and require "just and equitable compensation."[40] In reply, the Israeli ambassador charged that either Idi Amin had cooperated with the hijackers "or [Uganda] does not exercise sovereignty over its territory and was incapable of dealing with half a dozen terrorists."[41] He cited the obligations of Israel and Uganda as parties to the 1970 Hague Convention on Aerial Hijacking[42] and quoted Professor D.W. Bowett:[43]

The right of the State to intervene by the use or threat of force for the protection of its nationals suffering injuries within the territory of another State is generally admitted, both in the writings of jurists and in the practice of States.

He also cited Professor D.P. O'Connell's conclusion that traditional international law permitting such proportionate intervention by a national's state had not been repealed by the Charter and that "Article 2(4)... should be interpreted as prohibiting acts of force against the territorial integrity and political independence of nations, and not to prohibit a

---

[35] S/12124, Letter dated 5 July 1976 from the representative of Uganda to the President of the Security Council.
[36] S/12139 of 12 July 1976.   [37] S/12138 of 12 July 1976.
[38] S.C.O.R. (XXXI), 1939th Meeting, 9 July 1976, at 6, para. 44.
[39] S.C.O.R. (XXXI), 1939th Meeting, 9 July 1976, at 6, para. 46.
[40] S.C.O.R. (XXXI), 1939th Meeting, 9 July 1976, at 7, para. 53.
[41] S.C.O.R. (XXXI), 1939th Meeting, 9 July 1976, at 12, para. 98.
[42] Convention for the Suppression of Unlawful Seizure of Aircraft, 860 U.N.T.S. 105. Done on 16 December 1970.
[43] D.W. Bowett, *Self-Defense in International Law* 87–88 (1963).

use of force which is limited in intention and effect to the protection of a State's own integrity and its nationals' vital interests, when the machinery envisaged by the United Nations Charter is ineffective in the situation."[44] Acting in its capacity as authoritative interpreter of the Charter, the Council launched a serious debate on the modern legal status of states' historic right to intervene protectively on behalf of endangered citizens abroad.

The relatively few African states participating actively in the debate (Libya, Guinea, Mauritius, Benin, Somalia, Tanzania) and a few other third world countries (Guyana, India, Pakistan) as well as the Soviet bloc, all sided with Uganda, displaying varying degrees of vigor. Many countries, however, preferred not to participate at all. Panama, a member of the Council, spoke only to declare its intention to abstain in voting on both resolutions.[45] Romania firmly declared its conclusion that Israel's actions were illegal but called on the Security Council to "give more consideration" to the "dangerous spiral of violence and lawlessness in international life" and how to halt it by "joint, concerted action by all Governments..."[46] Japan took an equally ambivalent line.[47] France vehemently insisted that the general principle of non-intervention was not at stake, that the "Israeli intervention had the purpose and the effect of freeing certain Israeli citizens who, together with French citizens, were being subject to the most detestable blackmail [and]... threatened with immediate death..."[48]

Quite clearly, even in this instance, there was no agreement as to whether a state might use force to protect its citizens' lives overseas, in situations where neither their host-state nor the international system had been able to offer effective protection. The US[49] and Britain[50] clearly

---

[44] D.P. O'Connell, *International Law* 304 (2nd edn., 1970), quoted in S.C.O.R. (XXXI), 1939th Meeting, 9 July 1976, at 13, para. 108. To similar effect see Sir Humphrey Waldock, "The Regulation of the Use of Force by Individual States in International Law," 81 Recueil des Cours 455–514 (1952– II); Derek Bowett, *Self-Defence in International Law* 87–105 (1958); and Lord Arnold Duncan McNair, *Laws of Treaties* 209–10 (1961). For the contrary view see Ian Brownlie, "The United Nations and the Use of Force, 1945–1985," in *The Current Legal Regulation of the Use of Force* 492, 497–502 (A. Cassese ed., 1986).

[45] S.C.O.R. (XXXI), 1942nd Meeting, 13 July 1976, at 5, para. 33.

[46] S.C.O.R. (XXXI), 1942nd Meeting, 13 July 1976, at 6, para. 46.

[47] S.C.O.R. (XXXI), 1942nd Meeting, 13 July 1976, at 6–7, paras. 48–58.

[48] S.C.O.R. (XXXI), 1942nd Meeting, 13 July 1976, at 7, para. 43.

[49] S.C.O.R. (XXXI), 1942nd Meeting, 13 July 1976, at 11, para. 76.

[50] S.C.O.R. (XXXI), 1940th Meeting, 12 July 1976, at 13, paras. 103–109.

thought so, as did Sweden.[51] The Italian President of the Council, unable to discern any consensus, proposed referring the matter to the International Court, but no one took up his suggestion.[52]

At the end of a debate marked by extraordinary intensity and immoderation, but also by widespread ambiguity, the African resolution was not pressed to a vote and the US–UK resolution received 6 votes in favor (France, Italy, Japan, Sweden, UK, and US) with 0 against and 2 abstentions (Panama, Romania). However, 7 members (Libya, Pakistan, USSR, Tanzania, Benin, China, and Guyana) registered their opposition by boycotting the meeting.[53] (Under the rules of Charter Article 27(3), 9 votes were needed to pass the resolution, which thus failed.)

The Entebbe case is instructive because it posed the issue of the right to intervene on behalf of citizens in a situational context optimally favorable to the intervenor. Although Israel was not universally popular, neither was Idi Amin. The hostage predicament was manifestly one of great urgency. Israel's forces, moreover, had left Uganda promptly after rescuing the hostages and had taken care to inflict the least possible collateral damage. There was little question of Israel's pursuing any national interest other than rescue. The opposition of so many states, in this instance, thus illustrates the depth of fear of opening the door, however narrowly, to unilateral use of force, even where the justification for intervention is strong. But the considerable support Israel aroused also demonstrates the persuasive power of a well-presented and factually demonstrated case. Not only did the effort to chasten Israel fail in the Council, but, after a canvass of the prospects, Uganda made no effort to convene the General Assembly as it could have done under the "Uniting for Peace" procedure.

As a postscript, it is notable that, two years later, after an Egyptian cabinet minister was assassinated in Nicosia by Arab gunmen believed to be of the pro-Palestinian Abu Nidal group without encountering significant local opposition, and after those gunmen had seized a number of hostages in the Nicosia Hilton Hotel, Egyptian commandos entered Cyprus without permission and engaged the Cypriot National Guard in a gun battle, leading to a number of casualties. Following this attack, the guerrillas eventually surrendered to Cypriot authorities. They were placed on trial amidst severe deterioration in Egyptian–Cypriot

---

[51] S.C.O.R. (XXXI), 1940th Meeting, 12 July 1976, at 14, paras. 117–123.

[52] S.C.O.R. (XXXI), 1943rd Meeting, 14 July 1976, at 8–9, para. 56.

[53] 1977 U.N.Y.B. 320.

relations, but with Egypt insisting that it had acted strictly in self-defense of its citizens abroad.[54] The incident provoked no response from the UN political organs.

US–Grenada (1983)

In October 1983, military officers seized control of Grenada after killing leftist Prime Minister Maurice Bishop – himself installed by an earlier coup – as well as five members of his cabinet and other political leaders. Thereupon US forces intervened, supported by small contingents from Jamaica and Barbados. They acted, ostensibly, on the invitation of Sir Paul Scoon, the Governor-General and sole remaining legitimate institution of Grenada's government.

At its height this intervention involved 8,000 US troops with 300 military from other Caribbean states.[55] On October 25, the US ambassador to the United Nations, in a letter to the Secretary-General, stated that his country's action had responded to a request of the Organization of Eastern Caribbean States "to join with the people of Grenada in restoring government and order, and to facilitate the departure of those United States citizens and other foreign nationals who wish to be evacuated."[56]

When the situation was brought before the Security Council, fully forty-nine UN members not on that body asked to speak. Forty-three condemned the invasion as violative of the UN Charter, repeatedly citing evidence provided by Grenada's military coup leaders that "no danger to United States citizens existed..."[57] There was general disbelief that humanitarian rescue had been the real purpose of the invasion.

Skepticism about US intentions was reinforced when the representative of Jamaica, a partner in the invasion, volunteered that its principal purpose had been political rather than humanitarian: to prevent the military build-up introduced by Cuba into Grenada during the Bishop years from falling into the hands of even more extreme leftists.[58] Moreover, the Jamaican representative admitted that the force, including his

[54] *See Keesing's Contemporary Archives*, November 10, 1978, p. 29305.
[55] 1983 U.N.Y.B. 215.
[56] S/16076, Letter dated 25 October 1983, from the representative of the United States of America to the President of the Security Council.
[57] 1983 U.N.Y.B. 212. See also the statement of the representative of Guyana, S.C.O.R. (XXXVIII), 2487th Meeting, 25 October 1983, at 7, para. 7; representative of Grenada, S.C.O.R. (XXXVIII), 2487th Meeting, 25 October 1983, at 10, para. 90.
[58] S.C.O.R. (XXXVIII), 2489th Meeting, 26 October 1983, at 5, paras. 45–51.

country's troops, were not in Grenada to protect its citizens but to "assist the people of Grenada to free themselves from a military dictatorship and to establish conditions within which it might be possible for the will of the people to be deployed in free and fair elections."[59] He promised that the expeditionary force would withdraw "as soon as it is clear that such conditions have been established."[60]

This did not help and neither did the reticence of the US in adducing evidence of real danger to its nationals on the island. Virtually every speaker, whether from Europe, South America, Asia, or Africa, deemed the intervention unjustified. Even the representative of France aligned himself unqualifiedly with the critics:

The justifications put forward, relating to the internal situation of Grenada, do not seem to us to be admissible. They do not meet the conditions under which an intervention of this nature and magnitude could be considered. International law, in particular the Charter of the United Nations, authorizes intervention only in two eventualities: in response to a request from the legitimate authorities of the country, or upon a decision taken by the Security Council. I must add that France has never accepted certain interpretations of the Charter whereby other organs could authorize armed intervention without the approval of the Security Council.[61]

The South American states were especially vigorous in asserting their adherence to the rule barring any intervention without prior Security Council authorization.[62] Even the British ambassador reported that his "Government did not support these operations and that we wished a different course of action to be followed."[63] The Netherlands, too, held the action of the US and its allies incompatible with the law of the Charter.[64]

On October 27, the resolution proposed jointly by Guyana and Nicaragua was voted upon. It "deeply deplores the armed intervention in

---

[59] S.C.O.R. (XXXVIII), 2489th Meeting, 26 October 1983, at 6, para. 56.   [60] *Ibid.*
[61] S.C.O.R. (XXXVIII), 2489th Meeting, 26 October 1983, at 15, para. 146.
[62] S.C.O.R. (XXXVIII), 2491st Meeting, 27 October 1983, at 5, para. 43ff.; S.C.O.R. (XXXVIII), 2491st Meeting, 27 October 1983, at 11, para. 107ff. (Venezuela); S.C.O.R. (XXXVIII), 2491st Meeting, 27 October 1983, at 12, para. 111ff.; S.C.O.R. (XXXVIII), 2491st Meeting, 27 October 1983, at 24, para. 270ff. (Guatemala); S.C.O.R. (XXXVIII), 2491st Meeting, 27 October 1983, at 25, para. 275ff. (Trinidad and Tobago); S.C.O.R. (XXXVIII), 2491st Meeting, 27 October 1983, at 28, para. 310ff. (Colombia); S.C.O.R. (XXXVIII), 2491st Meeting, 27 October 1983, at 36, para. 395ff. (Chile); S.C.O.R. (XXXVIII), 2491st Meeting, 27 October 1983, at 36, para. 402ff. (Brazil).
[63] S.C.O.R. (XXXVIII), 2491st Meeting, 27 October 1983, at 20, para. 210.
[64] S.C.O.R. (XXXVIII), 2491st Meeting, 27 October 1983, at 33, para. 363ff.

Grenada, which constitutes a flagrant violation of international law and of the independence, sovereignty and territorial integrity of that State" and called for its "immediate cessation..."[65] The Council's vote was 11 in favor, 1 against (the US) and 3 abstentions (Togo, UK, Zaire).[66] The two African abstainers, far from supporting the US, argued that the resolution did not go far enough in condemning the intervention. Although Washington's veto formally prevented censure, the vote was a stinging rebuke to US policy and a powerful reassertion of the Charter's limits on self-defense under Article 51.

The matter was subsequently raised at the Thirty-Eighth session of the General Assembly, then in session. Guyana, Nicaragua, and Zimbabwe introduced a resolution[67] which almost exactly paralleled the one vetoed in the Security Council.[68] It was passed by an overwhelming vote of 108–9 with 27 abstentions.[69] Only Israel, El Salvador, and those Caribbean states that had joined the invasion voted with Washington. American combat forces withdrew by December 15.[70]

Throughout the Council and Assembly debates, it was apparent that the US had failed to demonstrate a credible threat to Americans in Grenada and that this, rather than a dogmatic rejection of a right to use force in defense of one's citizens abroad, had fashioned the near-unanimity with which states had responded.[71]

US–Egypt (1985–1986)

The key role played by credible evidence was further demonstrated on October 7, 1985, when Palestinian terrorists hijacked an Italian cruise liner, the *Achille Lauro*, and murdered an American passenger. Egyptian authorities subsequently negotiated the release of the ship and its passengers in return for allowing the hijackers to fly to Tunis on an Egyptian aircraft. American planes intercepted that flight,

---

[65] S/16077/Rev. 1 of 27 October 1983.

[66] S.C.O.R. (XXXVIII), 2491st Meeting, 27 October 1983, at 39, para. 431.

[67] A/38/L.8 and Add. 1.   [68] S/RES/38/7 of 2 November 1983.

[69] G.A. Res. 38/7 of 31 October 1983.

[70] Simon Chesterman, *Just War or Just Peace* 99 (2001).

[71] Christine Gray points out that the principles advanced (and rejected) in this instance trace their origins to those offered (also unsuccessfully) by Britain in 1956 for its invasion of Suez: (1) that there is an imminent threat of injury to nationals, (2) that there is a failure or inability on the part of the territorial sovereign to protect the nationals in question, (3) that the measures of protection are strictly confined to the object of protecting endangered nationals against injury. Gray, n. 6 above, at 110–11.

forcing it to land at a NATO base in Italy, where the hijackers were apprehended.

In this instance, the US countermeasure – taken against Egyptian state property – aimed not at rescue but at punishment and deterrence. In justifying its action, the US claimed to be enforcing Egypt's obligation under the 1979 Convention on the Taking of Hostages either to bring to trial, or to extradite, perpetrators, as well as exercising a right of reprisal for the killing of one of its citizens and the victimization of others on the ship.[72]

Although Egypt protested, joined by a few other Arab states, the response of most non-aligned and the Soviet bloc was distinctly muted[73] while most Western governments accepted the American justification.[74] Significantly, no effort was made to convene the Security Council or the General Assembly.

US–Libya (1986)

The claim to act in self-defense of citizens is asserted most strongly when the citizens are members of their nation's armed forces. A few months after the *Achille Lauro* sequence of events, on March 22–24, 1986, a US air and naval force entered the Gulf of Sidra in the Mediterranean in defiance of Libya's claim to enforce a "line of death" across the mouth of what it claimed to be its exclusive territorial sea. Most naval powers regarded the Gulf as international waters. As US ships approached, Libya responded with surface-to-air missiles and the despatch of a missile-armed patrol boat. In reply, US airmen bombed the missile sites and sank the Libyan boat. Although the Communist bloc, joined by some Arab states, accused the US of aggression, few actually supported the Libyan claim to be acting lawfully either in closing the Gulf of Sidra or in attacking the US ships. France, the UK, and Malta categorically rejected Libya's protests. The Security Council, when convened, took no action on a resolution in which Bulgaria and the Soviet Union sought unsuccessfully to condemn US "armed aggression."[75]

This encounter followed a series of Libyan moves, both overt and covert, against the US, Egypt, the Sudan, Chad, and Saudi Arabia as well as support for the Abu Nidal terrorist group which had struck at

---

[72] Antonio Cassese, *Terrorism, Politics and the Law* 23–39 (1989); Gregory V. Gooding, "Incident – Fighting Terrorism in the 1980's: the Interception of the Achille Lauro Hijackers," 12 Yale J. Int'l L. 158, 168–76 (1987).
[73] Weisburd, n. 17 above, at 291.   [74] *Ibid.*   [75] S/17954, 31 March 1986.

Rome and Vienna in 1985.[76] These had isolated Libya diplomatically. However, the vigorous US response to the Gulf of Sidra incident and the international community's failure to take up the Libyan cause appears to have provoked rather than chastened the authorities in Tripoli. On April 4, a bomb attributed to Libyan agents exploded in a Berlin nightclub frequented by American soldiers, killing three persons (two Americans) and injuring 229 (seventy-nine Americans). Ten days later, claiming that the government in Tripoli was planning more such attacks and that it was acting in self-defense,[77] the US launched a concerted aerial strike against various Libyan military targets, inflicting civilian as well as military casualties. One US plane and its crew were lost.

At the Security Council, the US characterized its action as intended to discourage future attacks on Americans. While it claimed to have persuasive evidence of Libya's involvement in the Berlin bombing, this, at the time, was more asserted than demonstrated. Only later did painstaking investigation by Berlin authorities give verisimilitude to Washington's allegations.[78] Moreover, even states inclined to accept that Libya was systematically targeting US overseas personnel also thought the US aerial strike disproportionate to that threat.[79] A draft resolution condemning the US attack was supported by 9 states – Bulgaria, China, Congo, Ghana, Madagascar, Thailand, Trinidad, the USSR, and the United Arab Emirates – with 5 opposed, including France, the UK, and the US.[80] The resolution thus was vetoed. But, even France, while nominally voting against the resolution, carefully distanced itself from the US "intervention."[81]

Oscar Schachter has pointed out that the UN regime has not obviated unilateral self-help and countermeasures. "General international law," he says, "allows counter-measures under certain conditions and within the limits of necessity and proportionality..." However, "State practice, although abundant, has not produced much clarity as to the circumstances in which retaliation may be used and the precise limits of counter-measures."[82] The response to the two US actions in 1986

---

[76] Weisburd, n. 17 above, at 293.   [77] S/17990, 14 April 1986.

[78] Weisburd, n. 17 above, at 294. On November 13, 2001, four persons linked to Libya were found guilty of the bombing. The German judge, Peter Marhofer, said that "Libya bears at the very least a considerable part of the responsibility for the attack." *New York Times*, November 14, 2001, at A8.

[79] S/17989, 14 April 1986; A/41/285; S/17996, 15 April 1986; A/41/287; S/17999, 15 April 1986.

[80] 1986 U.N.Y.B. 254.   [81] *Ibid.*

[82] Oscar Schachter, *International Law in Theory and Practice* 184 (1991).

support both observations. Nevertheless, these incidents do underscore the importance of clear evidence of provocation and of strict proportionality in shaping states' responses. After the Security Council was deadlocked by the veto, a resolution of condemnation passed the General Assembly by 79 to 28, with 51 states abstaining or absent.[83] Although some voted on purely ideological lines, most delegates appear to have reacted not in conformity with a general endorsement or rejection of a right to reprisal[84] for attacks on citizens abroad, but according to their assessment of the factual necessity and proportionality of the action taken.[85]

US–Panama (1989)

In 1989, US forces invaded Panama. The origins of this intervention go back to May 7 of that year, when, despite much fraud and violence, Presidential elections had been won by Guillermo Endara. However, the military dictator, General Manuel Noriega, refused to accept that result.[86]

As the US increased military deployment at its bases in the Canal Zone, Panama complained of provocation to the Security Council.[87] On December 15, Noriega publicly declared "a state of war with the United States."[88] Sporadic violence against Americans led to armed intervention. Five days later, America – speaking through Ambassador Thomas Pickering at the hastily convened Security Council – claimed the right to exercise its "inherent right of self-defence under international law ..."[89] Pickering explained the intervention's goals: "to safeguard the

---

[83] G.A. Res. 41/38 of 20 November 1986. The number of states abstaining or absent is cited in Weisburd, n. 17 above, at 296.

[84] Some authorities cite a Security Council resolution of 1964 as having declared all reprisals to be "incompatible with the purposes and principles" of the UN Charter. S.C. Res. 188 of 9 April 1964, sec. 1. The occasion was an attack by the British air force on Yemeni positions from which armed incursions against Aden allegedly originated. Since the passage of this resolution, such actions have not ceased but are usually no longer justified as reprisals but, rather, as acts of "self-defence" as defined by article 51 and its interpretation in state practice.

[85] A decade later, the importance of necessity and proportionality was reiterated by the International Court of Justice in its advisory opinion on the *Legality of the Threat or Use of Nuclear Weapons*, I.C.J. Reports, 1996, 226, paras. 141, 143.

[86] S/20627, 12 May 1989, Declaration of the members of the European Community.

[87] S.C.O.R., S/PV.2861, 28 April 1989, at 11–14; S/PV.2874, 11 August 1989, at 3–5.

[88] 1989 U.N.Y.B. 174. See also S.C.O.R., S/PV.2899, 20 December 1989, at 28 (Mr. Fortier, rep. of Canada).

[89] S.C.O.R., S/PV.2899, 20 December 1989, at 31.

lives of Americans, to defend democracy in Panama, to combat drug trafficking [by Noriega] and to protect the integrity of the Panama Canal Treaties."[90]

In this instance the supporting evidence of a threat was strong and well presented. Noriega's "declaration of a state of war" had been widely noted. Staged incidents involving threats to American troops, captured on television, had resulted in the death of a US officer. The foreign ministers of the Organization of American States had been spurned in their effort to "ensure the early transfer of power in accordance with democratic mechanisms."[91] Moreover, Panama's elected President, Guillermo Endara, vigorously defended the US invasion. Most states thus reacted in a decidedly muted manner, although Nicaragua's Sandinistas denounced this "pretext of protection of American citizens" as an "outrage against the conscience of the civilized peoples of the world"[92] and the Soviet ambassador wryly compared the US invocation of self-defense to "an explanation by a cat that it was chasing a mouse because it absolutely had to protect itself against it."[93]

What is striking about the Council's debates of December 20–23 is their restraint. Britain backed the US for an action taken "with the agreement and support of the Panamanian leader who had won last May's election" and in response to the killing of an unarmed American officer.[94] Canada "regretted" the US use of force but, on examining "the circumstances" found that "compelling reasons did exist" that justified recourse to Article 51 in self-defense.[95] France said that "for us, recourse to force is always deplorable and cannot be approved *per se*, whatever the causes"[96] but, then, "explicitly condemned" the Noriega regime as illegitimate and indicated France's "full and total support for the struggle against drugs..."[97]

Yugoslavia's representative appeared before the Council in his capacity as Chair of the Co-Ordinating Bureau of the non-aligned, made

---

[90] *Ibid.*

[91] S/20646, 18 May 1989, Letter of the Secretary-General of OAS to the UN Secretary-General.

[92] S.C.O.R., S/PV.2899, 20 December 1989, at 16.

[93] S.C.O.R., S/PV.2899, 20 December 1989, at 17–18.

[94] S.C.O.R., S/PV.2899, 20 December 1989, at 26–27.

[95] S.C.O.R., S/PV.2899, 20 December 1989, at 27–28.

[96] S.C.O.R., S/PV.2899, 20 December 1989, at 23–25.

[97] *Ibid.*

rather perfunctory remarks expressing his movement's "shock and dismay" at an action "which constitutes a violation of and disregard for the independence, sovereignty and territorial integrity of Panama."[98] He expressed the hope, "whatever one may think about the regime of General Noriega,"[99] that the US would speedily withdraw and allow the Panamanian people to set their own course. Similar sentiments were expressed by Nepal[100] and Ethiopia.[101] The representative of Finland thought America's "was a disproportionate response to the incidents in Panama, reprehensible as they were."[102] Brazil vaguely condemned "the use of force in international disputes" but also deplored "the events in Panama" and hoped for "a prompt and peaceful solution to the crisis."[103]

A resolution that "strongly deplores the intervention in Panama by the armed forces of the United States, which constitutes a flagrant violation of international law...,"[104] received 10 favorable votes, with 4 against and 1 abstention.[105] It was not adopted because of the negative votes of 3 permanent members. The action then shifted to the General Assembly, which, after an equally dispiriting debate, adopted essentially the resolution that had just been vetoed in the Security Council.[106] Its margin of approval was 75–20 with 40 abstentions.[107] Panama, now represented by an ambassador appointed by the Endara government, voted and spoke against it. Although most Latin American states, on principle, voted for the resolution, few spoke in its favor. Almost all sub-Saharan and many Caribbean nations abstained.

Several factors seem to have played a role in tempering UN opposition to the US action: the ill-repute of Noriega, the provocations against US personnel, the rash proclamation by Noriega of a state of war, endorsement of the American action by the duly elected Panamanian President, and the US forces' relatively speedy withdrawal. *The Economist* reported that "the standard excuse" of protecting American

---

[98] S.C.O.R., S/PV.2900, 21 December 1989, at 6.
[99] S.C.O.R., S/PV.2900, 21 December 1989, at 7.
[100] S.C.O.R., S/PV.2900, 21 December 1989, at 8–10.
[101] S.C.O.R., S/PV.2900, 21 December 1989, at 11–13.
[102] S.C.O.R., S/PV.2900, 21 December 1989, at 14–15.
[103] S.C.O.R., S/PV.2900, 21 December 1989, at 21.
[104] S/21048, 22 December 1989.
[105] *For*: Algeria, Brazil, China, Colombia, Ethiopia, Malaysia, Nepal, Senegal, USSR, Yugoslavia. *Against*: Canada, France, UK, US. *Abstaining*: Finland.
[106] G.A. Res. 44/240, 29 December 1989.   [107] 1989 U.N.Y.B. 175.

lives "was more justified than usual this time,"[108] that Panamanians themselves largely welcomed the US army's presence and that Latin American countries' reactions were muted and confined to "ritual" objections that barely concealed their passive assent.[109]

Overall, the system's response to this crisis – as to the others – suggests the primary importance not of doctrine but of the specific facts in each case and of the credibility of evidence adduced to justify recourse to force. This does not mean that there is no law, or that the law has been abandoned. Rather, it demonstrates that the system is flexible in weighing not only the legality but also the legitimacy of such interventions on a case-by-case basis.

US attack on Iraqi Intelligence Headquarters (1993)

After an alleged assassination attempt on ex-President George Bush by Iraqi agents in Kuwait, the US fired missiles at Intelligence Headquarters in Baghdad. It duly reported the action to the Security Council, justifying it as "self-defence" under Charter Article 51.[110] Washington claimed that the attack had been made only after having concluded that there was no reasonable prospect that new diplomatic initiatives or economic pressure could influence the Iraqi government to cease planning such attacks against Americans and that the target had been carefully chosen to minimize risk of collateral damage.[111] Evidence of the role of Iraqi agents was offered to the Security Council, which was convened at the instance of the US.[112] Only China criticized the US action, which most other states either supported or understood.[113]

US–Afghanistan and Sudan (1998)

On August 7, 1998, terrorists destroyed the US embassies in Nairobi, Kenya, and Dar-es-Salaam, Tanzania, killing hundreds and injuring thousands.

---

[108] *The Economist*, December 23, 1989, at 29 (UK edn. at 39).

[109] *The Economist*, January 6, 1990, at 25, 37 (UK edn. at 33, 49). But see the account of Simon Chesterman, who reports "the broad condemnation of the intervention by the international community." Chesterman, n. 70 above, at 103.

[110] S/26003, 26 June 1993.   [111] 1993 U.N.Y.B. 431.   [112] *Ibid*.

[113] N. Kritsiotis, "The Legality of the 1993 U.S. Missile Strike on Iraq and the Right of Self-Defence in International Law," 45 Int'l & Comp. L.Q. 162 (1994); L. Condorelli, "A Propos de l'Attaque Americaine Contre l'Iraq du 26 Juin 1993," 5 Eur. J. Int'l L. 134 (1994).

The Security Council without dissent "strongly condemned" the attacks and called for the perpetrators to be apprehended and brought "swiftly to justice" for these "cowardly criminal acts."[114] The Governments of Britain, Germany, Russia, France, Egypt, Canada, South Africa, Kenya, and Tanzania as well as the UN Secretary-General and the European Union all expressed their outrage.[115]

On August 21, the US, using cruise missiles, attacked a pharmaceutical plant in the Sudan and bombed a base in Afghanistan allegedly used as a training camp by Osama bin-Laden, the expatriated Saudi long associated with attacks on US overseas interests.[116] The US reported its action to the Security Council and claimed to have acted in self-defense under Article 51.[117]

Except for condemnation by Libya and Iraq, the US move was met with silence by other Arab mideast governments.[118] It was revealed that the US had obtained government approval to launch its attack on the Afghani base across the skies of Pakistan.[119] The Russians labelled the attacks "unacceptable" but quickly added that "international acts of terrorism cannot go unpunished"[120] and that they would not affect a forthcoming visit by President Clinton to Moscow. French Prime Minister Lionel Jospin said that "[w]herever terrorism is launched from, we must respond with a decisive and firm answer"[121] and British Prime Minister Tony Blair declared that "the USA must have the right to defend itself against terrorism."[122] This left protesting Sudanese and Taliban leaders somewhat isolated. Sudan's formal complaint was not inscribed on the agenda of the Security Council, although its purport was subsequently supported in a resolution of the non-aligned.[123]

The Security Council, far from censuring the US, unanimously adopted a resolution charging the Taliban with serious violations of international law by sheltering and permitting the training of terrorists on its territory. It demanded bin-Laden's extradition to stand trial in a

---

[114] S/RES/1189 (1998), 13 August 1998. [115] *New York Times*, August 8, 1998, at A8.

[116] *New York Times*, August 21, 1998, at A1. [117] S/1998/780.

[118] *New York Times*, August 21, 1998, at A12.

[119] *New York Times*, August 21, 1998, at A10.

[120] *New York Times*, August 22, 1998, at A6. [121] *Ibid.*

[122] *New York Times*, August 22, 1998.

[123] See Africa Research Bulletin 1998, 13268. Final Document of the XIIth Summit of the Non-aligned Movement, 2–3 September 1998, Durban, South Africa, S.159. *See also* Nico Krisch, "Unilateral Enforcement of the Collective Will: Kosovo, Iraq and the Security Council," 3 Max Planck Yearbook of United Nations Law 59 at 60 (1999).

country where he had been indicted and adopted its first sanctions against Taliban air transport and financial resources.[124]

Conclusions

Although the evidence adduced by the US against Osama bin-Laden was credible, that against the Sudanese pharmaceutical plant was not. Nevertheless, the system evidently regarded the provocations as extremely serious and the response as reasonably proportionate. Notably, there was no effort in the UN to argue that such recourse to force was *ipso facto* illegal.

This mirrors the general UN practice. When the facts and their political context are widely seen to warrant a pre-emptive or deterrent intervention on behalf of credibly endangered citizens abroad, and if the UN itself, for political reasons, is incapable of acting, then some use of force by a state may be accepted as legitimate self-defense within the meaning of Article 51. Military action is more likely to be condoned if the threat to citizens is demonstrably real and grave, if the motive of the intervening state is perceived as genuinely protective, and if the intervention is proportionate and of short duration and likely to achieve its purpose with minimal collateral damage. In practice, whether an action is deemed lawful or not has come to depend on the special circumstances of each case, as demonstrated to, and perceived by, the political and legal institutions of the international system. Of course, in any debate on the use of force, some states will respond solely to the factor of ideology, political alignment, national self-interest, or historical imperatives. Many others, however, will consider evidence of the circumstances and manner in which force was deployed.

These instances of UN-based state practice may be thought to be random, leaving the law indeterminate. However, the practice may also be read to yield either a narrow, or a broad, clarification of applicable law. Narrowly, recourse to armed force in order to protect nationals abroad may be said to have been condoned as legitimate in specific mitigating circumstances, even though that recourse is still recognized as technically illegal. Or, in a broader interpretation of practice, the system may be said to have adapted the concept of self-defense, under Article 51, to include a right to use force in response to an attack against nationals, providing there is clear evidence of extreme necessity and the means chosen are proportionate.

[124] S/RES/1267 of 15 October 1999.

7

Anticipatory self-defense

The typology

Earlier chapters of this study have employed a typology for examining the UN system's response to states' "unauthorized" resort to force, i.e. in circumstances in which the state has not been the victim of a traditional armed attack and the Security Council has not voted to invoke collective measures under Charter Chapter VII. Chapter 3 has identified five clusters of justification advanced in support of such unauthorized recourse to force. Using this analytic typology, the study seeks to ascertain the extent to which each kind of unconventional justification has been validated in systemic practice.

From the foregoing examination of some of this practice, it appears that the principal organs of the United Nations have responded in accordance with the nuanced situational merits of each crisis, rather than in compliance with any general redefinition of the concept of "self-defence" contained in Article 51. Although the role of political horse-trading cannot be discounted, it appears that most countries have reacted with integrity, instance-by-instance, to the weight of factual and contextual evidence presented by advocates and critics of each use of force. This is also true in those instances in which the use of force has been justified as "anticipatory self-defence."

Anticipatory use of force in self-defense as a legal concept

Anticipatory self-defense has a long history in customary international law. As early as 1837, it was canvassed by US Secretary of State Daniel Webster in the *Caroline* dispute. In a classical attempt to define but also to limit it, Webster concluded that such a right arises only when there is a "necessity of self-defence ... instant, overwhelming, leaving no choice of means and no moment for deliberation." He cautioned that it permits "nothing unreasonable or excessive."[1]

Has recourse to such anticipatory self-defense in circumstances of extreme necessity been preserved, or repealed, by the Charter?[2] Common sense, rather than textual literalism, is often the best guide to interpretation of international legal norms. Thus, Bowett concludes that "no state can be expected to await an initial attack which, in the present state of armaments, may well destroy the state's capacity for further resistance and so jeopardise its very existence."[3] In 1996, the International Court of Justice indirectly touched on this question in its *Advisory Opinion on the Legality of the Use of Nuclear Weapons in Armed Conflict*. A majority of judges was unable to conclude that first-use of nuclear weapons would invariably be unlawful if the very existence of a state were threatened.[4] Despite its ambiguity, the Court appears to have recognized the exceptional nature and logic of a state's claim to use means necessary to ensure its self-preservation. The same reasoning can lead to the logical deduction that no law – and certainly not Article 51 – should be interpreted to compel the *reductio ad absurdum* that states invariably must await a first, perhaps decisive, military strike before using force to protect themselves.

On the other hand, a general relaxation of Article 51's prohibitions on unilateral war-making to permit unilateral recourse to force whenever a state feels potentially threatened could lead to another *reductio ad absurdum*. The law cannot have intended to leave every state free to resort to military force whenever it perceived itself grievously endangered by actions of another, for that would negate any role for law.[5] In practice, the UN

---

[1] For a discussion see Sir Robert Jennings and Sir Arthur Watts, 1 *Oppenheim's International Law* 420–27 (9th edn., 1992).

[2] See generally Derek Bowett, *Self-Defense in International Law* 118–92 (1958); Yoram Dinstein, *War, Aggression and Self-Defense* (1988).

[3] Bowett, *Self-Defence in International Law* at 185–86.

[4] *Legality of the Threat or Use of Nuclear Weapons (Request by the United Nations General Assembly for an Advisory Opinion)*, 1996 I.C.J. 26 at 265, para. 105(2)E: "The Court cannot conclude definitively whether the threat or use of nuclear weapons would be lawful or unlawful in an extreme circumstance of self-defence, in which the very survival of a State would be at stake."

[5] This is the valid point made by Ian Brownlie, *International Law and the Use of Force by States* 275 (1963).

system has sought, with some success, to navigate between these two conceptual shoals. Three instances may be indicative: the US (and OAS) blockade against Cuba during the 1962 missile crisis, Israel's attack on its Arab neighbors in 1967, and Israel's raid on the Iraqi nuclear reactor in 1981. These provide some evidence by the UN system – what was said, what was done, and what was left unsaid or undone – of its way of responding to a claim of "anticipatory self-defence."[6]

Anticipatory self-defense: post-Charter practice

The Cuba missile crisis (1962–1963)

On October 22, 1962, President John F. Kennedy announced his intention to impose a naval quarantine on Cuba to compel the removal of secretly emplaced Soviet missiles said to pose an imminent threat to US national security.[7] A day later, the Council of the OAS supported this US resort to force. It "recommended" that members "take all measures, individually and collectively including the use of armed force which they may deem necessary" to prevent the missiles "from ever becoming an active threat to the peace and security of the Continent."[8]

The US argued that this military action, carefully called a "quarantine," did not constitute use of force in violation of Article 51. Since no ship had actually tried to run its blockade,[9] none had been seized.

---

[6] It may be significant, for example, that states that could have been expected to seek approval for a normative enunciation of a right to anticipatory self-defense chose not to do so during the drafting of key resolutions of the General Assembly such as the *Declaration on Friendly Relations*, the *Definition of Aggression* and the *Declaration on the Non-Use of Force*, or during the International Law Commission's work on State Responsibility. Christine Gray, *International Law and the Use of Force* 112 (2000). See also Pierre Cot and Alain Pellet (eds.), *La Charte des Nations Unies* 779 (1991). This may simply demonstrate that states prefer to argue, case by case and in the context of specific facts, that an anticipatory recourse to self-defense was demonstrably necessary as a measure of self-preservation or, even better, that the defensive recourse to force was not anticipatory but in response to hostile actions analogous to an armed attack, such as a blockade. *See* Malcolm Shaw, *International Law* 694–95 (3rd edn., 1991).

[7] Presidential Proclamation 3504 of October 23, 1962, 57 Am. J. Int'l L. 512 (1963).

[8] Resolution on the Adoption of Necessary Measures to Prevent Cuba from Threatening the Peace and Security of the Continent, OAS Council, Annex A, OEA/Ser.G/V/C-d-1024 Rev. 2 (23 October 1962).

[9] On October 26, a Soviet-chartered Lebanese vessel was boarded peacefully in the only physical encounter between the adversaries.

Moreover, Washington argued, the "quarantine," had been legitimated by endorsement of the regional organization.[10]

In the Security Council, US Ambassador Adlai Stevenson relied less on such technical legal arguments than on the right of the US and the OAS to respond preventively to "this transformation of Cuba into a base for offensive weapons of sudden mass destruction,"[11] mounted on missiles "installed by clandestine means"[12] in pursuit of a Soviet "policy of aggression."[13] Despite "categorical assurances"[14] by Moscow that its missile deployment was solely of a "defensive character,"[15] Stevenson insisted that it was "clearly a threat to [the Western] hemisphere. And when it thus upsets the precarious balance in the world, it is a threat to the whole world."[16] He characterized America's role as standing firm against "this new phase of aggression...,"[17] and sought to place the quarantine in a posture of national and regional self-defense against a threatening, hostile new deployment of armed force by Moscow.

The weakness in this claim was that the Soviet missile deployment in Cuba could quite credibly be explained in defensive, rather than offensive, terms. A year earlier, the US had sponsored an attempt to invade Cuba at the Bay of Pigs. The Soviet representative, pointedly referring to that "April fiasco,"[18] reiterated his country's pledge to ensure against further such efforts to overthrow the Castro regime. Asserting "that [the new] arms and military equipment are intended solely for defensive purposes"[19] in response to "continuous threats and acts of provocation by the United States,"[20] he added:

No State, no matter how powerful it may be, has any right to rule on the quantity or types of arms which another State considers necessary for its defence. According to the United Nations Charter, each State has the right to defend itself and to possess weapons to ensure its security.[21]

---

[10] See L. Meeker, "Defensive Quarantine and the Law," 57 Am. J. Int'l L. 515, 518–24 (1963); A. Chayes, "The Legal Case for U.S. Action in Cuba," 47 Department of State Bull. 763 (1962); A. Chayes, "Law and the Quarantine of Cuba," 41 For. Aff. 550, 553–57 (1963).

[11] S.C.O.R. (XVII), 1022nd Meeting, 23 October 1962, at 3, para. 14.

[12] S.C.O.R. (XVII), 1022nd Meeting, 23 October 1962, at 12, para. 61.

[13] S.C.O.R. (XVII), 1022nd Meeting, 23 October 1962, at 6, para. 29.

[14] S.C.O.R. (XVII), 1022nd Meeting, 23 October 1962, at 14, para. 71.

[15] *Ibid.*   [16] S.C.O.R. (XVII), 1022nd Meeting, 23 October 1962, at 15, para. 74.

[17] S.C.O.R. (XVII), 1022nd Meeting, 23 October 1962, at 15, para. 77.

[18] S.C.O.R. (XVII), 1022nd Meeting, 23 October 1962, at 28, para. 146.

[19] S.C.O.R. (XVII), 1022nd Meeting, 23 October 1962, at 30, para. 155.

[20] *Ibid.*   [21] S.C.O.R. (XVII), 1022nd Meeting, 23 October 1962, at 35, para. 178.

Three draft resolutions were put before the Security Council, proposed, respectively, by the United States, the Soviet Union, and by Ghana with the United Arab Republic (UAR). The US draft called for UN supervision of "the withdrawal from Cuba of all missiles and other offensive weapons."[22] The Soviet resolution condemned the quarantine and demanded its revocation,[23] while the Ghana–UAR draft studiously refrained from taking sides but called on the Secretary-General to mediate and on the parties "to refrain . . . from any action which might . . . further aggravate the situation."[24] Acting UN Secretary-General U Thant, supporting the African lead, called on the US and USSR to negotiate a peaceful solution and on Cuba to halt construction and development of new missile installations. None of the three resolutions was put to a vote while vigorous bilateral negotiations were pursued. On January 7, 1963, the US and USSR, having worked out a settlement, sent a joint letter to the Secretary-General thanking him for his efforts and "in view of the degree of understanding between them" requesting deletion of the item from the Security Council's agenda.[25]

What little the crisis revealed about states' attitude to anticipatory self-defense seemed to indicate that very few, outside the Soviet bloc, relied on a strict interpretation of Articles 2(4), 51, and 53.[26] Instead Western European and Western Hemisphere states rallied behind the US action while many of those in Africa and Asia supported the neutral initiative of the Secretary-General.[27]

Israeli-Arab War (1967)

On May 18, 1967, the Secretary-General received a message from Cairo's Foreign Minister requesting withdrawal of the United Nations' Emergency Force (UNEF) that had served as a buffer between Israelis and Egyptians in the Sinai since the war of 1956.[28] Although expressing his misgivings, U Thant felt required to comply. Immediately, UAR

---

[22] S/5182 of 22 October 1962.   [23] S/5187 of 23 October 1962.
[24] S/5190 of 24 October 1962.   [25] S/5227, 7 January 1963.
[26] Sean D. Murphy, *Humanitarian Intervention: The United Nations in an Evolving World Order* 342–43 (1996).
[27] For example, twelve Francophone African states communicated this position of support to the Secretary-General, 1962 UN Yearbook 108. See also A. Mark Weisburd, *Use of Force: The Practice of States Since World War II* 215–18 (1997).
[28] The letter is reproduced in A/6669 and Add.1, special report of the Secretary-General to General Assembly's 22nd session, 18 May 1967.

forces redeployed to occupy the former buffer zone and thereby directly confronted Israeli forces.[29] This confrontation spread from land to sea. With UN forces withdrawn from their Sinai base at Sharm El Sheikh, Cairo declared the Gulf of Aqaba and Strait of Tiran closed to Israeli shipping.[30] At the same time, there was an ominous increase in Palestinian forces' infiltration along the border between Israel and Syria, where peacekeepers of the UN Truce Supervisory Organization (UNTSO) were still uncomfortably positioned.[31] An orchestrated Arab assault on Israel seemed inevitable and, as Professor Malcolm Shaw points out, it "could of course, be argued that the Egyptian blockade itself constituted the use of force, thus legitimising Israeli actions without the need for 'anticipatory' conceptions of self-defence."[32]

At approximately 3 a.m. on June 5, 1967, Israel and Egypt each notified the President of the Security Council that an armed attack had been launched by the other. When, a few hours later, the Security Council met in emergency session, the Secretary-General reported that, since his personnel had been evacuated at Egypt's request, he could not ascertain which party had initiated hostilities. Fighting quickly spread to Israel's other fronts, including Jerusalem.[33] On the following day the Council unanimously passed a resolution placing blame on none of the parties, but calling on all "to take forthwith as a first step all measures for an immediate cease-fire..."[34]

Israel argued that it was merely responding as victim of a concerted armed attack by forces of the UAR, Jordan, and Syria. This argument was difficult to credit, given its forces' large successes in the first days of fighting. Alternatively, Israel argued a right of anticipatory self-defense: that the sudden withdrawal of UNEF from the Sinai at Cairo's insistence had gravely prejudiced Israel's vital interests, leaving it with few options but to pre-empt an Arab attack by launching one of its own.

The Council took no position on this argument. Its second resolution, introduced by the Soviet Union, and passed unanimously on June 7, again demanded a cease-fire but carefully refrained from either apportioning blame or granting exculpation. It notably did not call for the withdrawal of Israeli troops from newly occupied territory.[35] Israel and Jordan mutually accepted this demand on condition that all other parties

---

[29] 1967 U.N.Y.B. 166.   [30] 1967 U.N.Y.B. at 168.   [31] 1967 U.N.Y.B. at 164.
[32] Shaw, n. 6 above, at 694; Gray, n. 6 above, at 112.   [33] 1967 U.N.Y.B. 175.
[34] S. Res. 233 of 6 June 1967.   [35] S. Res. 234 of 7 June 1967.

follow suit. Egypt hesitated for two days, then accepted conditionally.[36] A few parties to the conflict (Syria, Iraq, Kuwait) altogether rejected, or failed to accept, the cease-fire[37] even as Israeli forces occupied Gaza, the West Bank, Sinai, and Golan Heights. On June 9, Syria signalled its acceptance of the two cease-fire resolutions, yet fighting continued. Meanwhile, inside and outside the Council, the Soviet Union, with increasing stridency, called for condemnation of Israel and a roll-back of the parties to the *status quo ante*. Nevertheless, a unanimous Security Council, on June 11, again impartially demanded all-party observance of the cease-fire, the freezing of the combatants' positions, but not a roll-back of the gains made by Israel.[38]

In his study of these events, Professor Weisburd has concluded that the war had begun with "a preemptive air strike" by Israel against Egypt's airfields that completely destroyed the Egyptian air force. A misguided effort to come to Egypt's aid then led to the annihilation of Jordan's air force. The land war ended with Israeli occupation of territories more than four times its previous size. "Israel initially justified its actions before the United Nations," he reports, "by claiming, falsely, that it had been attacked first, though it subsequently reinforced this argument by stressing both the character of the Egyptian blockade [of the Strait of Tiran] as an act of war and the very dangerous situation in which Israel found itself on June 5."[39]

Although Israel also based its justification on actual self-defense against such aggressive acts as the closure of the Strait of Tiran, its words and actions clearly asserted a right to anticipatory self-defense against an imminent armed attack. It is difficult not to conclude that the Council members gave credence to this latter argument, since none of its resolutions spoke of the return of captured territory or censured the Israeli action despite urgent demands to that effect by the Soviet Union and its Eastern European allies.[40] The Soviet resolution condemning Israel and demanding return of all captured territory garnered only 4 of 15 Council votes, with even a bare-bones call for simple withdrawal supported by only 6 states.[41]

At the Fifth Emergency Special Assembly, convened at Soviet insistence on 17 June, 1967,[42] only a resolution regarding humanitarian

---

[36] S/7953, 8 June 1967 (UAR).
[37] S/7945, 7 June 1967 (Israel); S/7946, 7 and 8 June 1967 (Jordan); S/7948, 8 June 1967 (Kuwait).
[38] S. Res. 236 of 11 June 1967.   [39] Weisburd, n. 27 above, at 137.
[40] 1967 U.N.Y.B. 110–11.   [41] 1967 U.N.Y.B. 179, 190.   [42] A/6717 of 13 June 1967.

assistance and another calling on Israel to rescind its annexation of East Jerusalem were able to round up the requisite two-thirds majority.[43] Numerous condemnatory resolutions and demands for pull-back proposed by the Soviet Union[44] and Albania[45] failed to be adopted. A similar non-aligned initiative was voted down with the help of states in Western Europe, the Western Hemisphere, and Africa.[46]

In the ensuing period, as Weisburd summarizes it, "the international consensus that emerged was, in effect, that while Israel could not be permitted to retain the land seized from the Arabs, any return of the land had to be linked to satisfaction of Israel's reasonable security concerns." Thus, "the international community was unwilling to focus solely on the fact that Israel acquired the Arab lands by force without reference to the underlying political situation that led up to the use of force."[47]

On July 9, the Security Council, by consensus, authorized the Secretary-General to "work out with the Governments of the United Arab Republic and Israel...the necessary arrangements to station United Nations military observers in the Suez Canal sector...,"[48] thereby, for the time being, *de facto* accommodating the Israeli gains. On November 22, it unanimously adopted a further resolution that, while confirming the "inadmissibility of the acquisition of territory by war," linked withdrawal of Israeli forces to the "[t]ermination of all claims or states of belligerency" against Israel and respect for its "right to live in peace within secure and recognized boundaries free from threats or acts of force..."[49] Professor Malcolm Shaw concludes that in this instance the system "apportioned no blame...and specifically refused to condemn..." the Israeli recourse to force.[50] While some experts have pointed out that neither the Council nor the Assembly formally embraced the principle of anticipatory self-defense – indeed, that the Israelis did not exclusively justify their action as such, but also claimed to be acting in *actual* self-defense[51] – the primary facts speak for themselves. Israel had not yet been attacked militarily when it launched its first strikes. As for

---

[43] G.A. Res. 2253 (ES-V) and G.A. Res. 2252 (ES-V).

[44] A/L.519 rejected 4 July 1967, paragraph by paragraph. 1967 U.N.Y.B. 209.

[45] A/L.521 rejected 4 July 1967 by 71 against to 22 for with 27 abstentions.

[46] A/L.522 rejected 4 July 1967 by 53 in favor, 46 against and 20 abstentions (a two-thirds majority being necessary to adoption).

[47] Weisburd, n. 27 above, at 139.   [48] S/8047, S.C. Meeting 1366 of 9 July 1967.

[49] S. Res. 242 of 22 November 1967.   [50] Malcolm Shaw, *International Law* 429 (1977).

[51] Professor Christine Gray asserts that, while the Israeli action "was apparently a pre-emptive strike against Egypt, Jordan and Syria,...it did not seek to rely on

the Straits of Tiran, Israel had not begun to exhaust its diplomatic remedies. Its attack on Egypt was in anticipation of an armed attack, not a
reaction to it. Most states, on the basis of evidence available to them,
did however apparently conclude that such a armed attack was imminent, that Israel had reasonably surmised that it stood a better chance
of survival if the attack were pre-empted, and that, therefore, in the circumstances, it had not acted unreasonably. This does not amount to an
open-ended endorsement of a general right to anticipatory self-defense,
but it does recognize that, in demonstrable circumstances of extreme necessity, anticipatory self-defense may be a legitimate exercise of a state's
right to ensure its survival.

Israel–Iraq (nuclear reactor) (1981)

On June 7, 1981, nine aircraft of the Israeli air force bombed the
Tuwaitha research center near Baghdad. In a note to the Secretary-
General, the Israeli Government claimed to have destroyed the "Osirak"
(Tamuz-1) nuclear reactor[52] which, it said, was developing atomic bombs
that were to be ready for use against it by 1985.[53]

Iraq, in asking for an immediate meeting of the Security Council,
described the attack as a grave act of aggression, pointing out that
it, unlike Israel, was a party to the 1968 Treaty on Non-Proliferation
of Nuclear Weapons (NPT) and that its reactor, registered with the
International Atomic Energy Agency (IAEA), was subject to IAEA
inspection, and had never been found in violation of the nuclear
safeguards agreement.[54] Israel, however, claimed that Iraq's uranium
purchases were more consistent with weapons production than with
peaceful use and that its government's bellicose rhetoric had confirmed
an intent to use the weapons.[55] As for the IAEA inspections, Israel argued that these were easy to circumvent,[56] making the pre-emptive strike
necessary.

States' reactions, however, were highly negative. On June 19 the
Council unanimously adopted a strongly condemnatory resolution that
affirmed Iraq's inalienable "sovereign right" to develop a peaceful

---

anticipatory self-defence." Gray, n. 6 above, at 112. She surmises that states acting in
this way are reluctant to invoke anticipatory self-defense as a principled justification
because "they know [it] will be unacceptable to the vast majority of states." *Ibid.*
[52] A/36/313, S/14510, 8 June 1981.   [53] A/36/610, S/14732, 19 October 1981.
[54] 1981 U.N.Y.B. 275–76; Weisburd, n. 27 above, at 287–89.
[55] Weisburd, n. 27 above, at 288.   [56] *Ibid.*

nuclear capacity and called on Israel to place its own nuclear reactors under IAEA control by adhering to the NPT.[57] In November, the General Assembly endorsed an even stronger resolution containing a "solemn warning" against repetition of such action.[58] It received 109 votes in favor with only the US and Israel opposed and 34 abstentions.

In stating its case, Israel was not able to demonstrate convincingly that there was a strong likelihood of an imminent nuclear attack by Iraq. The negative response reflected this, as well as a sense that Israel – a nuclear power deliberately remaining outside the NPT safety network – was trying to dictate to another sovereign state whether it could develop a nuclear capability. Even so, neither the Council nor the Assembly imposed any sanctions. The Assembly's only action was to request the Secretary-General "to prepare with the assistance of a group of experts, a comprehensive study of the consequences of the Israeli armed attack against the Iraqi nuclear installations devoted to peaceful purposes..."[59]

The attack on Iraq can be seen in the same legal context of anticipatory self-defense as other instances noted in this chapter. Israel claimed to have acted to pre-empt an imminent, crippling, use or threat of use of a nuclear weapon against it by Iraq – a state which still regarded itself as at war with "the Zionist state." Iraq, to the contrary, denied any intent to produce, let alone to deploy, weapons of mass destruction. No conclusive, or even highly probabilistic, evidence was produced by Israel to support its claim of extreme necessity, although, for both Israel's supporters and opponents, the question less concerned Iraq's nuclear-weapons capability than its propensity to use it. Propensities, however, are obdurately unamenable to conclusive proof.[60]

Sometimes views of the probity of evidentiary proof change with the passage of time and as more evidence comes to light. By the time Iraq invaded Kuwait in 1990, the UN's harsh judgment of Israel's anticipatory strike was being reappraised, especially as it became apparent that Baghdad, possessing a sophisticated medium-range ballistic delivery system, indeed had developed an extensive array of nuclear, biological, and chemical weapons and that its *animus* evidently was not peaceful.

---

[57] S.C. Res. 487 of 19 June 1981.   [58] G.A. Res. 36/27 of 13 November 1981.

[59] G.A. Res. 37/18 of 16 November 1982.

[60] The distinction is clarified by Weisburd, n. 27 above, at 299. He states that anticipatory self-help differs from reprisal in that the state asserting it must show "that it had reason to believe that it was to be the target of future actions by the group against whom retaliatory action had been taken and that the attack was to deter these future attacks."

Had Israel not struck in 1981, the reversal of Iraq's invasion of Kuwait a decade later might well have been impossible.

Again, however, evidence, rather than abstract principle, seems to determine the response to each instance in which a state claims the right to use force in anticipatory self-defense. States seem willing to accept strong evidence of the imminence of an overpowering attack as tantamount to the attack itself, allowing a demonstrably threatened state to respond under Article 51 as if the attack had already occurred, or at least to treat such circumstances, when demonstrated, as mitigating the system's judgment of the threatened state's pre-emptive response. This is made more likely if the response is proportionate and avoids collateral damage. The practice of UN organs also makes clear, however, that it is for them – collectively responding to the evidence – and not for an attacking state to determine the propriety or culpability of such anticipatory use of force.

Conclusions

The problem with recourse to anticipatory self-defense is its ambiguity. In the right circumstances, it can be a prescient measure that, at low cost, extinguishes the fuse of a powder-keg. In the wrong circumstances, it can cause the very calamity it anticipates. The 1967 Israeli "first-strike" against Egypt's air force was widely seen to be warranted in circumstances where Cairo's hostile intention was evident and Israel's vulnerability patently demonstrable. In the end, the UN system did not condemn Israel's unauthorized recourse to force but, instead, sensibly insisted on its relinquishing conquered territory in return for what was intended to be a securely monitored peace. The system balanced Egypt's illegitimate provocations against Israel's recourse to illegal preventive measures. Most states understood that a very small, densely populated state cannot be expected to await a very probable, potentially decisive attack before availing itself of the right to self-defense.

In the case of the Cuba missile crisis, the international system appears to have been less than convinced that the Soviets' introduction of nuclear-armed missiles – albeit stealthy – genuinely and imminently threatened the US. It was apparent, for example, that deployment of nuclear-armed missiles on US and Russian submarines off each other's coasts had not engendered similar claims to act in "anticipatory self-defence." Still, the covert way Soviet missiles were introduced in Cuba and the disingenuousness with which their deployment had at first been denied, strengthened the US claim to be responding to an imminent threat. That claim was so strongly supported by other states in the Americas as to impede the usual third world rush to judgment against the US. Most important, the forceful countermeasures taken, although probably an act of war in international law and a violation of the literal text of Articles 2(4) and 51, was also seen as cautious, limited, and carefully calibrated. No shots were fired by the ships implementing the blockade. In the end, the outcome – the withdrawal of Soviet missiles from Cuba in return for a reciprocal dismantling of US missiles on the Turkish–Soviet border, together with Washington's promise not again to attempt an invasion of Cuba – was seen by most states (except Cuba) as a positive accomplishment.

Only in the instance of Israel's aerial strike against the Iraqi nuclear plant did the system categorically condemn and deny both the legality and legitimacy of recourse to anticipatory self-defense. In doing so, however, even vociferous critics of Israel made clear that they were not opposed to a right of anticipatory self-defense in principle but, rather that they did not believe that Iraq's nuclear plant was being used unlawfully to produce weapons and that a nuclear attack on Israel was neither probable nor imminent. In this conjecture they may have been wrong, but they were surely right in subjecting to a high standard of probity any evidence adduced to support a claim to use force in anticipation of, rather than as a response to, an armed attack.

8

Countermeasures and self-help

The "self-help" dilemma

When a right is denied, it is natural to turn to the authority that is the source of that right in the expectation that it will be enforced. When that expectation is not met, there is moral force to the argument that those aggrieved by the failure should themselves be allowed to enforce their legal entitlement as best they can.

In international law, the issue of the legality of countermeasures and self-help arises when, a state having refused to carry out its legal responsibilities and the international system having failed to enforce the law, another state, victimized by that failure, takes countermeasures to protect its interests. "Its interests" in this context denotes the peaceful enjoyment of rights accruing to a state, of which it is deprived by the continuing wrongful acts of another state. It may also be, however, that the notion of a transgressed state interest has expanded to include not only violations of its rights as a sovereign, but also of rights held derivatively as a member of the international system. Thus, for example, every state may enjoy the right *erga omnes* not to have the earth's "commons" – the seas, the air – polluted in violation of globally applicable norms. Along similar lines, every state may have a right to act to prevent a genocide that, even if not directed at its own people, violates the treaty-based common conscience of humanity. Some recognition has been given to this more extended notion of a state's self-interest by the International Law Commission's Restatement of the Law of State Responsibility.[1] That there are such *erga*

[1] Text of Articles, State Responsibility, 31 May 2001, International Law Commission, article 48: "Any State other than an injured State is entitled to invoke the responsibility

109

omnes norms in international law which, if violated, give rise to a claim by any or all states does not of course resolve the vexed issue of what remedial steps states may take to protect their violated rights against further breaches. Normally, redress would have to be sought through the peaceful means provided by the treaty establishing the violated right or by general international law. The Draft Articles on State Responsibility, in Article 49, permits countermeasures "against a State which is responsible for an internationally wrongful act in order to induce that State to comply with its obligations" but, it adds, such countermeasures "shall not affect (a) The obligation to refrain from the threat or use of force as embodied in the United Nations Charter..."[2]

What, exactly, is that "obligation...as embodied in the...Charter"? Is there an inexorable obligation "to refrain from...use of force," when does it arise and what countermeasures are precluded by it? How relevant is the practice of UN organs in construing this limitation on the right to take countermeasures?

These questions are all too relevant because of severe imperfections in the capacity of the international legal system to ensure compliance with its norms and to guarantee a remedy for violations. Reason suggests that self-help and countermeasures remain necessary remedies of last resort. Nevertheless, the text and context of the UN Charter seem to indicate otherwise. Article 2(4)'s ban on resort to force brooks no exception for states' enforcing their rights when UN collective measures have not been taken or have failed. Indeed, the Charter does not seem even to recognize any duty on the part of the UN system itself to enforce international legal rights against violators unless the breaches rise to the level of a threat to the general peace of nations within the meaning of Article 39. Nowhere does the Charter specifically license the Security Council, let alone states acting on their own, to enforce international law, although, exceptionally, Article 94(2) does authorize a party to a case decided by the International Court of Justice, if the other party fails to carry out a judgment against it, to "have recourse to the Security Council, which may, if it deems necessary, make recommendations or decide upon measures to be taken to give effect to the judgment."

Footnote 1 (*cont.*)
of another State...if: (a) The obligation breached is owed to a group of States including that State, and is established for the protection of a collective interest of the group." The Convention on the Prevention and Punishment of the Crime of Genocide, 78 U.N.T.S. 277 of 1951 is the leading example of a wrong *erga omnes* that accords a right to all states *qua* any violation.
2 State Responsibility, 31 May 2001, International Law Commission article 50.

However, this provision is so weak that it has proven all but impossible to implement.[3]

How, then, is a state to secure its rights in international law against a stubborn violator? To be sure, if the violation rises to the level of a threat to the peace, breach of the peace, or act of aggression, the victim may apply to the Security Council under Charter Article 39. Less dramatic violations of law are potentially subject to pacific settlement procedures (Charter Chapter VI), but none of these envisages enforcement. Consequently, under a strict interpretation of the Charter, states, individually and, in all but extreme cases even collectively, may be said to have renounced the option to enforce their rights, even when the UN system fails to do it for them. If that is indeed the law, it tilts peace far away from justice.

Weak enforcement, of course, is a general problem of the international system. "The most common complaint about international law," Professor Schachter has written, "is that it lacks effective enforcement. Its obvious deficiencies from this standpoint are the absence of compulsory judicial process and the limited capability of international institutions to impose sanctions on a violator."[4] The UN Charter, he adds, deliberately "accords priority to the peaceful resolution of disputes rather than to the enforcement of law..." That bargain, he observes, does not go unchallenged in practice. "Inevitably, the victims of violations have resorted to self-help..."[5]

This has sometimes met with approval or tacit acquiescence, sometimes not. As usual, the facts matter as does the clarity with which they are put forward. In its Advisory Opinion on Namibia, the International Court of Justice declared illegal South Africa's usurpation of that territory's administration and went on to encourage states to act so as to deprive South Africa of the fruits of its illegal occupation by economic measures, if not by military action.[6] The General Assembly, however,

---

[3] See, for example, the failure of the Security Council to overcome a US veto in order to comply with Nicaragua's effort to enforce the decision of the ICJ in its favor in its dispute with the US. Letter of Nicaragua to the President of the Security Council, S/18230, 22 July 1986; Resolution calling for full compliance with the ICJ decision, S/18250 of 31 July 1986. This resolution received 11 votes in favor, 1 against (US), with 3 abstentions. It is notable that, in contradiction to Charter article 27(3), the US vote was counted as a veto even though it was "a party to [the] dispute..." and, arguably, the draft resolution would have constituted a "decision... under Chapter VI..." If action to enforce an ICJ decision were to be proposed under Chapter VII, however, the veto would apply.

[4] Oscar Schachter, *International Law in Theory and Practice* 184 (1991).   [5] *Ibid.*

[6] 1971 I.C.J. 16.

went further: calling on members to give *military* support to "front-line states" confronting South Africa.[7] The large majority voting to recommend[8] direct military action obviously believed that the taking of such remedial action would be lawful.[9]

Despite the paucity of judicial and political *opinio juris*, it appears that recourse to self-help remains an option not entirely foreclosed by the Charter, at least as interpreted or implied by state practice. Among the instances in which armed force has been used to give effect to a state's assertion of a legal right, several have involved long-standing wrongs which the system had previously recognized as such, but nevertheless had failed to redress. In these circumstances, the state using force to assert its rights has sometimes resorted to creative fictions: alleging that it was responding to an armed attack or to something closely analogous to an armed attack such as foreign subversion, or a massive, foreign-induced flow of refugees across its borders. In a few instances, however, the victimized state has bluntly justified its recourse to countermeasures as self-help, pleading extreme necessity. The reaction of the international system in these exceptional instances lends further credence to the thesis that state recourse to force may be tolerated, perhaps even specifically approved, in circumstances not anticipated by the drafters of the Charter. Among such circumstances is the failure of the UN system to redress an egregious wrong recognized as such in international law. Protracted failure may give rise to a limited right of self-help on the part of a *bona fide* injured party, even when the injury does not rise to the threshold of an "armed attack."

Self-help: post-Charter practice

Israel–Argentina (1960)

Adolf Eichmann, who had long been sought to stand trial for massive crimes against humanity, was kidnapped by Israeli agents in Argentina

---

[7] G.A. Res. 36/121A of 10 December 1981. The resolution was adopted by 120–0 with 27 abstentions. G.A. Res. 2151 (XXI) of 17 November 1966. This resolution was passed by 89 votes to 2 with 17 abstentions. See, to same effect, E.S.C. Res. 2101 (LXIII) of 3 August 1977.

[8] See UN Charter Articles 10, 11(2), 14.

[9] G.A. Res. 36/121A of 10 December 1981. This call to states to resort to self-help was couched in general terms of resisting "aggression," which would place such countermeasures within the ambit of permissible recourse to force created by Article 51, rather than as enforcement of an ICJ decision.

on May 23, 1960 and flown to Israel. While the Israeli government expressed "regret" for having "violated Argentine law or interfered with matters within the sovereignty of Argentina"[10] it claimed that it had acted solely "to bring to trial the man responsible for the murder of millions of persons..."[11]

Argentina convened the Security Council,[12] where it demanded "appropriate reparations."[13] Its representative called on Israel to punish those who had violated its sovereignty,[14] arguing that Israel's actions "impaired" a "principle" of "supreme importance": the "unqualified respect which States owe to each other and which precludes the exercise of jurisdictional acts in the territory of other states."[15] If that principle were not upheld, Buenos Aires warned, "international law would soon be replaced by the law of the jungle."[16] Argentina did not oppose bringing Eichmann to account and agreed that "the circumstances are exceptional." But it insisted that this could not justify Israel's resort to force. "If a breach, a single breach, is made in the fabric of the law," its representative insisted, "the whole structure may fall in ruins."[17] In essence, Argentina wanted Eichmann back, and his captors punished.

Israel's representative, Golda Meir, cited the finding of the International Military Tribunal at Nuremberg that Eichmann, as head of Section B4 of the Gestapo, had organized the "final solution" of the Jewish "problem,"[18] the killing of 6 million Jews, 4 million of them in extermination camps.[19] She asked: "would Argentina have admitted Adolf Eichmann into its territory had it known his true identity? Would asylum have been accorded him? Surely not."[20]

It remained for the Soviet representative to say what must have been on others' minds: that "many of the war criminals have succeeded in evading just retribution" and that "some of them, as is well known, have found refuge in Argentine territory. By omitting to take measures for the timely arrest and extradition of Eichmann as a war criminal" Argentina had violated its international legal obligations.[21] The Polish

---

[10] S/4342 of 21 June 1960.   [11] *Ibid.*
[12] S.C.O.R. (XV), 865th Meeting, 22 June 1960, at 2, para. 5.
[13] S/4334 of 8 June 1960.
[14] S.C.O.R. (XV), 865th Meeting, 22 June 1960, at 5, para. 24.
[15] S.C.O.R. (XV), 865th Meeting, 22 June 1960, at 7, para. 34.
[16] *Ibid.*
[17] S.C.O.R. (XV), 865th Meeting, 22 June 1960, at 9, para. 42.
[18] S.C.O.R. (XV), 866th Meeting, 22 June 1960, at 5, para. 22.
[19] S.C.O.R. (XV), 866th Meeting, 22 June 1960, at 7, para. 28.
[20] S.C.O.R. (XV), 865th Meeting, 22 June 1960, at 9, para. 42.
[21] S.C.O.R. (XV), 865th Meeting, 22 June 1960, at 12, para. 60.

representative added that, "were it not for the attitude taken by certain states towards Nazi war criminals, we most certainly would have no dispute today on Eichmann."[22] The US[23] and British[24] representatives, while generally endorsing Argentina's call to reassert the UN Charter's principle prohibiting states' unilateral recourse to force, thought the claim to "appropriate reparation" had already been satisfied by Israel's apology.

At the end of the debate, the Security Council passed a resolution reiterating the principle of respect for national sovereignty,[25] to which Israel duly expressed its adherence,[26] and declaring that "acts such as that under consideration, which affect the sovereignty of a Member State and therefore cause international friction, may, if repeated, endanger international peace and security."[27]

The members of the Security Council, clearly, endorsed the general principle that no state has a right to employ self-help on the territory of another. At the same time, it was equally evident that there was widespread understanding of Israel's action in the light of Eichmann's well-established culpability and the suspicion that Argentina had been less than wholehearted in the pursuit of war criminals hiding in its territory. These *mitigated*[28] whatever wrong had been done by recourse to this unilateral countermeasure. The Council thus upheld legality but exercised leniency in responding to the facts and circumstances of its violation, supporting the general applicability of Argentina's normative claim, but giving it no other satisfaction and imposing on Israel neither penalties nor any obligation to make restitution for resorting to self-help in such exceptional circumstances.

India–Portugal (1961)

Ever since its admission to the United Nations in 1955, Portugal had refused to accept responsibility for applying to its territories in Africa and Asia the legal obligation in Charter Article 73(e), which required it to make periodic reports on "non-self-governing territories" and to

[22] S.C.O.R. (XV), 867th Meeting, 23 June 1960, at 3, para. 14.
[23] S.C.O.R. (XV), 867th Meeting, 23 June 1960, at 1–2, para. 5.
[24] S.C.O.R. (XV), 867th Meeting, 23 June 1960, at 8, para. 36.
[25] S. Res. 138 (1960) of 23 June 1960, para. 1.
[26] S.C.O.R. (XV), 868th Meeting, 23 June 1960, at 16, para. 90.
[27] S. Res. 138 (1960) of 23 June 1960, para. 1.
[28] For a discussion of mitigation in international law, see chapter 10.

develop their capacity for self-government. Instead, Lisbon argued, these territories were not colonies but an integral part of Portugal.[29] It insisted that the "political rights of the inhabitants of overseas Portugal were identical with those of the inhabitants of metropolitan Portugal."[30] In practice, however, since Portugal was a dictatorship, neither the people of one or the other enjoyed any political rights.

The General Assembly deplored Lisbon's failure to live up to its Charter obligations. In 1960, it adopted the "declaration on the granting of independence to colonial countries and peoples"[31] which specifically found the Portuguese overseas possessions to come within the category of colonies to which the right of self-determination applied.[32] Goa was the first of these colonies where Portugal confronted a direct challenge to its scoff-lawish behavior by another state that claimed for itself the right to take forceful countermeasures.

With a population of 650,000, Goa had been governed by Portugal for 450 years and was overwhelmingly Christianized, although its people, primarily, were of Indian ethnicity. Geography, history, and culture were cited by India as imbuing it with a special interest in vindicating the right of decolonization. From the time of its own independence, India had vociferously demanded the return of Goa and several other foreign-ruled enclaves in the subcontinent, a demand to which France acceded in 1954 by relinquishing Pondichery, but which Portugal flatly rejected. In December, 1961, 30,000 Indian troops massed on Goa's borders and Lisbon appealed to the Security Council to stop this "provocation."[33]

India's legal claim to Goan emancipation may not have been as clean-cut as Israel's claim to have Eichmann brought to justice. Indeed, a year earlier, in a related matter, the International Court had seemed to accept Portuguese sovereignty over its subcontinental enclaves.[34] Nevertheless, India argued forcefully that Portuguese colonial rule violated the Charter rights of both India and of the Goan people. Efforts to enforce these rights peacefully through the UN system had come to naught. The Indian

---

[29] G.A.O.R. (XI), 618th Meeting, 31 January 1957, at 341, para. 3. Statement of Mr. Norgueira.

[30] G.A.O.R. (XI), 618th Meeting, 31 January 1957, at 341, para. 6.

[31] G.A. Res. 1514 (XV) of 14 December 1960.

[32] G.A. Res. 1542 (XV) of 15 December 1960.

[33] S/5018, 11 December 1961, at 1.

[34] *Case concerning Right of Passage over Indian Territory (Portugal v. India)* (Merits), Judgment of 12 April 1960, 1960 I.C.J. 6. Although Goa was not in contention in this case, its status was indistinguishable from that of the two enclaves, Dadra and Nagar-Aveli, that were involved in the dispute.

representative pointed out that New Delhi had tried for fourteen years to negotiate a peaceful end to this illegal occupation, but that Portugal had refused even to discuss the matter,[35] leaving India with no recourse but to resort to military self-help.[36]

US Ambassador Adlai Stevenson called on the Council to condemn India.[37] "What is at stake today is not colonialism," he said, "it is a bold violation of one of the most basic principles of the United Nations Charter,...Article 2, paragraph 4..."[38] Few followed his lead. The UK representative merely called for a negotiated settlement.[39] Liberia joined Russia and Egypt in strongly supporting India's right to take countermeasures.[40] The Egyptian President of the Security Council noted that the "use of force has not so far been abjured by any nation represented here. Indeed, many nations in this Council maintain today vast armies and great inventories of weapons as testimony to the fact that force is a distinct and accepted element in international life. India has undoubtedly used force in this case – minimum force... – [but] necessary force...after fourteen years of patient waiting...to liberate Indian national territory."[41] At the end of this debate, India's Ambassador Jha summed up:

> The use of force, in all circumstances, is regrettable but so far as the achievement of freedom is concerned, when nothing else is available, I am afraid that it is a very debatable proposition to say that force cannot be used at all.[42]

A resolution supporting India,[43] and another demanding an immediate cease-fire[44] both failed to be adopted. After the vote, Ambassador Stevenson said: "[W]e have witnessed tonight an effort to rewrite the Charter, to sanction the use of force in international relations when it suits one's own purposes. This approach can only lead to chaos and to the disintegration of the United Nations."[45] Ambassador Zorin took

---

[35] S/5020, 13 December 1961, at 1–2.
[36] S.C.O.R. (XVI), 987th Meeting, 18 December 1961, at 9–10, paras. 41–43.
[37] S.C.O.R. (XVI), 987th Meeting, 18 December 1961, at 15, paras. 65ff.
[38] S.C.O.R. (XVI), 987th Meeting, 18 December 1961, at 16, para. 75.
[39] S.C.O.R. (XVI), 987th Meeting, 18 December 1961, at 18, paras. 81ff.
[40] S.C.O.R. (XVI), 987th Meeting, 18 December 1961, at 19, paras. 89ff. (Liberia); at 21, paras. 104ff (Soviet Union); at 25, paras. 120ff (United Arab Republic).
[41] S.C.O.R. (XVI), 987th Meeting, 18 December 1961, at 28, paras. 136–138.
[42] S.C.O.R. (XVI), 988th Meeting, 18 December 1961, at 16, para. 78.
[43] S/5032. This resolution was defeated by 7 votes to 4.
[44] S/5033. This resolution was supported by 7 votes to 4, but vetoed by the Soviet Union.
[45] S.C.O.R. (XVI), 988th Meeting, 18 December 1961, at 27, paras. 130–131.

the opposite view: that the Council had refused to support the forces of unlawful colonial oppression and thus had proven "the merit of the Council, not its weakness."[46]

After its successful annexation of the Portuguese territory, India extended citizenship and rights of full participation in its democratic political system to Goa's population. Portugal itself, and its remaining overseas possessions for fifteen more years remained under fascist rule. Clearly, most nations did not seem to share Ambassador Stevenson's dire assessment of the precedent-setting effects on the UN system of India's unilateral recourse to self-help. In the next Assembly, no effort was made to censure India, which suffered little loss of moral authority, especially among the non-aligned. Rather, the incident seemed to confirm a degree of systemic tolerance for recourse to military force when used to redress what was widely perceived as an egregious, long-standing and amply demonstrated wrong for which the UN system had provided no other redress.

Turkey–Cyprus (1974)

As we noted in chapter 6, Turkey had justified its 1964 attack on Greek-Cypriot military positions as a defence of embattled Turkish-Cypriots. The introduction of neutral UN peacekeepers (UNFICYP) did not resolve this simmering conflict. On July 15, 1974, with the support of the military junta then ruling Greece, the Greek-led Cypriot National Guard overthrew the government of Archbishop Makarios,[47] replacing it with the junta's own surrogate, Nikos Sampson, who promised to effect a union with Greece. Such a union, however, had been expressly forbidden by the terms of the international agreement under which Cyprus had attained its independence.[48] That regime further provided:

In the event of a breach of the provisions of the present Treaty, Greece, Turkey and the United Kingdom undertake to consult together with respect to the representations or measures necessary to secure observance of those

---

[46] S.C.O.R. (XVI), 988th Meeting, 18 December 1961, at 28, para. 139.
[47] S/11353 and Add.1–33, July 21, 1974. Report of the Secretary-General on developments in Cyprus. See also A. Mark Weisburd, *Use of Force: The Practice of States Since World War II* 153 (1997).
[48] Treaty of Guarantee, 16 August 1960, article 1. U.N.T.S., vol. 382, no. 5475 (1960), esp. Article IV.

provisions. In so far as common or concerted action may not prove possible, each of the three guaranteeing powers reserves the right to take action with the sole aim of re-establishing the state of affairs created by the present treaty.

Turkey, invoking the Tripartite Treaty of Guarantee, sought British military intervention. After London demurred, Turkish forces invaded Cyprus on July 20, claiming the right to protect "compatriots."[49] Hastily convened, the Security Council unanimously adopted a resolution calling for the withdrawal of all "foreign military personnel," and respect for "the sovereignty, independence and territorial integrity" of Cyprus together with "an immediate end to foreign military intervention..."[50] On July 22, both the Greek junta in Athens and its Cypriot puppet regime collapsed. Turkey nevertheless continued to reinforce its expedition and to expand its area of control, ultimately occupying a third of the island.

In defence of its invasion, Turkey argued that its forces had undertaken "a peace operation" in fulfillment of "its legal responsibilities as co-guarantor of the independence and constitutional order of Cyprus" in the face of a coup "manufactured by the dictatorial regime of Athens."[51] The Council's response was neither to condone nor to condemn. On July 23 it unanimously "demanded" a cease-fire and, on August 15 unanimously "insist[ed]" on compliance.[52] On August 16 it "record[ed] its formal disapproval of the unilateral military actions undertaken against the Republic of Cyprus" but – since both Greece and Turkey fitted the bill – named no wrong-doer and took no action.[53]

By July 30, agreement among the Greek, Turkish, and British authorities had been reached in negotiations at Geneva.[54] UNFICYP was redeployed along a line separating the ethnic communities in such a

---

[49] S/PV.1783, 23 July 1974, at 7.   [50] S. Res. 353 (1974) of 20 July 1974.

[51] S/PV.1781, July 20, 1974, at 20, para. 224.

[52] S. Res. 354 of 23 July 1974; S. Res. 358 of 15 August 1974.

[53] S. Res. 360 of 16 July 1974. The vote was 11–0 with Byelorussia, Iraq, and the Soviet Union abstaining. The change in the operational mandate of UNFICYP was raised by the Secretary-General in his appearance before the Security Council on July 27, 1974. He noted that the UN force's original mandate did not envisage its interposition between the armed forces of Turkey and those of Cyprus. 1974 U.N.Y.B. 269. The creation of a "security zone" between the two ethnic communities in Cyprus, agreed at a conference of the parties in Geneva, July 25–30, 1974, placed UNFICYP in the new role of patrolling this disengagement.

[54] S/11398, Letter from the UK transmitted by the Secretary-General to the Security Council, July 30, 1974. See also S/PV.1788 of 31 July 1974, pp. 1–2, paras. 1–10.

way as to ratify the *de facto* partition of the island achieved by Turkey's intervention.[55] As if to balance this *de facto* effect with a *de jure* posture, both the Security Council[56] and the General Assembly[57] overwhelmingly endorsed the "territorial integrity" of Cyprus, even as UNFICYP, in the face of continued violence,[58] began to patrol the new line that belied the island's "integrity."

The Security Council's reaction to Turkey's use of force may be summarized as benevolent neutrality. Turkey had acted in response to a ruthless Greek attempt to seize the island-nation in violation of the internationally guaranteed constitutional rights of its Turkish minority. Once its objective had been achieved by the collapse of the Greek junta, however, Turkey went on to occupy a disproportionate part of the island, precipitating large-scale ethnic cleansing. The UN system, although of necessity positioning its peacekeepers along the resultant line of demarcation forged by events beyond its control, firmly rejected – and, almost three decades later still rejects – the island's forcible partition in violation of the "territorial integrity" endorsed both by the Council and Assembly.[59] Nevertheless, a Turkish Federated Republic within Cyprus was declared on February 13, 1975.[60] In November, 1983 an independent Turkish Republic of Northern Cyprus was proclaimed unilaterally.[61] This move was deplored by a Security Council vote of 13–1 (Pakistan) with 1 abstention (Jordan), in a resolution declaring the secession "invalid" and calling for its "withdrawal."[62] A further Council resolution called on all states not to recognize the independence of the Turkish entity,[63] a decision met with widespread compliance.

In several ways, these events foreshadowed dilemmas that continue to be central to the UN's overall peacekeeping mission, yet remain unresolved: (1) that the oppression of a state's minority by its majority

---

[55] S/113980. UNFICYP was unanimously renewed for a further six-month period by S. Res. 364 (1974) of 13 December 1974.

[56] S. Res. 355 of 1 August 1974.

[57] G.A. Res. 3212 (XXIX) of 1 November 1974. This resolution was adopted unanimously at the Assembly's 2275th Plenary Meeting.

[58] S/11444, 13 August 1974. Letter from the Representative of Cyprus to the President of the Security Council alleging "renewed acts of naked aggression against my country by Turkey." See also S/PV.1792 of 14 August 1974.

[59] S. Res. 353 (1974) of 20 July 1974, para. 1; S. Res. 355 (1974) of 1 August 1974, preamb. para. 1.

[60] Declaration of 13 February 1975, establishing a Turkish Federated State in Cyprus. S/11624 of February 18, 1975, Annex II.

[61] S/PV.2497 of 17 November 1983, pp. 2, 10, paras. 8, 88, 96.

[62] S/RES/541 of 18 November 1983.   [63] S/RES/550 of 11 May 1984, para. 3.

is more likely to be opposed effectively by one or more directly concerned nations acting alone than collectively by a UN system in which many states are primarily concerned to preserve, above all, the principle (or myth) of state sovereignty over "domestic" matters; and (2) that benevolent forcible measures taken to emancipate an oppressed minority are likely, if successful, to lead to demands for partition and secession that the UN's state-centered system is understandably reluctant to endorse, but which it also cannot muster the requisite resolve to suppress.

In this instance, the Greek junta's attempt to achieve union with Cyprus against the wishes both of the Greek-Cypriot government of Archbishop Makarios and of the Turkish-Cypriot minority, as well as in violation of the 1960 Tripartite Treaty of Guarantee, made inevitable the UN system's initially mild reaction to Turkish self-help countermeasures. The mildness of the response by the Security Council to that use of force is made even more striking when one considers that these countermeasures, claimed to be validated by the 1960 Tripartite Treaty of Guarantee, were facially unlawful not only under Charter Article 2(4) but also under a literal reading of Article 103, which provides that in the event of a conflict between obligations of a Member under the Charter and any other treaty (i.e. the Tripartite Treaty of Guarantee), the former "shall prevail." Nevertheless, for peacekeeping purposes, and in consideration of all the circumstances, the system initially accommodated the Turkish invasion and its demographic consequences – mitigating the consequences of their illegality, yet refusing *de jure* to recognize their finality.

In this instance, as in other examples, the UN system sought to reconcile the conflicting demands of legality and legitimacy. Concern for legitimacy caused the states constituting the Security Council to balance Turkey's well-founded concern for the violated rights of Turkish-Cypriots against longer-range concerns for the stability of a system based on states' obligation not to resort to force in self-help. In respect of Cyprus, this balance gradually shifted as the situation evolved. At first, the facts were that a fascist regime in Greece had succeeded in overthrowing the legitimate Cypriot government of Archbishop Makarios, abrogating the nation's constitution and the international treaty regime guaranteeing Cypriot independence and minority rights. In these specific circumstances, legitimacy concerns outweighed considerations of strict legality, *mitigating* the system's response to the illegal Turkish invasion. Once, however, the Colonels' regime in Greece had fallen and with it the puppet authority installed in Cyprus, Turkey's continuing territorial encroachment quickly lost its legitimacy and made inevitable UN reversion to unqualified support for the requisites of legality: withdrawal of Turkish military forces and restoration of Cypriot territorial integrity.

Morocco (Mauritania)–Spain (1975)

In 1975, Morocco (with Mauritania) forcefully annexed a neighboring colonial territory it had long asserted to be part of its patrimony. It claimed to be acting to remedy a long-standing colonial wrong that the international system had failed to redress. This time, however, recourse to self-help engendered greater resistance from the UN system than had India's comparable action in Goa fifteen years earlier. The reasons for this are instructive in that they illustrate some of the limits to the legitimacy of claims based on self-help and recourse to forceful counter-measures.

There are similarities, as well as differences, between the annexation of Goa and that of the Western Sahara. Like Goa, the Western Sahara had been colonized by a European power which long resisted implementing the Charter-based legal obligations of self-determination. But Spain, un-like Portugal, had eventually agreed to UN demands,[64] accepting "the inalienable right of the people of Spanish Sahara to self-determination" and, however belatedly, cooperating with its recommendations on imple-mentation. In 1968, Madrid agreed to the visit of a UN mission "for the purpose of recommending practical steps for the full implementation" of "self-determination" and UN participation in the "preparation and supervision" of a referendum to determine the wishes of the colony's population.[65]

With Spain declaring its imminent intent to release its grip on its North-West African colony,[66] Morocco to the north, and Mauritania to the south, both pressed claims based on historic title.[67] The for-mer, which had gained its independence from France in 1957, spoke in terms almost identical to those used by India with respect to Goa: that the Spanish colony was part of historic Morocco and that all offers to negotiate its peaceful return had long been rebuffed by Spain. Unlike India, however, Morocco sought to validate its right to the territory by

---

[64] See, for example, G.A. Res. A/7419(II) of 18 December 1968.   [65] *Ibid.*
[66] A/10095, 28 May 1975.
[67] A/10097, 28 May 1975 (Morocco); A/10101, 30 May 1975 (Mauritania).

enlisting the General Assembly in a request for an advisory opinion to the International Court of Justice.[68] To Rabat's surprise, the Court found that neither the internal nor the international acts adduced by Morocco to demonstrate its historic title supported the existence, prior to the era of colonization, of any legal tie of territorial sovereignty between the Western Sahara and the pre-colonial Moroccan state.[69] The Court came to the same conclusion in dismissing a parallel Mauritanian claim. As to both claims, the Court reiterated the importance of the peoples' right to self-determination.

This judicial rejection of Morocco's claim surprised King Hassan II, who promptly announced plans to lead a "peaceful" march of 350,000 persons to reclaim the southern territories.[70] Spain responded with an appeal to the Security Council, claiming that the march "constitutes an act of force, prepared and carried out by Moroccan subjects and authorities in order to jeopardize the territorial integrity of the Sahara and to violate an internationally recognized border."[71] Its ambassador denounced "the intolerable threats of the Government of Morocco" and requested "that the Council act immediately."[72] Morocco's representative responded that it was doing no more than using self-help to redress a long-standing wrong inflicted on it in violation of the law; that, moreover, the "Western Sahara has never existed as a legal entity and... had always been an integral part" of his country.[73] Rabat argued that it had been ready to negotiate the colony's peaceful reintegration "but was unable to do so because of the inertia evinced by Spain."[74] The march, he said, "is simply a question of Moroccans returning to their homeland."[75]

As these events were unfolding, the General Assembly, then in session, received the report of a Visiting Mission it had sent to examine the facts prevailing in the colony. It reported that almost everyone encountered in the Western Sahara had been categorically in favor not of

---

[68] It prompted the General Assembly to request the ICJ to render an advisory opinion regarding the validity of "legal ties between this territory and the Kingdom of Morocco and the Mauritanian entity." G.A. Res. 3292 (XXIX) of 13 December 1974.

[69] *Western Sahara* (advisory opinion), International Court of Justice, October 16, 1975. 1975 I.C.J. 12.

[70] S/11852, 18 October 1975.   [71] S/11851, 18 October 1975.

[72] S.C.O.R. (XXX), 1849th Meeting, 20 October 1975, at 1, para. 6.

[73] S.C.O.R. (XXX), 1849th Meeting, 20 October 1975, at 6, para. 36.

[74] S.C.O.R. (XXX), 1849th Meeting, 20 October 1975, at 7, para. 47, 51.

[75] S.C.O.R. (XXX), 1849th Meeting, 20 October 1975, at 8, para. 60.

joining Morocco but of independence.[76] The Security Council, through its President, appealed to the King "to put an end forthwith"[77] to his planned invasion, and, when this failed, "deplore[d] the holding of the march" and "call[ed] upon Morocco immediately to withdraw from the Territory of Western Sahara…"[78]

With Generalissimo Franco on his deathbed, the Government of Spain, in disarray, capitulated. On November 18, it notified the United Nations of a tripartite agreement secretly reached four days earlier transferring Spanish colonial title to Morocco and Mauritania.[79] With considerable bitterness, the General Assembly "took note" of these developments[80] while "reaffirm[ing] the inalienable right to self-determination…of all the Saharan populations…"[81]

Unlike the question of Goa, that of the Western Sahara has remained on the international agenda, prodded by neighboring Algeria,[82] which long provided sanctuary for the Frente Popular para la Liberacíon de Saguia el Hamra y de Rio del Oro (POLISARIO). The Assembly has recognized this insurgency against Morocco as the "national liberation movement of the Sahara" and accepts that it enjoys "the support of the vast majority of its inhabitants."[83] In the words of the Chair of the Assembly's Fourth Committee: "the struggle of the Frente POLISARIO was a just one and, sooner or later, would be victorious."[84] Nigeria, as Africa's strongest power, appealed to Morocco and Mauritania "to respect the same tenets thanks to which they [themselves had]…acceded

---

[76] A/10023/Rev.1. Report of Special Committee on Situation with regard to implementation of Declaration on Granting of Independence to Colonial Countries and Peoples (covering its work during 1975). Chapter XIII, Annex: Report of United Nations Visiting Mission to Spanish Sahara, 1975. Adopted 7 November 1975, Meeting, 1023.

[77] S/11869, 6 November 1975.

[78] S.C. Res. 380 (1975) of 6 November 1975. This resolution was adopted by consensus.

[79] S/11880, 19 November 1975. Under this agreement, Spain announced that its authority over the Western Sahara would terminate "by 28 February 1976, at the latest" and that, in the interim, its administering power would be transferred by its Governor-General and two Deputy Governors to be appointed by Morocco and Mauritania.

[80] G.A. Res. 3458B (XXX) of 10 December 1975, para. 1.

[81] G.A. Res. 3458B (XXX) of 10 December 1975, para. 2.

[82] G.A.O.R. (XXX), Fourth Cttee, Trusteeship, 11 September–11 December 1975, Question of Spanish Sahara. Mr. Rahal (Algeria), at 222–24, paras. 29–72.

[83] G.A.O.R. (XXX), Fourth Cttee, Trusteeship, 11 September–11 December 1975, at 251, para. 81 (the Chairman).

[84] G.A.O.R. (XXX), Fourth Cttee, Trusteeship, 11 September–11 December 1975, at 251, para. 82.

to independence"[85] and charged Spain with setting "a dangerous precedent by... abdicating its colonial responsibilities."[86] The tattered legitimacy claim advanced by Morocco was outweighed, on the facts, by the legality-based claim made on behalf of the people of the Western Sahara. "Let our African brothers study the implications [of their recourse to force] ... very carefully," the Nigerian representative cautioned Morocco, "in terms of its consequences for other colonial countries."[87]

After Franco's death, even the new Spanish Government showed no enthusiasm for defending the tripartite settlement. On February 26, 1976, it formally notified the United Nations that its responsibilities were terminated but added "the decolonization of Western Sahara will reach its climax when the views of the Saharan population have been validly expressed."[88]

This has yet to occur. On April 14, 1976, Mauritania and Morocco signed an agreement formally dividing the Western Sahara between them. Algeria commented that this reflected "the policy of aggression and fait accompli pursued by those two governments..." and that it would regard the agreement as "null and void."[89] The General Assembly at its 1976 meeting, again "reaffirm[ed] its commitment to the principle of self-determination..." and welcomed the taking up of the matter by the Organization of African Unity.[90] The call for self-determination has been reaffirmed by subsequent Assemblies,[91] which have kept the matter "under active review..."[92]

With pressure from the United Nations, the OAU, and from an active POLISARIO insurgency within the territory, Mauritania concluded an agreement with the POLISARIO on August 10, 1979, renouncing its claims and withdrawing its forces.[93] Morocco immediately occupied the relinquished region, an action widely criticized in the Assembly, which "deeply deplor[ed] the aggravation of the situation resulting from the continued occupation of Western Sahara by Morocco and the extension of that occupation to the territory... evacuated by Mauritania."[94] This passed by a vote of 85 to 6 with 41 abstentions.[95] Almost all the votes

---

[85] G.A.O.R. (XXX), Plen. Meetings, vol. III, 2418th Meeting, 26 November 1975, at 1013, para. 16 (Harriman).
[86] *Ibid.*   [87] *Ibid.*   [88] A/31/56, 26 February 1976.   [89] *Ibid.*
[90] A/RES/31/45 of 1 December 1976, paras. 1 and 2.
[91] A/RES/32/22 of 28 November 1977, paras. 1 and 2; S/RES/33/31 of 13 December 1978, paras. 1–4.
[92] S/RES/33/31, para. 4.   [93] A/34/427, S/13503, 20 August 1979.
[94] A/RES/34/37 of 21 November 1979.   [95] 1979 U.N.Y.B. 1062.

in favor were cast by third world members, with the abstentions coming primarily from states that were in one way or another allied with the Moroccan dynasty: members of NATO and conservative monarchies of the Islamic group.

The efforts to reverse the Moroccan resort to self-help have continued. The OAU's Implementation Committee, in August, 1981, decided "to organize and conduct a general and free Referendum in the Western Sahara" that would give the population a choice between independence and integration with Morocco.[96] This was adopted by its Assembly of Heads of State and overwhelmingly welcomed by the UN General Assembly.[97] By 1982, despite outrage expressed by Morocco, the "Saharan Arab Democratic Republic," represented by POLISARIO, was welcomed as a member of the OAU.[98] The UN Secretary-General indicated his approval and support, promising to co-operate "closely with [the OAU] with a view to implementation of the pertinent decisions of our two organizations."[99]

Even as Morocco's King Hassan continues to declare his intention not to reopen the question, the issue has refused to recede. On the ground, POLISARIO for years continued to harass the far stronger Moroccan forces, compelling them to retreat to coastal enclaves behind hastily constructed walls of sand. On 12 June 1983, the African Heads of State asked the United Nations to deploy a peacekeeping force in the territory and to create conditions for holding a self-determination referendum.[100] The UN General Assembly instructed the Secretary-General to take the necessary steps.[101]

In November 1987, following consultation with the OAU, the UN Secretary-General despatched a special representative and a joint UN–OAU team to the Western Sahara to formulate proposals for a cease-fire and the holding of the referendum. This was followed in the spring of 1988 by consultations between the UN and OAU Secretaries-General and King Hassan.[102] By August, peace proposals had been finalized[103] which, in September, appeared to have been accepted by Morocco and

---

[96] A/36/512, S/14692, 16 September 1981.
[97] A/RES/36/46 of 24 November 1981. [98] A/37/99, Annex II, 24 February 1982.
[99] A/38/555, 2 November 1983.
[100] A/39/680, Annex, 21 November 1984; A/RES/38/40 of 7 December 1983, para. 1.
[101] A/RES/38/40 of 7 December 1983, para. 2. *See also* A/RES/39/40 of 5 December 1984; A/RES/40/50 of 2 December 1985; A/RES/42/78 of 4 December 1987.
[102] A/43/680, 7 October 1988, at 4, paras. 3–7.
[103] A/43/680, 7 October 1988, at 4, para. 9.

the POLISARIO.[104] These "provide a framework for the conclusion of a cease-fire and the establishment of conditions necessary for the organization of a credible referendum that will make it possible for the people of the Western Sahara to exercise its inalienable right to self-determination..."[105] The proposal called for POLISARIO to agree to a cease-fire, for the Moroccan forces to withdraw and deploy at selected sites, and for the United Nations to provide observers to monitor this disengagement. During the transition between cease-fire and referendum, "the Secretary General's Special Representative [would] be the sole and exclusive authority, particularly with regard to all questions pertaining to the referendum, including [its] organization, monitoring and conduct..."[106] The Security Council quickly and unanimously endorsed this initiative.[107]

After protracted further negotiations, in April 1991, the Council established the United Nations Mission for the Referendum in Western Sahara (MINURSO),[108] followed by a cease-fire on September 6.[109] The next steps were clear: identification and registration of voters, return of refugees, and holding of a referendum set for January.

By 1992, although the cease-fire continued to hold, problems regarding voter registration began to delay MINURSO. The January referendum was rescheduled for May,[110] then became bogged down in differences regarding voter "eligibility criteria."[111] The Council repeatedly extended the term of MINURSO deployment[112] in the hope of holding the referendum eventually and, meanwhile, prolonging the cease-fire.

Despite the indecisive actions taken by the system to reverse Morocco's use of military force, it is clear from these events that King Hassan II's justification – that he had used force only as a countermeasure of last resort to end foreign occupation of Moroccan territory – has been emphatically rejected by a large majority of UN (and OAU) members. Slowly, the UN system has continued to exert pressure against an unlawful annexation achieved by force, while not rejecting the claim that decolonization by force in some instances may be legitimate.

---

[104] A/43/680, 7 October 1988, at 5, para. 13.   [105] *Ibid.*
[106] A/43/680, 7 October 1988, at 6, para. 13.   [107] S. Res. 621 of 20 September 1988.
[108] S. Res. 690 of 29 April 1991. See also, for financing of MINURSO, A/RES/45/266 of 17 May 1991.
[109] S/22779, 10 July 1991.   [110] S/23662, 28 February 1992, at 6–8.
[111] S/1994/283 of 10 March 1994.
[112] E.g., S/RES/1228 of 11 February 1999; S/RES/1301 of 31 May 2000.

That Morocco has failed to justify itself where India, in its annexation of Goa, had succeeded, is due to various contextual factors. Most important is that, in seizing Goa, India was extinguishing the territorial claim of a European colonial power which, over a prolonged period, had continued to exhibit no interest in carrying out its clear legal obligation toward the people of the disputed territory. This gave India's action a degree of legitimacy as a countermeasure of last resort. The technical illegality of its action was mitigated by the legitimacy of the cause it espoused. In the instance of the Western Sahara, by contrast, Morocco could make no such credible claim to legitimacy.

Indonesia–East Timor (1975)

The same analysis holds for Indonesia's resort to self-help in asserting its claim to East Timor. In 1975, with the fall of the dictatorship in Lisbon, four of the five remaining Portuguese overseas territories became independent and joined the United Nations: Angola, Mozambique, Cape Verde, and Sao Tomé–Principe.[113] Portugal also announced the imminent decolonization of East Timor and claimed that it was seeking to bring this about in accordance with applicable UN principles.

By late 1975, however, efforts to introduce an orderly process of Timorese self-determination were failing. On November 28, FREITILIN, the territory's leading nationalist movement, unilaterally declared East Timor's independence.[114] Other, smaller, political parties favoring integration with Indonesia reacted by calling for Jakarta's intervention.[115]

Indonesia took essentially the same posture as had Morocco towards the Western Sahara, asserting that it had used force only as a last resort to vindicate a legal right the UN system had failed to protect. Jakarta said that it had reluctantly but "firmly resolved to exercise its legitimate right to defend its territorial integrity, sovereignty and its right to protect the security of the life and property of its citizens"[116] and it promised to take "necessary measures" to "protect the people"[117] with whom there were "strong links of blood, identity, ethnic and moral culture": links that had been forcibly frustrated "by the colonial power . . . for more than 400 years . . ."[118]

---

[113] 1975 U.N.Y.B. 853. [114] A/10402, S/11887, 29 November 1975.
[115] A/10403, S/11890, 1 December 1975.
[116] A/C.4/808, 4 December 1975, at 1, paras. 2–6.
[117] A/C.4/808, 4 December 1975, at 3, para. 12(d).
[118] A/C.4/408, 4 December 1975, at 4, Annex, Enclosure: Proclamation.

On December 7, Indonesia launched a powerful naval, air, and land attack. Portugal, unable to mount an effective defence, called for the convening of the Security Council.[119] The dispute was also brought before the General Assembly, which was then in session. The verdict against Indonesia was not ambiguous. On December 22, the Council unanimously "deplore[d] the intervention of the armed forces of Indonesia in East Timor" and "call[ed] upon [them] to withdraw without delay..." It summoned all parties "to respect the territorial integrity of East Timor as well as the inalienable right of its people to self-determination..."[120] In the General Assembly, a similar yet stronger resolution was approved on December 12.[121] It "strongly deplored" the Indonesian invasion and specifically "call[ed] upon the Government of Indonesia to desist from further violations of the territorial integrity of Portuguese Timor..."[122] India, no doubt recalling its own seizure of Goa, was one of only nine members to vote against this condemnation.[123]

For twenty-four years the UN system persisted.[124] It absolutely rejected "the claim that East Timor has been integrated into Indonesia, inasmuch as the people of the Territory have not been able to exercise freely their right to self-determination and independence..."[125] In 1998, after the collapse of the Suharto dictatorship, the new government in Jakarta reluctantly agreed to a UN-supervised plebescite. An operation to organize this "consultation" was created in June, 1999.[126] When the resultant endorsement of independence was confronted with armed resistance, the Council authorized a multinational force to restore peace[127] and established a Transitional Administration (UNTAET) to oversee the territory's development to peace and independence.[128]

The failure of Indonesia to prevail in this case stands in marked contrast to India's success in winning acceptance of its seizure of Goa. By exerting force and justifying it as "self-help" to redress a long-standing wrong, India was able to benefit from the manifest unwillingness of Portugal to allow the inhabitants of Goa any meaningful say – as required by the law of the Charter – in determining their political future. This contrasted unfavorably with the robust democracy that union with India offered Goans. After becoming a part of the Indian Federation

---

[119] S/11899, 8 December 1975.   [120] S. Res. 384 (1975) of 22 December 1975.
[121] 1975 U.N.Y.B. 860.   [122] G.A. Res. 3485 (XXX) of 12 December 1975, para. 5.
[123] The vote was 72 in favor, 9 against with 4 abstentions.
[124] See, for example, S. Res. 389 of 22 April 1976; A/RES/31/53 of 1 December 1976.
[125] A/RES/32/34 of 28 November 1977.   [126] S/RES/1246 of 11 June 1999.
[127] S/RES/1264 of 15 September 1999.   [128] S/RES/1272 of 25 October 1999.

the Goans were able to enter freely and fully into the public life of their community, unlike the East Timorese, who were forced to live under Indonesian military dictatorship.

Once again, the specific context and facts of a situation, rather than strict adherence to legal doctrine, appeared to determine the UN system's willingness to accommodate a member state's unauthorized use of force in self-help. These facts, or the perception of them, determined the balance struck between considerations of legitimacy and legality. In the instance of East Timor, this weighing of the relevant facts deprived the Indonesian authorities of the crucial element of legitimacy that had muted systemic reaction to India's technically illegal conduct while leaving Jakarta in a public posture widely regarded both as substantively illegal *and* illegitimate.

Argentina–UK (Malvinas/Falklands) (1982)

The same kind of rhetoric as had been used to good effect by India in 1961 to justify use of force in self-help against Portugal's stubborn colonial policy in Goa was also invoked, in 1982, by Argentina when it invaded the British Falkland Islands (Malvinas), a colony off its coast. That incident, like Morocco's and Indonesia's resort to self-help, demonstrate that the system neither dogmatically accepts nor rejects a state's right to use force in vindication of a long-claimed right. Rather, it is the specific circumstances that determine the response.

On April 1, with Argentine personnel already landed on another regional British dependency, South Georgia, and with an attack on the Falklands imminent, Britain convened the Security Council. It argued that the 1,900 Falklanders were mainly of British origin and that their families had lived for generations in these lands, which had been British since early in the nineteenth century.[129]

Argentina, in response, insisted that what it called the Malvinas Islands "have been part of the national territory since the independence of the [Argentine] Republic, through natural succession to the unquestionable rights which the Spanish Crown had over them...since 1811."[130] Britain had forcibly deprived Argentina of the islands in 1833 "when its struggle for independence had just concluded" and when "the Republic could not oppose militarily the plundering to which it had

---

[129] S.C.O.R. (XXXVII), 2345th Meeting, 1 April 1982, at 1, para. 6.
[130] S.C.O.R. (XXXVII), 2345th Meeting, 1 April 1982, at 4, para. 31.

been subjected."[131] Its ambassador referred to General Assembly resolutions passed in 1966, 1967, 1969, and 1971 that had urged Britain and Argentina to resolve their dispute through negotiations. He added that the non-aligned movement had twice (in 1975 and 1979) decided that the purpose of these negotiations should be "to restore the ... territory to Argentine sovereignty ..."[132] Throughout, Britain had remained obdurate, leaving, at last, no option but recourse to military self-help.[133]

The Security Council did not accept this argument. In the face of impending war, it called on Argentina and the UK "to exercise utmost restraint ... and ... refrain from the use or threat of force ..."[134] Notwithstanding, Argentina's forces landed the next day. Britain demanded that the Security Council condemn this "wanton act" which, its representative said, sought "to impose ... a foreign and unwanted control over 1,900 peaceful agricultural people who have chosen in free and fair elections to maintain their links with Britain and the British way of life."[135]

Argentina did not win this encounter. It was defeated militarily by a British expeditionary force. Its diplomatic effort at justification fared just as badly. On the first day after its invasion, the Security Council, by 10 votes to 1 with 4 abstentions, demanded the withdrawal of Argentine forces.[136] Only Panama accepted the argument that the Islands, being legally Argentine, could lawfully be regained by forceful countermeasures.[137]

As the military conflict continued, so did the debate about the legality of Argentina's recourse to military force, the relative strengths of Argentine and British title, and, ultimately, the relative weight of such claims as against the legitimate interests of the inhabitants and their right to self-determination.[138] Most, but not all Latin American states supported Argentina (Brazil and Chile, notably, did not), while most African and Western European states, with the US, supported Britain. The Soviet Union and its satellites, as well as China, supported the Buenos

---

[131] S.C.O.R. (XXXVII), 2345th Meeting, 1 April 1982, at 4, para. 34.
[132] S.C.O.R. (XXXVII), 2345th Meeting, 1 April 1982, at 5, paras. 44–45.
[133] S.C.O.R. (XXXVII), 2345th Meeting, 1 April 1982, at 4–5, paras. 39–43.
[134] S.C.O.R. (XXXVII), 2345th Meeting, 1 April 1982, at 8, para. 74.
[135] S.C.O.R. (XXXVII), 2346th Meeting, 2 April 1982, at 1, para. 5.
[136] S/RES/502 (1982) of 3 April 1982. Those voting for the resolution were France, Guyana, Ireland, Japan, Jordan, Togo, Uganda, the UK, US, and Zaire. Panama voted against. China, Poland, Spain and the USSR abstained.
[137] S.C.O.R. (XXXVII), 2350th Meeting, 3 April 1982, at 29, para. 275.
[138] See 1982 U.N.Y.B. 1320–1347.

Aires junta: somewhat oddly, given its right-wing politics and ruthless repression of suspected leftists. On the other side, many states joined in imposing sanctions on Argentina.

On 14 June, after heavy casualties on both sides, Brigadier-General Mario Benjamín Menéndez, the Commander of the Argentine Land, Sea and Air Forces in the Malvinas, signed an Instrument of Surrender.[139] The General Assembly's resolution of 4 November, passed by 90 votes to 12 with 52 abstentions, noted the cease-fire and requested the parties "to resume negotiations in order to find as soon as possible a peaceful solution to the sovereignty dispute . . ." while reaffirming their obligation not to use force, or to threaten its use.[140]

While many factors and interests no doubt determined the reaction of states and the interstatal system to Argentina's recourse to forceful self-help, the junta in Buenos Aires never succeeded in convincing the UN majority of the legitimacy of its cause. States were divided about the relative weight to be accorded legitimacy claims based on historic title and anti-colonialism, on the one hand, and those of self-determination on the other, with the majority leaning towards the priority of self-determination. Further, in seeking endorsement of its invasion, Argentina was hindered by the fascist cast of its governing junta.

Conclusions

The UN Charter makes no exception to the rule barring states' recourse to violence, not even in situations where an evident and serious wrong has been done that the system, over a protracted period, has failed to redress. The Charter makes no provision for individual or collective military enforcement of legal rights of states and peoples, as such. In this sense, the Charter may be said to have abrogated states' historic right to deploy force in self-help and to have restricted countermeasures to actions not involving "the threat or use of force" prohibited by Charter Article 2(4). It thus seems to have tilted the balance in the direction of peace and away from justice or, alternatively, in favor of the enunciation of rights but away from their muscular implementation.

On the other hand, a limited right to self-help has long been recognized in customary international law and practice. This has not been specifically repealed by the Charter. It can be argued that, in the absence

---

[139] S/15231 of 17 June 1982.   [140] A/RES/37/9 of 4 November 1982.

of new ways to defend or effectuate legal rights, the Charter should not be read to prohibit countermeasures as the remedy of last resort. Indeed, UN practice seems to offer some latitude for states' resort to countermeasures in self-help. In some instances this tolerance has been manifest in UN passivity when faced with actual recourse to force. Israel's capture of Eichmann in Argentina, India's invasion of Goa, as well as Turkey's intervention in Cyprus were met with comparative equanimity, the specific circumstances of each case lending an aura of legitimacy to a recourse to unilateral force and mitigating the system's judgment of self-help in those instances.

On the other hand, those instances in which the UN organs rejected claims of a right to self-help demonstrate that the system mitigates or acquiesces only reluctantly. Self-help may be acknowledged as a remedy of last resort in a situation in which all alternatives for the peaceful vindication of a recognized legal right have been exhausted and the law and the facts indisputably support a plea of extreme necessity. It has not been recognized when used to press less legally convincing claims such as those solely based on geographic contiguity and historic title, especially when the claimed rights are opposable by rights of equal or greater weight, such as that of self-determination.[141]

Nevertheless, in exception cases the use of force in self-help, while prohibited by the Charter text, may be justified by the evident legitimacy of the cause in which self-help is deployed; and a widespread perception of that legitimacy is likely to mitigate, if not actually to exculpate, the resort to force. This may be recognized implicitly by the International Law Commission's Report on State Responsibility which, although prohibiting countermeasures taken in derogation of the "obligation to refrain from the threat or use of force as embodied in the Charter of the United Nations"[142] leaves open recourse to such measures when not actually prohibited by the Charter. The practice of UN organs demonstrates that while the prohibition on forcible self-help is absolute in theory, the

---

[141] Instances include the resistance of a population to their absorption by a neighboring state. These include territories such as Gibraltar, Kaliningrad, Nagoro-Karabakh, St. Helena, St. Pierre et Miquelon, St. Martin/St. Maartens, St. Thomas, Western Samoa, and numerous other Pacific and Caribbean territories. In none of these instances has practice justified a right on the part of neighbors to liberate these "dependent territories."

[142] Report of the International Law Commission, Fifty-second session, 1 May–9 June and 10 July–18 August 2000, G.A.O.R., 55th Sess., Supp. No. 10 (A/55/10), State Responsibility, Draft Articles, article 51.

principle is more textured in practice. This paradox is the subject of further inquiry in chapter 10.

Obviously, the law of countermeasures and self-help is in flux. The ICJ, in the *Corfu Channel* case, did not regard as lawful the military countermeasures taken by the British navy in self-help, but it did accept that extreme necessity could mitigate the legal consequences of the illegality of those acts if necessity were demonstrable by clear contextual evidence.[143] This, too, is approximately the conclusion to be drawn from state practice in the institutions of the UN system. Like the Court, the political organs of the United Nations have carefully avoided giving a broad, dogmatic answer to the issues posed by states' recourse to armed countermeasures. Doctrine and principle, here, too, appear subservient to narrower reasons of contextual justice and legitimacy, with the specific facts being given appropriate weight. The invasion of Goa was perceived as the democratic liberation of a part of geographic and cultural India long ruled by a remote and stubborn Iberian dictatorship. The Turkish military occupation of Northern Cyprus in 1974 at first seemed a legitimate reaction to the subterfuge of a despised and expansionist Greek military junta. In the Eichmann case, the strength of Israel's justification was generally acknowledged. The Israelis had argued that a great wrong may sometimes have to be redressed by a much smaller one, and that definition of mitigating circumstances found considerable resonance.

Other arguments based on self-help have fallen on stonier ground. This is exemplified by the rejection of efforts by Argentina's junta to legitimize its invasion of the Falklands, of Indonesia's occupation of East Timor, and of Morocco's suppression of self-determination in the Western Sahara. Each of these cases is different. Each confirms only (but importantly) the systemic recognition of a margin of flexibility that cannot as yet be precisely defined, but which, in practice, seems to converge upon something approximating consensus. Each demonstrates the importance of facts, evidence and sensitivity to political context in shaping the systemic response to a claim of self-help, whether that claim is advanced as a legal right or in mitigation of the consequences of a technical wrong.

A larger conclusion may also be teased from this evidence of practice. In interpreting the normative principles of the Charter, the principal organs have made an effort to act as a sort of jury: determining the probative value of alleged facts, assessing claims of extreme necessity,

---

[143] *Corfu Channel case*, Judgment of April 9, 1949. I.C.J. Reports, 1949, p. 4, at 34–35.

and weighing the proportionality of specific action taken by a party that might otherwise be deprived of any remedy for a serious delict committed against it. This quasi-jury has demonstrated concern to apply the United Nations' quasi-constitution as a "living tree." And, like juries everywhere, the principal organs have tried to bridge the gap, when it appears, between legality and legitimacy, so that the legal order is not seen to suffer from the deficiency that arises when that gap becomes too wide.

This approach encounters its most difficult test when a state or group of states engages in an unauthorized military action that is sought to be justified by evidence of extreme humanitarian necessity: the subject of chapter 9.

9

The "purely humanitarian" intervention

[W]hile there may be reason to support vigilante justice in some lawless situations, this is a far cry from conceding that sheriff's badges should be handed out to any right-minded person with a gun.

> Simon Chesterman *Just War or Just Peace?* 56 (2001)

Necessity is the mother of intervention.

> Devika Hovell Research Paper (2000, unpublished)

Definition

When a government turns viciously against its own people, what may or should other governments do? The events of the recent past do not permit this to be dismissed as an "academic question."

If the wrong being perpetrated within a state against a part of its own population is of a kind specifically prohibited by international agreement (e.g. the Genocide Convention and treaties regarding racial discrimination, torture, the rights of women and children, and the International Covenant on Civil and Political Rights, as well as agreements on the humanitarian law applicable in civil conflict), humanitarian intervention against those prohibited acts may be thought of as a subspecies of self-help. This is conceptually more persuasive if the wrongful acts have been characterized explicitly or implicitly by the applicable universal treaties as offenses *erga omnes*: that is, against any and all states party to the agreement defining and prohibiting the wrong. In such circumstances, it is possible to argue that every state may claim a right of self-help as a vicarious victim of any violation, at least after exhaustion of institutional and diplomatic remedies. Analogous universal rights to self-help

135

might also arise in the event of violations of certain rules of customary law.

On the other hand, it is clear from the negotiating record that the Charter's Articles 2(4) and 51 were intended to circumscribe, and perhaps even abrogate, unilateral recourse to force except in response to an armed attack by one state on another. This makes it hard to construe those texts as anything but a prohibition of any humanitarian intervention that involves the use of military force, since even egregious violation by a government of the fundamental human rights of its own citizens does not evidently cross the original "armed attack" threshold.

Nevertheless, "humanitarian intervention" has been used by states, and by regional organizations, to justify their use of force (without prior Security Council authorization) in various circumstances. Such interventions have rid a state of a despot wreaking carnage on his own people, ended a bloody civil war, and stopped genocide against a group, tribe, or class. In a few situations, several such tragedies seemed to be occurring simultaneously. In this chapter we will examine several of these technical violations, the Charter system's response to them, and the effect those systemic responses may have had on the evolution of law.

A "right of humanitarian intervention" was mooted at San Francisco[1] and is much discussed in legal literature.[2] However, no such right made its way into the UN Charter. Even though its text does "reaffirm faith in fundamental human rights,"[3] it does not make provision for using force to implement that commitment.

Has this been modified by practice? Initially, a distinction must be made between Security Council-authorized collective humanitarian interventions and interventions by states or groups of states acting at their own discretion. Although the Charter text does not specifically authorize the Council to apply Chapter VII's system of collective measures to prevent gross violations of humanitarian law and human rights, in practice it has done so occasionally; for example by authorizing members to use coercive measures to counter apartheid in South Africa and revoke Rhodesia's racially motivated Unilateral Declaration of Independence

---

[1] See chapter 3 (p. 47).

[2] Christine Gray, *International Law and the Use of Force* (2000); Independent International Commission on Kosovo, *The Kosovo Report: Conflict, International Response, Lessons Learned* (2000); Danesh Sarooshi, *The United Nations and the Development of Collective Security* (1999); A. Mark Weisburd, *Use of Force: The Practice of States Since World War II* (1997); Sean D. Murphy, *Humanitarian Intervention* (1996); Oscar Schachter, *International Law in Theory and Practice* 106–201 (1991).

[3] Preamble, para. 2. See also Article 1, para. 3.

(UDI), as well as to help end egregious ethnic conflicts in Yugoslavia, Somalia, and Kosovo and to reverse a Haitian military coup that sought to undo a UN-supervised democratic election.[4] Invoking Article 39 in each of these instances, the Council found a sufficient "threat to the peace, breach of the peace, or act of aggression" to warrant the taking of collective measures. In none, however, did the humanitarian justification for action stand alone. Additional factors were cited to legitimate Council action, including the threat to peace caused by massive out-flows of refugees and the danger of wider involvement by other states in response to wrongful acts committed by an offending regime or faction.

Some of these Council authorizations of recourse to force have stretched the literal text of Chapter VII, but they violated no explicit Charter prohibition. While Article 2(7) does purport to exclude UN "intervention in matters which are essentially within the domestic jurisdiction of any state..." that constraint is inapplicable when the Organization is engaged in "enforcement measures under Chapter VII." Thus, each of the instances in which the Council has used, or authorized coalitions of the willing to use collective measures in situations of civil war or against regimes engaged in egregious human rights violations can be fitted into Charter text. Even when occurring wholly within one state, a civil war, oppression, or humanitarian outrage, as well as its byproducts such as massive flows of refugees into neighboring countries, or the engagement of external intervenors, may reasonably be judged by the Council to threaten international peace and security, thereby legitimating coercive measures by the United Nations, or a UN-authorized coalition of the willing.

It is much more difficult conceptually to justify in Charter terms the use of force by one or several states acting without prior Security Council authorization, even when such action is taken to enforce human rights and humanitarian values. The Charter's Article 2(4), strictly construed, prohibits states' unilateral recourse to force. The text makes no exception for instances of massive violation of human rights or humanitarian law when these occur in the absence of an international aggression against another state. In the strict Charter scheme, states are not to use force except in self-defense[5] and regional organizations may not take

---

[4] See, for example, S. Res. 232 of 16 December 1966 (Rhodesia); S. Res. 418 of 4 November 1977 (South Africa); S/RES/713 of 25 September 1991 (Yugoslavia); S/RES/794 of 3 December 1992 (Somalia); S/RES/940 of 31 July 1994 (Haiti); S/RES/1160 of 13 March 1998 (Kosovo).

[5] UN Charter, articles 2(4) and 51.

"enforcement action... without the authorization of the Security Council..."[6]

A state using military force without Council authorization against another in "humanitarian intervention" is thus engaging in an action for which the Charter text provides no apparent legal authority. Many governments, understandably, have been reluctant to see any relaxation of this prohibition. They fear that even if a humanitarian action were effective, it would still constitute a dangerous precedent contributing to the gradual erosion of the Charter's basic rule requiring "[a]ll Members [to] refrain in their international relations from the threat or use of force against... any state..."[7] Weaker states, in particular, still cleave to Article 2(4) as their best defense against the historically demonstrated proclivity of the strong to teach manners to the weak. The more cynical may even believe that there is no such thing as a "purely humanitarian intervention": that using this pretense, states merely pursue their national self-interest. Scholars thus are deeply and vociferously divided.[8]

However, as with other instances examined in earlier chapters that also involve the use of force, the institutional history of the United Nations – as distinct from the Charter's text – and record of state practice, neither categorically precludes nor endorses humanitarian intervention. Rather, the history and practice support a more nuanced reconciling of the pursuit of peace (as evidenced by Charter Article 2(4)) and of justice

---

[6] UN Charter, article 53.   [7] UN Charters, article 2(4).

[8] Among many writings generated by recent events: Philip Allott, "Kosovo and the Responsibility of Power," 13 Leiden J. Int'l L. 83 (2000); Antonio Cassese, "A Follow-Up: Forcible Humanitarian Countermeasures and *Opinio Necessitatis*," EJIL (1999), vol. 10, 791; Christine Chinkin, "The State That Acts Alone: Bully, Good Samaritan or Iconoclast?" EJIL (2000), vol. 11, 31; Pierre-Marie Dupuy, EJIL (2000), vol. 11, 19; Christopher Greenwood, "International Law and the NATO Intervention in Kosovo," 4 Int'l & Comp. L.Q. 926 (2000); Vera Goulland-Debbas, The Limits of Unilateral Enforcement of Community Objectives in the Framework of UN Peace Maintenance EJIL (2000), vol. 11, 361; Vaughn Lowe, "International Legal Issues Arising in the Kosovo Crisis," 4 Int'l & Comp. L.Q. 934 (2000); Jules Lobel, "Benign Hegemony? Kosovo and Article 2(4) of the UN Charter," 1 Chicago J. Int'l L. 19 (2000); Shinya Murase, "Unilateral Measures and the Concept of Opposability in International Law," in 28 Thesaurus Acroasium 402 (2000) (concerning countermeasures generally); Georg Nolte, "Kosovo und Konstitutionalisierung: zur humanitären Intervention der NATO-Staaten," ZaöRV 59/4, 941 (1999); Mary Ellen O'Connell, "The UN, NATO, and International Law After Kosovo," 22 Human Rights Quarterly 57 (2000); Michael Reisman, "Unilateral Action and the Transformations of the World Constitutive Process: The Special Problem of Humanitarian Intervention," EJIL (2000), vol. 11, 3; Ruth Wedgwood, "Unilateral Action in the UN System," EJIL (2000), vol. 3, 349.

through the protection of human and humanitarian rights (as evidenced by the canon of rights-creating universal agreements). In this practical reconciliation we can detect a pragmatic range of systemic responses to unauthorized use of force, depending more on the circumstances than on strictly construed text. This patterned practice suggests *either* a graduated reinterpretation by the United Nations itself of Article 2(4) or the evolution of a subsidiary adjectival international law of mitigation, one that may formally continue to assert the illegality of state recourse to force but which, in ascertainable circumstances, mitigates the consequence of such wrongful acts by imposing no, or only nominal, consequences on states which, by their admittedly wrongful intervention, have demonstrably prevented the occurrence of some greater wrong.

In the remainder of this chapter we will examine eight instances of states' use of force in overtly or implicitly humanitarian interventions. In four of these, an individual state used force without prior Security Council authorization: (India–Pakistan, 1971, Tanzania–Uganda, 1978–79, Vietnam–Kampuchea, 1978–79, France–Central African Empire, 1979). In one, several states jointly participated in such enforcement (France, UK, US–Iraq, 1991–93). In three instances it was regional or collective security organizations that used force in humanitarian crises without prior Council authorization (ECOMOG–Liberia, 1989, ECOMOG–Sierra Leone, 1991, NATO–Yugoslavia (Kosovo), 1999). The calibrated response of the UN system to these eight initiatives may give some indication of the way the principal organs have sought, in interpreting the Charter, to reconcile its systemic – but not always congruent – desiderata of peace and justice.

Humanitarian intervention: post-Charter practice

India–Bangla Desh (1971)

In December, 1971, India's armed forces invaded East Pakistan and thereby facilitated that province's secession from Pakistan. New Delhi acted after its neighbor had used severe military repression for nine extremely violent months in an effort to end a civil insurrection. Already in April, the Indian Government had advised the United Nations that the scale of human suffering in Pakistan's eastern province had grown to the point where it ceased to be a matter only of domestic concern. New Delhi's representative spoke of "gross violation of basic human rights" by the Pakistani military "amounting to genocide, with the object of stifling the democratically expressed wishes of a people."[9] During this period, an estimated 8 million refugees fled to India in response to draconian measures taken against them.[10] The UN Secretary-General, confirming the extent of the human disaster, warned of the intolerable burden on India's resources.[11]

Pakistan's representative denied allegations of his country's culpability, although admitting that several million East Bengalis had fled to India. He rejected the theory which, he said, "had been invented by India, that an influx of refugees constituted aggression against the country that haboured them," noting, rather, that under international law it was India's duty to ensure that these refugees did not use their encampments to subvert law and order in Pakistan.[12]

When large-scale fighting erupted between India and Pakistan on December 3, the Secretary-General informed the Security Council, under Article 99 of the Charter, that the situation constituted a threat to international peace and security.[13] It convened the next day.

The Indian representative told Council members that "there is neither normalcy nor peace in East Pakistan, and as a result, we have suffered aggression after aggression."[14] He spoke of Pakistan's "campaign of genocide"[15] and, as 120,000 Indian troops poured in, announced his country's recognition of an independent People's Republic of Bangla Desh.[16] Rejecting the charge that India's actions violated Pakistani sovereignty and territorial integrity, he argued that these were not the only norms of the Charter system. "I wonder why we should be shy about speaking of human rights," he said. "What happened to the Convention on genocide? What happened to the principle of self-determination?"[17] Recalling that 1–2 million East Bengali lives had been lost to military repression, New Delhi's representative invoked the justification of humanitarian necessity. "No country in the world can remain unconcerned," he said. "Inaction and silence in the face of this human tragedy could be interpreted by all those who suffer as helplessness, if not indifference, of the outside world."[18]

[9] 1971 U.N.Y.B. 140.   [10] 1971 U.N.Y.B. 137.

[11] A/8401/Add.1. Introduction to report of Secretary-General on work of the Organization, 21 September 1971, at 7–8, paras. 177–191.

[12] 1971 U.N.Y.B. 140.   [13] 1971 U.N.Y.B. 146.

[14] S.C.O.R. (XXVI), 1606th Meeting, 4 December 1971, at 14, para. 153.

[15] S.C.O.R. (XXVI), 1606th Meeting, 4 December 1971, at 16, para. 167.

[16] S.C.O.R. (XXVI), 1608th Meeting, 6 December 1971, at 7, para. 70.

[17] S.C.O.R. (XXVI), 1608th Meeting, 6 December 1971, at 27, para. 262.

[18] G.A.O.R. (XXVI), 2003rd Plen. Meeting, 7 December 1971, at 14, para. 156.

Pakistan, with more than half its population in revolt, insisted that, despite the flow of refugees into Indian territory "there was no warrant for India's claim that the invasion of Pakistan was justified by recourse to the right of self-defence."[19] He insisted that the crisis was "internal."[20] China, agreeing, called for censure of India and demanded the immediate withdrawal of the invading forces,[21] a position essentially supported by the United States, which condemned intervention by India "across its borders in the affairs of another member state in violation of the United Nations Charter."[22] Britain and France, however, took a more conciliatory tone, arguing that the Indian invasion and Pakistani repression of its East Bengali population could only be considered together: that addressing one without the other ignored their intimate connection and was bound to fail.[23]

On December 4, a US resolution calling on the Governments of India and Pakistan for "an immediate cessation of hostilities" and "an immediate withdrawal of armed personnel present on the territory of the other" – obviously aimed at India – received 11 votes, with 2 opposed (Poland, USSR) and with Britain and France abstaining. All third world members of the Council (Argentina, Burundi, China, Nicaragua, Sierra Leone, Somalia, and Syria) voted in its favor, a strong rejection of the justification offered by India, even though the resolution was vetoed by the Soviet Union.[24]

When the debate re-emerged in the General Assembly, India argued that the dumping of millions of Pakistani refugees on its territory constituted a form of "civil aggression" that damaged India as surely as if it had been a military assault. "Not only did 10 million refugees come to us as a result," India's representative told the General Assembly, "but our security was... threatened, our social and economic fabric endangered and international tension increased. There was hardly any response from the international community which seemed paralyzed and did not take any action to prevent the massive extinction of human rights and genocide."[25]

---

[19] S.C.O.R. (XXVI), 1606th Meeting, 4 December 1971, at 9, para. 102.
[20] S.C.O.R. (XXVI), 1606th Meeting, 4 December 1971, at 10, para. 105.
[21] China draft resolution, S/10421 of 5 December 1971. The resolution was not adopted.
[22] S.C.O.R. (XXVI), 1606th Meeting, 4 December 1971, at 18–19, para. 194.
[23] S.C.O.R. (XXVI), 1606th Meeting, 4 December 1971, at 21–22, paras. 220–227 (France); at 30, paras. 325–330.
[24] S/10416, S.C.O.R. (XXVI), 1606th Meeting, 4 December 1971, at 33, para. 371.
[25] G.A.O.R. (XXVI), 2003rd Plen. Meeting, 7 December 1971, at 15, para. 165.

On December 7, the Assembly, by a lop-sided majority of 104 to 11 with 10 abstentions decided that the hostilities constituted "an immediate threat to international peace and security" and called for "withdrawal of... armed forces...."[26] Notably, however, the resolution did not accuse India of aggression, as Pakistan and its ally, China, had demanded. It also recognized the "the need to deal appropriately at a subsequent stage, within the framework of the Charter of the United Nations, with the issues that have given rise to the hostilities."[27] Although couched in diplomatic parlance, this constituted a recognition of linkage between the Charter's prohibition on unilateral recourse to force (Article 2(4)) and other humanitarian and human rights requisites of the Charter.

Not every government has acquiesced in this linkage. Even as the newly created People's Republic of Bangla Desh presented its application for membership in the United Nations, it was vetoed by China.[28] Not until 1974 was the new state admitted.[29] This undoubtedly reflected not only China's, but also some other members' ambiguity in reacting to the countervailing requisites of justice and peace and of legitimacy and legality. What kind of precedent had been set by the success of India's action, and should its outcome be endorsed by the UN system? On the one hand, there was little doubt that democratic India had put a welcome stop to a terrible carnage in East Pakistan being perpetrated by Pakistan's junta, composed as it was primarily of the Western-province's military officers. Chesterman concludes that the humanitarian factor "mitigate[d] India's position" even if it did not make the remedy acceptable.[30]

On the other hand, India's motives were not exactly above suspicion. The dismemberment of Pakistan and the carving out of a new state deeply reliant on it did undoubtedly serve India's most important national security concerns and strengthened its dominance of the subcontinent. Understandably, unease competed with relief at what the Indian military had accomplished in defiance of strictly construed Charter text. In particular there was evident reluctance to accept humanitarian necessity and the flow of refugees as being tantamount to an armed attack for purposes of releasing powerful states from the obligation not to use force in the absence of Security Council authorization.

---

[26] G.A. Res. 2793 (XXVI) of 7 December 1971.   [27] *Ibid.*

[28] S/10771, rejected by 11 votes in favor to 1 against (China) and 3 abstentions (Guinea, Somalia, Sudan), 25 August 1972. 1972 U.N.Y.B. 219.

[29] S. Res. 351 (1974) of 10 June 1974 and G.A. Res. 3203 (XXIX) of 17 September 1974.

[30] Simon Chesterman, *Just War or Just Peace* 75 (2001).

And yet, many wondered, how high a price in justice could be exacted for the sake of preserving the primacy of peace? And how well was peace being preserved by permitting such injustice?

Tanzania–Uganda (1978)

Seven years later, this same set of concerns – reconciling peace with justice and legitimacy with legality – seemed to pose a less formidable dilemma. The conflict between Uganda and Tanzania began in October, 1978, with a series of border incursions by Field Marshal Idi Amin's forces into Tanzanian territory.[31] Tanzania seized on this provocation to end Amin's atrocious rule.

The Field Marshal, characteristically, did not go gentle into that good night. On February 14, 1979, he complained to the United Nations that Tanzanian troops had attacked and occupied 350 square miles of Ugandan territory. The Organization treated this communication with supreme indifference.[32] One day later, Libya, Amin's principal supporter, wrote the UN Secretary-General:

We find President Amin's announcement that Tanzanian troops have crossed the borders and entered Uganda a matter of great danger [to] the peace and security of Africa . . . Therefore we deem it necessary and urgent to act in order to bring about a peaceful evacuation of the Tanzanian troops [and] . . . we hope that you will act quickly to end this dispute, guided by the principle that no State has the right to overthrow the regime of another by forceful or any other means.[33]

This communication, too, met with no response, either from the Secretary-General or the Security Council. Desultory efforts at OAU mediation came to naught as Tanzania demanded that Uganda first be censured for aggression.[34] As the combined forces of the Tanzanian army, accompanied by Ugandan exiles, continued their advance on Kampala, Idi Amin renewed his call for UN "good offices"[35] but, even with Libya providing Amin a measure of diplomatic and military

---

[31] In October, Uganda, ostensibly to prevent infiltration of men and arms in support of its domestic opponents, seized and then annexed the Kagera Salient, a Tanzanian area on its border.

[32] *New York Times*, February 15, 1979, at 3.

[33] S/13087, Letter dated 15 February 1979 from the representative of the Libyan Arab Jamahiriya to the Secretary-General.

[34] *Le Monde*, 2 March 1979, at 4.   [35] *Le Monde*, 4–5 March 1979, at 5.

support,[36] the Security Council and the Secretary-General studiously avoided addressing Uganda's complaint.

On March 28, Kampala's envoy requested "an urgent meeting of the Security Council," asserting that this "act of aggression and violation of the sovereignty and territorial integrity of my country is a serious threat to regional as well as international peace and security."[37] Only a few days later, however, the invading force had reached the capital[38] and the Ugandan representative, seeing the direction of events, withdrew his as-yet unanswered request for a Council meeting.[39]

In Kampala, a new provisional government was quickly formed as Marshal Amin fled to Libya.[40] By mid-April, Tanzanian troops had pacified the entire country and its UN mission had realigned itself to the new realities.[41] Others – the UK, the US, Zambia, Mozambique, India, China, the Soviet Union, and Ethiopia – soon extended formal diplomatic recognition.

Undoubtedly, this case must be appreciated in the context of an un-usually widespread contempt for the extravagant human rights abuses of the Amin regime. Some 300,000 deaths have been attributed to it.[42] Its foolhardy military provocations against Tanzania not only reinforced the bad image of a regime that had strayed far beyond the bounds of tolerable governmental behavior, but also provided a legal cover of sorts for Tanzania's response,[43] although the "proportionality" of Tanzania's countermeasure – occupying all of Uganda – is at least problematic. The truth of the matter, however, is simpler. With a few exceptions, states of the international community had concluded that it was time for Amin to go, citing both his atrocities against his own people and bellicosity

---

[36] Libya was reported to have sent "more than three thousand troops," *Le Monde*, 4 April 1979, at 1.

[37] S/13204, Letter dated 28 March 1979 from the representative of Uganda to the President of the Security Council.

[38] *Le Monde*, 6 April 1979, at 4.

[39] S/13228, Letter dated 5 April 1979 from the representative of Uganda to the President of the Security Council.

[40] *Le Monde*, 17 April 1979, at 3.   [41] *Le Monde*, 14 April 1979, at 3.

[42] Murphy, n. 2 above, at 105.

[43] The heads of government of Botswana, Mozambique, Zambia, Angola, and Tanzania, in a communiqué of 4 March 1979, had spoken of the "unprovoked and unpremeditated war of aggression launched by Idi Amin against the United Republic of Tanzania, . . ." S/13141, Letter dated 5 March 1979 from the representative of Angola to the Secretary-General. Annex. Press communiqué issued by the Front Line States on 4 March 1979.

towards his Tanzanian neighbor. That the task of removing him was performed by Tanzania, a leading member of the non-aligned movement, seems to have made the questions of principle and precedent – the violation of a member state's sovereignty – less salient than had the invader been a large (or, worse, a former colonial) power. It was also apparent to the international community that Tanzania had no territorial ambitions. The last Tanzanian troops withdrew in May 1981, after order had been restored by the new Ugandan government.

This crisis is noteworthy not only for the lack of outrage expressed by states on behalf of the Charter's violated principles, but also for the way the system expressed its assent in silence. The Secretary-General ignored Uganda's and Libya's calls for the United Nations to take notice. The Security Council passed over in silence the several efforts to have it convened. It is also notable that Tanzania, to the extent it made any effort to justify its use of force, relied on a right of self-defense against Ugandan aggression and not on Amin's egregious offenses against humanitarian law and human rights, even though "self-defence" under Article 51 could not possibly justify the disproportionate Tanzanian reaction to a relatively minor border provocation.

In this instance, a reading of the tea leaves of political history and institutional practice leads to the tentative conclusion that states simply but consciously decided to pass over in silent acquiescence what, in other circumstances, might vociferously have been deplored. This may well be less a matter of a double standard, as some critics have charged, than of deliberate and careful calibration, responsive to the specific context in which the action was taken. If recourse to a legal fiction – that Tanzania was acting in self-defense – made more palatable what was in all but name recognized as a necessary humanitarian intervention, then the system was quite willing to use that time-honored legal device to disguise under a thin veil of superficial consistency the significance of a gradually evolving pragmatic change in the way its rules were being applied.

Vietnam–Kampuchea (1978–1979)

Such careful calibration sometimes failed, however, during the Cold War when the interests of Big Powers were at stake. Reaction to Vietnam's invasion of Kampuchea strikingly illustrates this.

During their four-year rule, Kampuchea's governing Khmer Rouge, backed by China, emptied Cambodia's cities, killed a million people and destroyed the economy.[44] They also instigated incursions into neighboring Vietnam, whose regime was supported by the Soviet Union.[45]

On December 25, 1978, Vietnamese forces invaded Kampuchea, bringing to power a small group of exiles, headed by Heng Samrin, who had broken with the Khmer Rouge. At the United Nations, Kampuchea's representative charged Vietnam with "acts of aggression"[46] and the USSR with "supplying the invaders with military advisers and... equipment."[47] Although the Khmer Rouge's atrocious record on human rights was well known, the reaction, especially among third world states to Vietnam's action, was "almost uniformly negative."[48] China charged that Hanoi was seeking to annex its neighbor,[49] and told the Security Council:

The iron-clad fact is that, with Soviet support, Viet Nam has carried out a large-scale naked armed aggression against Democratic Kampuchea, seriously violating [its] independence, sovereignty and territorial integrity and gravely violating and menacing peace and security in South-East Asia, the whole of Asia and the world at large.[50]

Prince Norodom Sihanouk, invited to speak for the ousted regime, told the Council: "my country is the victim of a large-scale act of flagrant aggression by the Socialist Republic of Viet Nam... in *de facto* military alliance with the USSR,... drawing comfort from the total and unconditional support accorded it by the Powers of the Warsaw Pact,... respecting the 'good' old traditions of shamelessly swallowing up small neighbours whenever the opportunity presents itself..."[51] "[T]his war," he concluded, "is purely a war of aggression, annexation, colonization and regional hegemonism..."[52] launched by the "Hitlerite armed forces" of Vietnam and its Soviet sponsors.[53] Congratulating him, the Chinese ambassador referred to Vietnam as "the agent of Soviet hegemonism" and, in a piquant turn of phrase, as "the Cuba of Asia."[54]

[44] G. Klintworth, *Vietnam's Intervention in Cambodia in International Law* 19 (1989). *See also* Murphy, n. 2 above, at 103.

[45] Klintworth, *ibid.*   [46] S/12957, 7 December 1978.

[47] *Ibid.* See also 1978 U.N.Y.B. 281.   [48] Weisburd, n. 2 above, at 43.

[49] S/12962, 11 December 1978.

[50] S.C.O.R. (XXXIV), 2108th Meeting, 11 January 1979, at 2, para. 18; S.C.O.R. (XXXIV), 2108th Meeting, 11 January 1979, at 7, para. 73.

[51] S.C.O.R. (XXXIV), 2108th Meeting, 11 January 1979, at 7, para. 79.

[52] S.C.O.R. (XXXIV), 2108th Meeting, 11 January 1979, at 8, para. 83.

[53] S.C.O.R. (XXXIV), 2108th Meeting, 11 January 1979, at 7, para. 79.

[54] S.C.O.R. (XXXIV), 2108th Meeting, 11 January 1979, at 10, para. 104.

In reply, the Viet Nam representative argued that his country was acting in self-defense in a "border war started by the Pol Pot–Ieng Sary clique against Viet Nam" but that the overthrow of the Khmer Rouge had been the achievement not of Vietnamese military invasion but of "the revolutionary war of the Kampuchean people" against their government "which is an instrument in the hands of the reactionary ruling circles of Peking."[55] The US representative dryly observed that "this is as interesting a meeting as we have had in the Council for some time."[56]

Beneath this collision of flying invectives, Viet Nam, somewhat *soto voce*, did play the human rights card, its representative telling the Council:

the Pol Pot–Ieng Sary clique stripped the people of Kampuchea of all their rights, pursued inhumane policies and turned that happy people into slaves and the entire country into an immense concentration camp.[57]

He offered some details of Khmer Rouge atrocities, concluding that the country "became a living hell."[58] The point of these revelations, however, was not so much to justify Vietnam's invasion on humanitarian grounds as to support the fiction that there had inevitably been a spontaneous uprising by Cambodians against their oppressors: an assertion that fell on stony ground. It was left to Vietnam's East German allies to make the case more forcefully by using humanitarian arguments. The ouster of the Khmer Rouge its ambassador said, "should be welcomed and supported by all those who earlier spared no words to complain about the massive violations of human rights..." How one responds, he added, "is indeed a touchstone of one's seriousness about the struggle against massive violations of human rights."[59]

He did not succeed in his effort to move the public debate in this more candid direction. All Western and almost all non-aligned governments focused exclusively on the "peace" and "legality" issues raised by Hanoi's violation of its neighbor's state sovereignty, ignoring the "justice" and "legitimacy" issues raised by the Khmer Rouge's abuses of its citizens' human rights. Many baldly insisted that the deplorable human rights record of the ousted Kampuchean regime in no way justified resort

---

[55] S.C.O.R. (XXXIV), 2108th Meeting, 11 January 1979, at 12, para. 115.
[56] S.C.O.R. (XXXIV), 2108th Meeting, 11 January 1979, at 5, para. 56.
[57] S.C.O.R. (XXXIV), 2108th Meeting, 11 January 1979, at 13, para. 130.
[58] S.C.O.R. (XXXIV), 2108th Meeting, 11 January 1979, at 13, para. 131.
[59] S.C.O.R. (XXXIV), 2109th Meeting, 12 January 1979, at 8, para. 68.

to force by outsiders.[60] France's representative made this astonishing admonition:

The notion that because a régime is detestable foreign intervention is justified and forcible overthrow is legitimate is extremely dangerous. That could ultimately jeopardize the very maintenance of international law and order and make the continued existence of various régimes dependent on the judgment of their neighbours.[61]

Portugal engaged in an even more sweeping restatement of the principle of non-use of force:

In any case, there are no, nor can there be any, socio-political considerations that would justify the invasion of the territory of a sovereign State by the forces of another State; and not even provocative actions or the fear of an imminent attack could excuse such an act of aggression.[62]

Even the UK took essentially the same absolutist position.[63]

US Ambassador Andrew Young was almost alone in treating the crisis as one in which moral imperatives needed to be carefully weighed and balanced against the constraints of the international legal order.

The invasion by Viet Nam of Kampuchea presents to the Council difficult political and moral questions... It appears complex because several different provisions of the Charter are directly relevant to our deliberations. These are that: the fundamental principles of human rights must be respected by all Governments, one State must not use force against the territory of another

---

[60] S.C.O.R. (XXXIV), 2109th Meeting, 2 January 1979, at 2, para. 18 (Norway); S.C.O.R. (XXXIV), 2109th Meeting, 2 January 1979, at 4, para. 36 (France); S.C.O.R. (XXXIV), 2109th Meeting, 2 January 1979, at 6, para. 50 (Bangladesh); S.C.O.R. (XXXIV), 2109th Meeting, 2 January 1979, at 7, para. 59 (Bolivia); S.C.O.R. (XXXIV), 2109th Meeting, 2 January 1979, at 10, para. 91 (Sudan); S.C.O.R. (XXXIV), 2110th Meeting, 13 January 1979, at 2, para. 15 (Gabon); S.C.O.R. (XXXIV), 2110th Meeting, 13 January 1979, at 3, para. 25 (Portugal); S.C.O.R. (XXXIV), 2110th Meeting, 13 January 1979, at 4, para. 39 (Malaysia); S.C.O.R. (XXXIV), 2110th Meeting, 13 January 1979, at 5, paras. 48–49 (Singapore); S.C.O.R. (XXXIV), 2110th Meeting, 13 January 1979, at 6, para. 58 (New Zealand); S.C.O.R. (XXXIV), 2110th Meeting, 13 January 1979, at 6, paras. 65–66 (UK); S.C.O.R. (XXXIV), 2111th Meeting, 15 January 1979, at 3, para. 25 (Australia); S.C.O.R. (XXXIV), 2111th Meeting, 15 January 1979, at 4, paras. 34–36; S.C.O.R. (XXXIV), 2111th Meeting, 15 January 1979, at 7, para. 72 (Indonesia); S.C.O.R. (XXXIV), 2111th Meeting, 15 January 1979, at 13, para. 134 (Yugoslavia). There are numerous other examples.
[61] S.C.O.R. (XXXIV), 2109th Meeting, 12 January 1979, at 4, para. 36.
[62] S.C.O.R. (XXXIV), 2110th Meeting, 13 January 1979, at 3, para. 29.
[63] S.C.O.R. (XXXIV), 2110th Meeting, 13 January 1979, at 6–7, paras. 65, 67.

State, a State must not interfere in the affairs of another State, and, if there is a dispute between States, it must be settled peacefully.[64]

While insisting that the Council demand withdrawal of Hanoi's forces, Young did not ignore the United Nations' responsibility to deal with the human rights dimension:

Regarding the brutal violations of human rights which took place under the Pol Pot Government in Kampuchea, we believe the international community long ago should have brought the full weight of international condemnation to bear.[65]

Ambassador Young, however, shied away from concluding that, in such circumstances, the Vietnamese invasion, even if illegal, was much the lesser of the evils.

What can one deduce from all this? Was it necessary for humanity to suffer the death of a million Cambodians to reinforce the legal principle of non-intervention, or would it have been preferable – and should it have been legally permissible – for Vietnam, or a coalition of willing states, to have acted even earlier to put an end to this tragedy?

The UN system seemed incapable of producing an answer to this conundrum, treating it as an irresolvable conflict between values of peace and justice. On January 15, at the conclusion of the heated debate, the Security Council voted on a resolution introduced by the seven non-aligned members. Unlike an earlier, more vehement draft presented by China,[66] the seven-nation resolution only indirectly condemned the Vietnamese invasion. It called for "the preservation of the sovereignty, territorial integrity and political independence of" Cambodia and for "all foreign forces . . . to withdraw . . ."[67] It was vetoed by the Soviet Union in a vote of 13 to 2, with only Czechoslovakia siding with Moscow.

The question re-emerged in the General Assembly, which was faced with rival delegations: one representing the Khmer Rouge regime (Democratic Kampuchea), now relegated to fighting in border areas near Thailand, and the other sent by the new regime of a renamed Cambodia. By a vote of 6 to 3, the Assembly Credentials Committee accepted the credentials of the former and rejected the latter, a decision upheld in the Assembly's plenary session by a vote of 71 to 35, with 34

[64] S.C.O.R. (XXXIV), 2110th Meeting, 13 January 1979, at 7, para. 72.
[65] S.C.O.R. (XXXIV), 2110th Meeting, 13 January 1979, at 8, para. 78.
[66] S/13022, China: draft resolution, 11 January 1979.
[67] S/13027, Bangladesh, Bolivia, Gabon, Kuwait, Nigeria, and Zambia: draft resolution, 15 January 1979.

abstentions.[68] Most of the states that voted in favor of the report indicated that, despite their awareness of the deplorable record of the Khmer Rouge, they saw "no justification for the acceptance of the credentials of a régime installed through external intervention."[69] Rarely, at least since the Munich Pact of 1938 had dismembered Czechoslovakia to appease Hitler, were states so blatantly ready to choose the value of peace above that of justice. Seven weeks later, by a vote of 90–21 with 29 abstentions, the Assembly adopted the essentials of the draft resolution Moscow had vetoed in the Security Council the previous January.[70] As a sop to the values it was subordinating, the resolution added "that the people of Kampuchea should be enabled to choose democratically their own government, without outside interference, subversion or coercion."[71]

This support of most states for the rights of the Khmer Rouge is indicative of the strength of the system's residual adherence to the priority of peace and the non-use of force, absolute sovereignty, and territorial integrity. Indeed, the right of Pol Pot's fugitive regime to represent Cambodia continued to be recognized by the General Assembly until 1988.[72]

Several factors specific to the Cambodian episode probably helped shape the system's response. One was the extent to which the Vietnamese invasion was seen to serve geopolitical rather than humanitarian purposes. Vietnam's own human rights record, as several delegations pointed out, was hardly unblemished and there was not even a pretense by the invaders to institute any verisimilitude of governance by consent. Vietnam clearly failed to prove convincingly either of the two elements of its case: that it was, in fact, merely responding in self-defense to an armed attack, or that it was using force solely to avert a humanitarian catastrophe. If Hanoi had acted in self-defense, its response was seen evidently to fail the legal test of proportionality. As for averting a human tragedy in Cambodia, that, alas, had already happened, without Vietnamese protest, until such concern came to suit other purposes.

Moreover, Hanoi seemed in no haste to withdraw its forces, even years later, in part because it proved unexpectedly difficult for the regime it had installed to defeat remnants of the Khmer Rouge. Most important

---

[68] 1979 U.N.Y.B. 291. G.A. Res. 34/2A of 21 September 1979.
[69] 1979 U.N.Y.B. 292.   [70] G.A. Res. 34/22 of 14 November 1979.
[71] G.A. Res. 34/22 of 14 November 1979, para. 10.
[72] Vestigial resistance to Heng Samrin's government by the Khmer Rouge kept the civil war going and Vietnamese forces in Cambodia until an international accord in 1991 led to UN-supervised elections in 1993. Weisburd, n. 2 above, at 43.

to many, the opposing sides in Cambodia's prolonged ordeal seemed not so much bearers, respectively, of light and darkness but surrogates for China and the Soviet Union, locked in a bitter contest over their colliding spheres of influence. Observing this sorry spectacle, most governments could identify with neither protagonist, but only with the still widely valued principle prohibiting resort to force, no matter what.

Bangla Desh, Uganda, and Cambodia: when balancing these three cases, it is evident that each was decided by reference to its own special context. It is equally apparent that the Charter's Articles 2(4) and 51 establish a heavy burden of proof – an obligation to rebut a solid negative presumption – on those who, on their own initiative, would deploy force in the absence of, or disproportionate to, an armed attack on them. Vietnam clearly failed to discharge that evidentiary burden. One also detects a widespread and deep reluctance by governments to endorse humanitarian intervention openly, even while they do pay attention to humanitarian concerns in calibrating their reaction to each instance.

France–Central African Empire (1979)

If the UN system has sometimes looked the other way when one of the non-aligned has deployed unauthorized force, it has usually not given such a free pass to the Big Powers and former colonialists or, as in the case of Vietnam, their surrogates. This makes all the more remarkable the United Nations' lack of reaction against France's ouster of the head of the former Central African Empire.

Emperor Jean-Bedel Bokassa was overthrown on the night of September 20–21, 1979, during his state visit to Libya.[73] One month earlier, an OAU Commission of Inquiry composed of judges from five African states had determined that Bokassa had ordered, and participated in, the massacre of 100 school children.[74] There were many other reports of atrocities committed by the bizarre Emperor.[75]

Initially, the French Government denied involvement in the coup, claiming to have acted only in response to a request from the new government led by David Dacko.[76] *Le Monde*, however, reported that French military aircraft had landed in the capital, Bangui, during the night of the coup.[77] Dacko himself reported that the coup had been planned

[73] *New York Times*, September 21, 1979, at A1, A12.   [74] Weisburd, n. 2 above, at 41.
[75] Murphy, n. 2 above, at 108.   [76] *New York Times*, September 22, 1979, at A1, A4.
[77] *Le Monde*, 23–24 September 1979, at 3; *Le Monde*, 26 September 1979, at 1, 4; *Le Monde*, 28 September 1979, at 4.

and executed "with France," which had flown him home along with 800 troops.[78] The French Foreign Ministry, a few days later, admitted that, although it "did not install Dacko," it had let "a certain number of Central Africans know a few months ago" that if they deposed the Emperor they would get French aid.[79]

Libya, Benin, and Chad were alone among African states in criticizing France, supported only by the Soviet Union.[80] No government sought to convene the Security Council or to raise the matter before the General Assembly, which was in session. While France did not overtly play the "humanitarian intervention" card, it was quite clear that Bokassa's removal was widely welcomed on that basis. Paris averred that it had no intention of occupying the country or of acquiring territorial or other concessions. Accordingly, the system quietly, but eloquently, looked the other way. Scholars, in their post-mortems, have judged these events both as an example of humanitarian intervention "par excellence" (Fernando Teson)[81] and as just another instance of French paternalism at work in its former African domains (Simon Chesterman).[82]

France, UK, and US–Iraq (the Kurds, 1991)

In the wake of Iraq's 1991 defeat by Operation Desert Storm, its Shiite population in the south and the predominantly Kurdish areas of the north rose in revolt. The response from Baghdad was severe. Within days, 200,000 Kurds fled towards the Turkish border.[83] Initially, the Security Council did nothing, "a clear sign," according to Cambridge's Dr. Christine Gray, "that there was no well-established doctrine of humanitarian intervention at that time."[84] Perhaps not, but it took a divided Security Council only a few days to pass Resolution 688, which expressed grave concern at "the repression of the Iraqi civilian population... including most recently in Kurdish-populated areas, which led to a massive flow of refugees towards and across international

---

[78] *New York Times*, September 23, 1979, at A1, A6; *New York Times*, September 24, 1979, at A1.

[79] *New York Times*, September 28, 1979, at A1.

[80] *Le Monde*, 25 September 1979, at 3; *Le Monde* 26 September 1979, at 4; *Le Monde*, 28 September 1979, at 4; *Le Monde*, 30 September 1979, at 2.

[81] Fernando R. Teson, *Humanitarian Intervention: An Inquiry into Law and Morality* 150 (2nd ed., 1997).

[82] Chesterman, n. 30 above, at 81–82.   [83] *New York Times*, April 4, 1991, at A1, A11.

[84] Gray, n. 2 above, at 29.

frontiers and to cross-border incursions, which threaten international peace and security."[85] That, of course, is Charter Article 39 language, which is the condition precedent to an authorization to use collective force, although the resolution does not explicitly invoke Chapter VII. Still, the resolution, for good measure, also "condemn[ed] the repression...the consequences of which threaten international peace and security..."[86] and demanded that it end "immediately..."[87] It further called on states to aid humanitarian relief efforts to be organized by the Secretary-General and "demand[ed] that Iraq cooperate..."[88]

Yemen's representative, speaking for the Council's three dissenters, argued that, while there was undoubtedly a humanitarian problem, it did not threaten international peace and security but was a consequence of political unrest in Iraq. He asserted that "it is not within the Council's purview to address internal issues in any country."[89] Clearly, this was not the dominant view, although, behind the scenes, China threatened to veto any resolution that actually authorized military action to relieve the plight of the Kurds.

By mid-April, the Kurdish exodus had risen to more than a million persons.[90] The US, acting in concert with Britain and France, responded by declaring the area north of the 36th parallel out of bounds to Iraqi ground and air forces,[91] commencing aerial drops of food[92] and, on April 13, announcing the despatch of 10,000 troops[93] to protect and feed up to 700,000 Kurds.[94] Iraq's permission, Washington, London, and Paris said, was not required,[95] a posture that brought a quiet dissent from the UN Secretary-General[96] and from his Legal Counsel,[97] but no admonition either from the Security Council or the General Assembly. By late May 1991, the three-power intervention was superseded by an agreement between the Secretary-General and Baghdad authorizing deployment of 500 lightly-armed UN guards in the Kurdish region.[98]

---

[85] S/RES/688 of 5 April 1991. The resolution carried by 10 votes to 3 (Cuba, Yemen, Zimbabwe) with China and India abstaining.
[86] S/RES/688 of 5 April 1991, para. 1   [87] S/RES/688 of 5 April 1991, para. 2.
[88] S/RES/688 of 5 April 1991, paras. 6 and 7.
[89] S.C.O.R. 2982nd Meeting 5 April 1991, at 27.
[90] *New York Times*, April 11, 1991, at A10.   [91] *Ibid.*   [92] *Ibid.*
[93] *New York Times*, April 18, 1991, at A1.   [94] *New York Times*, April 11, 1991, at A10.
[95] *Ibid.*   [96] *New York Times*, April 19, 1991, at A1, A8.
[97] John Tessitore and Susan Woolfson (eds.), *A Global Agenda*: Issues Before the 48th General Assembly 42–43 (1993), citing A.P., 1/21/93.
[98] S/22663, 30 May 1991.

Impetus for the three-power operation had come primarily from the extensive worldwide television coverage of an unfolding humanitarian disaster. The United Nations' Special Rapporteur on Human Rights in Iraq, Max van den Stoel, soon confirmed the *bona fides* of the crisis[99] and the General Assembly registered its alarm at Iraqi repression.[100] China, although privately indicating that it would have felt obliged to veto a formal resolution permitting the three-power operation, kept silent when it occurred "off the books." Those states that participated in the intervention had promised that it would be of very short duration – which it was – and rather tentatively put forward the rationale that their action was "in support of" Resolution 688.[101] The international system responded primarily with benevolent silence. Even when the three Western powers imposed a no-fly zone on Iraq, and, again, after US aerial attacks on Iraqi missile bases in 1996 in response to the movement of Iraqi troops into Kurdish areas, none of these actions evoked much heat, although they were labelled "inappropriate and unacceptable"[102] by Russia.

Detectable in this period, however, is a worrisome hubris on the part of leading military powers when resorting to force without UN authorization. In late 1994, US Secretary of State Madeleine Albright said that "[w]hile Washington would prefer to have the Council behind it, it is prepared to take punitive action alone" when necessary.[103] This could not but reinforce fear that the world was embarking on a slippery slope, that silent acquiescence in the unauthorized use of force – even when force was being used only to carry out humanitarian initiatives in situations of demonstrable necessity – had potentially made it easier for powerful states to have their way whenever it suited their national interest.[104] That perception, whether or not correct, inevitably undercuts the case for a general doctrine of unilateral humanitarian intervention.[105]

---

[99] S/24386, 3 August 1992. See also E/CN.4/1994/58 (1994).

[100] *See*, for example, G.A. Res. 49/203 (1994).   [101] *See* Gray, n. 2 above, at 29.

[102] S/1996/712, 3 September 1996; S/1996/715, 4 September 1996, Annex.

[103] *New York Times*, October 15, 1994, at A1. Some US officials argued that these actions were pre-authorized by the Security Council's resolution (S/RES/687 of 3 April 1991) conditionally ending the use of force against Iraq.

[104] This is the central argument in Noam Chomsky's *The New Military Humanism* (1998).

[105] J. Loebel and S. Ratner, "Bypassing the Security Council: Ambiguous Authorization to Use Force, Cease-fires and the Iraqi Inspection Regime," 93 Am. J. Int'l L. 124 (1999). The UK also took the view that "extreme humanitarian need" justified a humanitarian intervention that "was entirely consistent with the objectives of SCR 688." UK Materials on International Law, 63 B.Y.I.L. 824 (1992).

While the US, during this period, chose rather to flaunt its power-based realpolitik, the UK did attempt to establish modest legal parameters justifying humanitarian interventions when undertaken without specific Security Council authorization. Gray summarizes the Foreign Office position as follows:

First, there should be a compelling and urgent situation of extreme humanitarian distress which demanded immediate relief; the other state should not be able or willing to meet the distress and deal with it; there should be no practical alternative to intervening in order to relieve the stress; and also the action should be limited in time and scope.[106]

Notably, although the US and UK conducted these military operations in close coordination, the same could not be said of their legal advisers. The State Department, too, had considered various legal pronouncements which, like those of their British counterparts, would have tried defining a limited right of humanitarian intervention. But, in the end, each draft was filed unused because none of the exculpatory legal theories seemed to establish the basis for a new reciprocal rights-based regime that was acceptable to the Americans, let alone to others.

ECOMOG–Liberia, Sierra Leone (1989–1999)

In December, 1989, a rebel force supported by several nearby African states entered Liberia under the leadership of Charles Taylor, a former minister in the dictatorship of Samuel Doe, who had gained power in 1980, after a violent coup against President William R. Tolbert. As fighting continued, with increasing casualties and growing flows of refugees, a third contender, Prince Yormie Johnson, entered the bidding with his own splinter army. By the summer of 1990, Doe's control was reduced to part of the capital, Monrovia, while Johnson's army controlled the rest of the embattled city and Taylor held sway over most of the countryside.[107] Some 5,000 persons had died and 500,000 had fled to neighboring states.[108]

These events were noted by the African regional organization to which Liberia belonged: the Economic Community of West African

---

[106] Gray, n. 2 above, at 30, citing UK Materials on International Law, 63 B.Y.I.L. 824 (1992) at 826–27.

[107] Murphy, n. 2 above, at 147. By March 1993, casualties were estimated to have reached 150,000 and 600,000 Liberians had fled to neighboring states. *Ibid.*

[108] *Keesing's Contemporary Archives*, 37644 (1990).

States (ECOWAS), which had been established in 1975.[109] Its governing Authority of Heads of State initiated negotiations among Liberia's warring parties, but to no avail. In June 1990, President Doe asked the Organization to send a peace-keeping force to help him re-establish control. The ECOWAS Mediation Committee, finding "a state of anarchy and the total breakdown of law and order... [with] hundreds of thousands of Liberians being displaced... and the spilling of hostilities into neighbouring countries"[110] decided to establish a neutral Cease-Fire Monitoring Group (ECOMOG) to enforce a truce.

This was not what Doe had requested, neither was it approved by the Taylor faction. ECOWAS decided to proceed nevertheless, imposing itself by force if necessary. Such a mission, by strict construction of Charter Article 53, requires the prior approval of the Security Council. Such permission, however, was neither sought nor given as ECOMOG, beginning on August 24, 1990, began deploying 15,000 troops, tanks and bombers in an effort to bring the parties to a settlement.[111] Although primarily Nigerian, the force included contingents from Ghana, Gambia, Guinea, and Sierra Leone.[112]

A cease-fire was agreed in November 1990,[113] after Doe had been captured and killed by troops led by Prince Johnson. Late in January 1991, fully five months after ECOMOG's military mission had begun, the Security Council issued a Presidential Statement in which "members... commend the efforts made by the ECOWAS Heads of State and Government to promote peace and normalcy in Liberia" and call on the warring parties to respect the cease-fire agreement.[114] It seemed to signal that the Council, in appropriate circumstances, could retroactively sanitize an action that may have been of doubtful legality at the time it was taken.

---

[109] Treaty of the Economic Community of West African States, May 28, 1975, 1010 U.N.T.S. 17; 14 I.L.M. 1200.

[110] M. Weller (ed.), *Regional Peace-Keeping and International Enforcement: the Liberian Crisis* 73 (1994).

[111] Murphy, n. 2 above, at 153. The force consisted primarily of Nigerian military, supported by units from Gambia, Ghana, Guinea, and Sierra Leone. It was commanded by General Arnold Quaindoo, a Ghanaian. Murphy, n. 2 above, at 151.

[112] Gray, n. 2 above, at 211.

[113] ECOWAS, Authority of Heads of State and Government, Decision A/DEC.1/11/90 Relating to the Approval of the Decision of the Community Standing Mediation Committee Taken During its First Session from 6 to 7 August, 1990, November 28, 1990. Reprinted in Weller, n. 110 above, at 111.

[114] S/22133 of 22 January 1991.

The breakdown of the cease-fire agreement and failure of an ECOWAS peace plan[115] led to renewed fighting in mid-1992, with ECOMOG now a principal combatant. As 600 of its troops were taken hostage by Charles Taylor's forces,[116] ECOWAS decided to impose an embargo on Liberia. To make it effective, however, international cooperation was needed, so, for the first time, the West African states approached the Security Council for formal authorization.[117] The Council agreed, finding that the situation was "a threat to international peace and security" and decided again to "commend" ECOWAS for its efforts. It thereupon invoked Chapter VII to impose a general and complete embargo on all military shipments except supplies for ECOMOG.[118] By mid-1993, the Council unanimously created a UN Observer Mission (UNOMIL)[119] to monitor ECOMOG's peacekeeping and peacebuilding operations. A peace agreement took effect in August 1996, leading a year later to an election that, paradoxically, was won by Charles Taylor.

The United Nations' response to ECOWAS' initiative in Liberia is instructive. Chapter VIII of the Charter spells out a subordinate role for regional organizations in any "enforcement actions." These, Article 53 specifies, are not to be taken "without the authorization of the Security Council..." This, we previously noted in chapter 2, had been the topic of intense debate during the drafting of the Charter. At the time, some American states, taking their cue from the new Inter-American security system established by the Act of Chapultepec, had sought broader regional enforcement powers. Some Arab states, too, envisaged a regional system of their own and even British Prime Minister Winston Churchill had imagined "three regional pillars" – in Europe, the Far East, and the Western Hemisphere – to constitute "a superstructure of some sort" for the proposed global organization."[120] Foreign Minister Anthony Eden added his support for "a European Organization which, under the guidance of the three major Allies might foster peaceful tendencies, heal the wounds of Europe and at the same time prevent Germany from again dominating the Continent." Eden made clear, however, that such

---

[115] Yamoussouko IV Accord, 30 October 1991, S/24815 (1992), Annex. Also in Weller, n. 110 above, at 175.

[116] Murphy, n. 2 above, at 154.

[117] S/24825, 18 November 1992.

[118] S/RES/788 of 19 November 1992.

[119] S/RES/856 of 10 August 1993; S/RES/866 of 22 September 1993.

[120] Memorandum by Leo Pasvolsky, Special Assistant to the Secretary of State, March 15, 1944, 1 Foreign Relations of the United States, 1944, 627. See also Winston S. Churchill, *The Second World War: The Hinge of Fate* 711–12, 802–07 (1950).

regional arrangements "should not conflict with the world-wide Organisation, but rather assist it to carry out its purpose."[121] In his caveat lay the seeds of one of the principal disputes to arise at San Francisco.

This conflict was not about Charter recognition of regional organizations but about whether, as Colombia urged, they should equally share with the Security Council responsibility for maintaining their regions' peace and security.[122] This was also strongly pushed by France, which complained that "it is incompatible with the conditions of security of some States, which demand immediate action, to defer, until such time as the Council has reached a decision, emergency measures for which provision has been made…by treaties of assistance…"[123] More support for this view came from Czechoslovakia and Turkey.[124] Initially, the US seemed to agree.[125] Nevertheless, in the end, it rallied a majority against such a co-equal regional role. While Washington conceded that "all regions are fully entitled to use all peaceful means of settling disputes without the permission of the Security Council"[126] it concluded that they should not be permitted to use force without prior Council authorization. Several Latin American states agreed.[127] In the end, Chapter VIII, Article 53, emerged from San Francisco unambiguously subordinating regional enforcement to prior Security Council authorization.

This drafting history makes it the more remarkable that the UN system directed virtually no criticism – and, eventually, widespread praise and endorsement – toward the ECOMOG initiative in Liberia, even though it had been taken without the requisite Council approval. Clearly, most nations were persuaded that Liberia's crisis was self-evident and required outside policing to restore a semblance of law and order. Since none of the Council members wished, themselves, to assume the task, they seemed grateful for the West Africans' initiative and unwilling to

---

[121] Tentative Proposals of the United Kingdom for a General International Organization, July 22, 1944, 1 Foreign Relations of the United States, 1944, 670 at 673.

[122] Minutes of the Thirty-Fifth Meeting of the United States Delegation, San Francisco, May 10, 1945, 1 Foreign Relations of the United States, 1945, 657 at 659–70.

[123] 12 U.N.C.I.O., Commission III, Committee 4, Doc. 269, III/4/5, 14 May 1945, 765 at 777.

[124] U.N.C.I.O., Commission III, Committee 4, Doc. 269, III/4/5, at 773, 781.

[125] United States Tentative Proposals for a General International Organization, July 18, 1944, 1 Foreign Relations of the United States, 1944, 653 at 653–54.

[126] Minutes of the Thirty-Fifth Meeting of the United States Delegation, San Francisco, May 10, 1945, 1 Foreign Relations of the United States, 1945, 660 (Harold Stassen).

[127] Bolivia, in particular, argued "that in no case should regional organizations or agencies be able to adopt sanctions without the express authority of the Security Council." *Ibid.*

cavil at its lack of requisite authorization. The thought was entertained by some, including the US government, that Liberia could be a useful precedent for more active policing of regional disputes by regional systems. Even China and Russia seemed to agree that, in situations such as this, intervention by regional organizations might be the most realistic recourse. Eventually, this sentiment was expressed in what was tantamount to a retroactive endorsement of the ECOWAS resort to force.[128]

The ECOMOG intervention thus established that, in the right circumstances, the UN system might tolerate a subregional humanitarian military intervention it had not authorized and might even join in carrying it out. As Professor David Wippman has pointed out, "the international community now appear[ed] willing not only to tolerate but to support a considerable degree of intervention in internal conflicts when necessary to restore order and save lives."[129]

The UN's response to the Sierra Leone crisis reinforces this interpretation. That country's civil war began in March 1991, when the Revolutionary United Front (RUF) revolted against President Joseph S. Momoh. The crisis accelerated and triangulated when Momoh was ousted, not by the RUF but by a military coup. As in Liberia, the conflict gradually generated hundreds of thousands of casualties and sent half the population into external or internal exile.[130] In the course of almost a decade of intermittent fighting, the country's infrastructure and social skein largely unraveled.

Briefly, elections restored a legitimate government. Then, on May 25, 1997, another military coup ousted the newly chosen President, Ahmad Tejan Kabbah. The Organization of African Unity thereupon appealed to ECOWAS "to help the people of Sierra Leone to restore the constitutional order..." The UN Security Council restricted its own response to welcoming ECOWAS' mediation efforts and expressing "support for the objectives of these efforts..."[131] However, in practice, ECOWAS went far beyond mediation. Against heavy resistance,

---

[128] For an earlier instance of an attempt to secure retroactive Security Council legitimation of an unlawful regional action see the Soviet initiative to win formal approval of an OAS enforcement action against the Dominican Republic, discussed in chapter 4 (p. 56).

[129] David Wippman, "Enforcing the Peace: ECOWAS and the Liberian Civil War," in *Enforcing Restraint, Collective Intervention in Internal Conflicts* 157 (Lori Fisler Damrosch, ed., 1993).

[130] S/1995/975, 21 November 1995, at 5, para. 32.

[131] S/PRST/1997/36, 11 July 1997.

it sent a military contingent to occupy Freetown, the Sierra Leone capital.[132]

On October 8, the Council unanimously "took note" of a further ECOWAS decision to impose sanctions on Sierra Leone. Acting under Chapter VIII of the Charter, it "authorize[d] ECOWAS... to ensure [their] strict implementation," including "halting inward maritime shipping in order to inspect and verify their cargoes and destinations..."[133] Nigeria, the lead-participant in the operation, ambiguously observed that "[a]lthough ECOWAS was sufficiently seized of the matter, the support and endorsement of the United Nations was needed."[134] It was apparent that, while the regional group – in violation of the strictly construed Charter text – had proceeded on its own authority, no member of the Security Council chose to object.[135] While not specifically authorizing the engagement of ECOMOG troops, it "commend[ed] the important role... ECOWAS has continued to play towards the peaceful resolution of this crisis."[136]

What ECOMOG troops did, in the week of 6–13 February, went far beyond effecting a "peaceful resolution."[137] They forcibly ousted the military junta, seized control of Freetown, and invited exiled President Kabbah to return.[138] The Security Council unanimously applauded this result.[139] It also, for the first time, tepidly offered to share the burden, authorizing the deployment of "up to ten United Nations military liaison personnel" to "coordinate closely" with ECOMOG.[140]

Still, the newly reinstalled government and its ECOMOG protectors found little respite. The RUF resumed its campaign, leaving ECOMOG to defend a regime without an army of its own. The Security Council, again commending ECOMOG, deplored the "continued resistance to the authority of the legitimate Government of Sierra

---

[132] S/PRST/1997/42, 6 August 1997.

[133] S/RES/1132 (1997) of 8 October 1997. The Council was presumably acting under Article 53.

[134] Press Release SC/6425, 8 October 1997, at 8.

[135] Russia, in the Security Council, did reiterate its view that the Charter required regional enforcement actions to be authorized by the Council. Gray, n. 2 above, at 229–30.

[136] Press Release, Presidential Statement, SC/6481, 26 February 1998.

[137] In its reporting to the Security Council, however, ECOMOG was careful to indicate that it was deploying force in self-defence or to enforce the arms and oil embargo. S/1997/895, S/1998/107, S/1998/123, S/1998/170.

[138] S/1998/249, 18 March 1998, at 2, para. 6; Press Release SC/6486, 16 March 1998.

[139] S/RES/1156 (1998) of 16 March 1998.

[140] S/RES/1162 of 17 April 1998, para. 5.

Leone..."[141] In June, it applauded ECOMOG's "positive role" in restoring "peace, security and stability throughout the country at the request of the Government of Sierra Leone" and authorized despatch of a 70-man United Nations Observer Mission (UNOMSIL) to monitor "the military and security situation"[142] and the combatants' compliance with human rights.[143]

Proclaiming that they were "fighting ECOMOG and the United Nations" the resilient RUF forces of Corporal Foday Sankoh staged a surprising advance in December 1999, reaching the center of Freetown again the next month. UNOMSIL was hastily evacuated,[144] but ECOMOG reinforcements from Nigeria, Ghana, Guinea, and Mali somewhat stabilized the situation. Freetown was recaptured in March.[145] On May 18, a cease-fire agreement was signed and dialogue initiated between the Government and the RUF,[146] followed by the signing of a peace agreement on July 7.[147]

This agreement was welcomed by the Council, despite expressions of distaste for the amnesty and power-sharing it afforded the rebels. In August, the Council again "commend[ed]" ECOMOG "on the outstanding contribution which it had made to the restoration of security and stability in Sierra Leone." It authorized the redeployment of 210 UNOMSIL military observers.[148] For the first time, the Council specifically approved "the new mandate for ECOMOG (S/1999/1073, Annex) adopted by ECOWAS on 25 August 1999."[149] In October, acting under Chapter VII of the Charter, the Council created a new United Nations Mission in Sierra Leone (UNAMSIL) with 6,000 military personnel to participate alongside ECOMOG in disarming and demobilizing insurgent forces.[150]

After only a few weeks of calm, fighting resumed,[151] with ECOMOG's casualties mounting and its resources increasingly strained. Nigeria's role became an issue in its presidential elections and, on December 7, its new President, Olusegun Obasanjo, notified the UN Secretary-General of his country's intention to withdraw its troops, prompting other West African governments with contingents in ECOMOG to follow suit.[152]

[141] Press Release, Presidential Statement, SC/6518, 20 May 1998.
[142] S/RES/1181 of 13 June 1998.   [143] S/1999/20, 7 January 1999, at 4, para. 21.
[144] S/1999/20, 7 January 1999, at 2, para. 10.   [145] S/1999/237, 4 March 1999.
[146] S/1999/645, 4 June 1999.   [147] S/1999/836, 30 July 1999.
[148] S/RES/1260, 20 August 1999, at 1, paras. 3 and 4.
[149] S/RES/1270, 22 October 1999, at 2, para. 7.
[150] S/RES/1270, 22 October 1999, at 2, para. 9.
[151] S/1999/1223, 6 December 1999.   [152] S/1999/1285, 28 December 1999.

With that, the situation in Sierra Leone again descended into chaos. The Council, acting under Chapter VII, responded by authorizing UNAMSIL to deploy 11,100 troops in place of ECOMOG.[153] In May 2000, this authorization was increased to 13,000.[154] Some Nigerian troops were "re-helmetted"[155] to join UNAMSIL and reinforcements were sent by India, yet the tide again turned in favor of the insurgents until Britain despatched a marine contingent that was able to lift the RUF's siege of Freetown.[156]

What conclusions regarding humanitarian intervention can be drawn? In both Liberia and Sierra Leone, the peacekeeping role had been undertaken by the regional force in circumstances which, from a humanitarian perspective, could be seen to have become intolerable. For most of the decade, the UN system had been unwilling to assume this task and ECOMOG's presence, if not pre-authorized in strict compliance with the Charter, had nevertheless been applauded by UN members who had commended ECOWAS peacemaking without, however, specifically authorizing it to use force as technically required by the Charter. Only much later had the Council itself begun to assume the role envisaged for it by the Charter's provision on collective security.

The ECOWAS interventions in Liberia and Sierra Leone can be said to have demonstrated the reticent UN system's increasing propensity to let regional organizations use force, even absent specific prior Security Council authorization, when that seemed the only way to respond to impending humanitarian disasters. While both interventions were eventually ratified and adopted by the Council – first in the form of resolutions "commending" them, and then by decisions making the United Nations a partner in those operations – such *ex post facto* approval effectively reinterprets the text of Article 53. That reinterpretation is further evident in the Council's response to civil conflict in the Central African Republic[157] and in Kosovo.

---

[153] S/RES/1289 of 7 February 2000, para. 9.

[154] S/RES/1299 of 19 May 2000, para. 1.

[155] Third Report of the Secretary-General on UNAMSIL, S/2000/186.

[156] UN Press Release SC/6857, 11 May 2000, at 4 (Ambassador Stewart Eldon).

[157] Army mutinies in the Central African Republic (CAR) were put down by unilateral French military intervention between April and November 1996. This could conceivably be construed as an intervention in response to a request by the CAR's legitimate government. In January 1997, the French forces were replaced by troops of Burkina Faso, Chad, Gabon, Mali, Senegal, and Togo operating (with French logistical support) under the authority of the Bangui Agreements (MISAB) and using force as necessary. UN Press Release SC/6407, 6 August 1997. Fighting continued into July 1997. Chesterman, n. 30 above, at 138. The regional intervention – if such it

NATO–Yugoslavia (Kosovo) (1999)

In important ways, the ECOWAS operations in Liberia and Sierra Leone were precursors of the NATO intervention in Kosovo. In each of these crises, a regional organization acted where the United Nations would not – or could not – rescue a population *in extremis*.[158] An important difference, however, is that, while the ECOWAS actions may not have been pre-authorized by the Security Council in strict compliance with the requirement of Charter Article 53, no significant opposition to them had arisen among its members. NATO's intervention, on the other hand, was strongly opposed by Russia and China, which would have vetoed it had the Council's approval been sought.[159] Despite these differences, the United Nations' response to the Kosovo crisis may be seen to have reinforced tendencies first evident during the earlier crises in West Africa.

The facts of Kosovo are well known, at least in outline.[160] Conditions there had begun to deteriorate in 1989, when Serb President Slobodan Milosevic rescinded the province's autonomous status, granted in 1974

is – was not approved by the Security Council under Chapter VII until August 1997 (S/RES/1125 of 6 August 1997): more than six months after the Banqui accord had initiated it and more than a year after the French intervention had begun. MISAB itself was eventually replaced by a UN force (MINURCA).

[158] Nevertheless, two differences should be noted. Liberia and Sierra Leone are both members of ECOWAS while Yugoslavia is not a member of NATO. ECOWAS, therefore, had jurisdiction under Article 52(1) of the UN Charter to "deal . . . with such matters relating to the maintenance of international peace and security as are appropriate for regional action . . ." while, formally, NATO had no comparable jurisdiction over Kosovo. Action in Kosovo can be said to have been taken *by* NATO but not *under* NATO, since Yugoslavia is not a member of the regional organization. NATO, in the strictly legal sense, had no special rights of enforcement and no privileged legal standing to deal with the matter other than such rights as evolving international law and practice may be said to accord to any states in the face of any large-scale violation of universal human and humanitarian rights. The Security Council did authorize regional action against the Federal Republic of Yugoslavia, however, even though that state was not a member of such implementing groupings as NATO and the Western European Union (WEU). For example, NATO and WEU helped enforce the arms embargo on Serbia and Montenegro under resolutions implicating Chapter VIII. See Gray, n. 2 above, at 234.

[159] In this sense, too, NATO's Kosovo operation was in sharp contrast to the NATO "double key" operations authorized by the Security Council in the former Yugoslavia and discussed in chapter 2 (pp. 39–40).

[160] See Independent International Commission on Kosovo ("The Goldstone Commission"), *Kosovo Report: Conflict, International Response, Lessons Learned* (2000); also, *Kosovo*, Foreign Affairs Committee, House of Commons (UK), Fourth Report, vol. 1, 23 May 2000. *See, also*, Vladimir-Djuro Degan, *Humanitarian Intervention (NATO Action Against the Federal Republic of Yugoslavia in 1999)*, ms., pp. 2–36, 2001.

by President Tito. The following year, Milosevic dissolved Kosovo's regional government and revoked the official status of the Albanian language used by 90 percent of the population. Albanian Kosovars reacted by creating an unofficial parallel system of schools, laws, judiciary, and taxation.

By 1997, however, this non-violent response began to fray as inter-ethnic violence raged elsewhere in the former Yugoslavia. Late in 1997, large-scale student protests in Pristina, the capital, were harshly suppressed and an underground Kosovo Liberation Army (KLA) began operating. Belgrade responded by deploying troops, attacking villages with helicopters, and using tanks and armored personnel carriers in maneuvers designed to cow any civilians seen as supporting the insurgents. On March 5, 1998, fifty Kosovars were killed in the Drenica area, including twenty-five women and children. Terrified civilians fled into the mountains as villages suspected of harboring KLA elements were pounded by artillery.[161] The UN Secretary-General, in October 1998, reported that the "level of destruction" by Serb forces "points clearly to an indiscriminate and disproportionate use of force against civilian populations"[162] and to "appalling atrocities, reminiscent of recent past events in the Balkans." The "great majority" of these were "committed by security forces...of the Federal Republic of Yugoslavia."[163]

On March 31, the Security Council "condemn[ed] the use of excessive force by Serbian police... against peaceful demonstrators in Kosovo" but also "all acts of terrorism by the Kosovo Liberation Army...and all external support for terrorist activity in Kosovo..."[164] The resolution expressed "support for an enhanced status for Kosovo which would include a substantially greater degree of autonomy and meaningful self-administration."[165] It "emphasiz[ed] that failure to make constructive progress towards the peaceful resolution of the situation...[would] lead to the consideration of additional measures."[166] Acting under Charter

---

[161] These and related events are reported in *Kosovo/Kosova, As Seen, as Told: An Analysis of the Human Rights Findings of the OSCE Kosovo Verification Mission*, October 1998 to June 1999, OSCE Office for Democratic Institutions and Human Rights (1999), pt. I, ch. 1.

[162] S/1998/912, 3 October 1998.

[163] S/1998/912, 3 October 1998. *See also* S/1999/99, 30 January 1999, annex II, table 1 for documentation of atrocities the vast majority of which the Secretary-General attributed to Serb forces.

[164] S/RES/1160 of 31 March 1998.   [165] S/RES/1160 of 31 March 1998, para. 5.

[166] S/RES/1160 of 31 March 1998, para. 19.

Chapter VII, the Council reimposed the recently suspended arms embargo on Yugoslavia.[167]

As the situation continued to deteriorate, the Council expressed grave concern "at the recent intense fighting in Kosovo and in particular the excessive and indiscriminate use of force by Serbian security forces and the Yugoslav Army which have resulted in numerous civilian casualties and, according to the Secretary-General, the displacement of over 230,000 persons"[168] (out of a total population of approximately 2 million). It demanded that immediate steps be taken by both sides "to avert the impending humanitarian catastrophe"[169] and that Yugoslavia not "carry out any repressive actions against the peaceful population" but "resolve existing problems by political means on the basis of equality for all citizens and ethnic communities in Kosovo."[170] Brandishing its Chapter VII enforcement powers, the Council foresaw that if these and other measures were not complied with, it would "consider further action and additional measures to maintain or restore peace and stability in the region."[171]

As the summer wore on, Yugoslav army units continued their campaign against an increasingly hostile civilian population, torching 300 villages, burning down mosques and driving out another 300,000 civilians.[172] In September, expressing "deep alarm," the Council called for granting Kosovo "a substantially greater degree of autonomy and meaningful self-administration"[173] and commended efforts by the Organization for Security and Cooperation in Europe (OSCE) to verify compliance with humanitarian norms. In a Presidential Statement in January 1999, the Council "strongly condemn[ed] the massacre of Kosovo Albanians in the village of Racak" and expressed "deep concern...that the victims were civilians, including women...and at least one child."[174]

In mid-March, Yugoslavia rejected an agreement proposed by the Contact Group (France, Germany, Italy, UK, US) at Rambouillet. It would have provided Kosovo with greater autonomy, required the

---

[167] S/RES/1160 of 31 March 1998, para. 8.
[168] S/RES/1199 of 23 September 1998, para. 2.
[169] S/RES/1199 of 23 September 1998, para. 2.
[170] S/RES/1199 of 23 September 1998, para. 5.
[171] S/RES/1199 of 23 September 1998, preamble and para. 16.
[172] "The Balkans 2000," paper prepared for Ditchley Conference by Conflict Management Group 1999, at 6.
[173] S/RES/1203 of 24 October 1998, preamble and para. 1.
[174] S/PRST/1999/2, 19 January 1999.

withdrawal of Yugoslav troops, and deployed international peacekeepers. Less than one week later, on March 24, NATO forces began their air strikes. Simultaneously, Yugoslav troops began a well-planned campaign of ethnic cleansing. By then, more than 600,000 Kosovars had fled into neighboring states and an additional 850,000 persons were internally displaced and homeless.[175]

As NATO attacks got underway, the Russian ambassador demanded the convening of the Security Council.[176] The debate, on that occasion, demonstrated that there were essentially three camps: those who defended the NATO action as a necessary response to the extreme humanitarian disaster, those who considered NATO to be in flagrant violation of the UN Charter, and those who somehow managed to hold both these positions simultaneously.

The first camp consisted primarily of NATO states, together with Arab and Islamic nations. In the words of US Ambassador Peter Burleigh:

We and our allies have begun military action only with the greatest reluctance. But we believe that such action is necessary to respond to Belgrade's brutal persecution of Kosovar Albanians, violations of international law, excessive and indiscriminate use of force, refusal to negotiate to resolve the issue peacefully and recent military build-up in Kosovo – all of which foreshadow a human catastrophe of immense proportions.[177]

He also cited the pressure on neighboring countries of flows of refugees, "threatening the stability of the region"[178] and the Security Council's previous recognition that the situation constituted a threat to world peace.[179] In essence, he argued that NATO's action was "justified and necessary to stop the violence and prevent an even greater humanitarian disaster."[180] "Humanitarian considerations underpin our actions," Canada's Ambassador Robert Fowler added. "We cannot simply stand by while innocents are murdered, an entire population is displaced, villages are burned and looted, and a population is denied its basic rights... We remain deeply concerned about further atrocities..."[181] Ambassador Danilo Türk of Slovenia added: "all diplomatic means have been exhausted..."[182] The point was made even more sharply by the Netherlands representative:

[175] Conflict Management Group 1999, n. 172 above, at 6.
[176] S/1999/320, 24 March 1999.
[177] S.C.O.R. (LIV), 3988th Meeting, 24 March 1999, at 4.   [178] Ibid.
[179] Ibid. Burleigh cited to S/RES/1199 and S/RES/1203 of 1998.
[180] S.C.O.R. (LIV), 3988th Meeting, 24 March 1999, at 5.
[181] S.C.O.R. (LIV), 3988th Meeting, 24 March 1999, at 6.   [182] Ibid.

The Secretary-General is right when he observes... that the Council should be involved in any decision to resort to the use of force. If, however, due to one or two permanent members' rigid interpretation of the concept of domestic jurisdiction, such a resolution is not attainable, we cannot sit back and simply let the humanitarian catastrophe occur.[183]

The representative of Gambia declared that "at times the exigencies of a situation demand, and warrant, decisive and immediate action."[184] He thought this was such a time.

Notably, the defenders of NATO's action were reluctant to use the traditional legal fictions. It could have been claimed that law permitted a forceful response in self-defense to end that which had engendered the flow of refugees flooding into Albania and Macedonia. It would have been arguable that massive violations of human rights justified states taking military countermeasures when these violations had been recognized and condemned by the Security Council but it had been unable to muster an effective collective response. However, it was evident that among NATO members opinion was divided as to whether to seek a principled legal justification, and, if so, which one. Rather, the emphasis was on the particular facts and the extreme necessity for acting to prevent something far worse than a use of force in technical violation of Article 2(4). "The action being taken is legal," proclaimed Britain's Sir Jeremy Greenstock. "It is justified as an exceptional measure to prevent an overwhelming humanitarian catastrophe."[185] His position was later endorsed by the Foreign Affairs Committee of Britain's House of Commons, which, after hearing from governmental and non-governmental experts, concluded that "a humanitarian emergency existed before NATO intervened" and that "a humanitarian catastrophe would have occurred... if intervention had not taken place."[186]

In the second camp were the Russians, Chinese, Namibians, and, although not members of the Council, the Indians. Ambassador Sergei Lavrov of Russia put his country's position thus:

Attempts to justify the NATO strikes with arguments about preventing a humanitarian catastrophe in Kosovo are completely untenable. Not only are these attempts in no way based on the Charter or other generally recognized rules of

---

[183] S.C.O.R. (LIV), 3988th Meeting, 24 March 1999, at 8.

[184] S.C.O.R. (LIV), 3988th Meeting, 24 March 1999, at 8.

[185] S.C.O.R. (LIV), 3988th Meeting, 24 March 1999, at 12.

[186] *Kosovo*, Fourth Report, vol. 1, House of Commons (UK) Foreign Affairs Committee (2000), para. 138.

international law, but the unilateral use of force will lead precisely to a situation with truly devastating humanitarian consequences.[187]

What was happening would create "a dangerous precedent that could cause acute destabilization and chaos on the regional and global level" with "the virus of illegal unilateral approaches" spreading "not merely to other geographical regions but to spheres of international relations other than questions of peace and security."[188] He insisted that "the potential of political and diplomatic methods to yield a settlement in Kosovo has certainly not been exhausted."[189]

Ambassador Qin Huasun of China took an even more absolutist position in reliance on Charter text. "The question of Kosovo," he said, "as an internal matter of the Federal Republic of Yugoslavia, should be resolved among the parties concerned in the Federal Republic... We oppose interference in the internal affairs of other States, under whatever pretext or in whatever form."[190] The representative of Namibia, although acknowledging the "degree of brutality perpetrated on the civilian population" of Kosovo, insisted that "[m]ore violence and destruction cannot salvage peace."[191] India took a similar position:[192]

The attacks against the Federal Republic of Yugoslavia... are in clear violation of Article 53 of the Charter... Among the barrage of justifications we have heard, we have been told that the attacks are meant to prevent violations of human rights. Even if that were to be so, it does not justify unprovoked military aggression. Two wrongs do not make a right.[193]

The third camp consisted of a few states which sought to have it both ways. "As a matter of principle," the representative of Malaysia said, "my delegation is not in favour of the use or threat of use of force to resolve any conflict situation... If the use of force is at all necessary, it should be... sanctioned by the Security Council..." He then went on to "regret that in the absence of Council action on this issue it has been necessary for action to be taken outside of the Council."[194] The

---

[187] S.C.O.R. (LIV), 3988th Meeting, 24 March 1999, at 2–3.

[188] S.C.O.R. (LIV), 3988th Meeting, 24 March 1999, at 3.

[189] *Ibid.*

[190] S.C.O.R. (LIV), 3988th Meeting, 24 March 1999, at 12.

[191] S.C.O.R. (LIV), 3988th Meeting, 24 March 1999, at 10.

[192] S.C.O.R. (LIV), 3988th Meeting, 24 March 1999, at 16.

[193] He was reminded by Ambassador Danilo Türk of Slovenia that India had used force in just such circumstances of extreme humanitarian crisis when it intervened in Pakistan's repression of East Bengal in 1971 without Security Council authorization.

[194] S.C.O.R. (LIV), 3988th Meeting, 24 March 1999, at 10.

Gabonese ambassador simply noted for the record that his government "is in principle opposed to the use of force to settle local or international disputes."[195]

After two days of debate, Russia offered a draft resolution declaring that NATO's "unilateral use of force constitutes a flagrant violation of the United Nations Charter." Invoking Chapter VII, it demanded the "immediate cessation"[196] of NATO aggression. The resolution was defeated by an overwhelming margin of 3 in favor and 12 – including Malaysia and Gabon – against.[197]

During May, Russian Prime Minister Viktor Chernomyrdin and former Finnish President Martti Ahtisaari brokered the agreement between NATO and Belgrade which ended the conflict. The Kumanovo Military Technical Agreement of June 9, 1999 required Yugoslav forces to withdraw from Kosovo and provided for deployment of an international peacekeeping force and civil administration, while reaffirming Yugoslav titular sovereignty over the region.[198] The Security Council in Resolution 1244, with 14 favorable votes and none opposed, "welcome[d]" this agreement[199] and endorsed its "general principles"[200] while putting the full force of Chapter VII behind its implementation[201] and demanding "the full cooperation" of the Yugoslav Republic[202] by the immediate withdrawal from Kosovo of its military police and paramilitary forces.[203] It also authorized deployment of a UN "international civil and security presence"[204] with civil responsibility[205] alongside NATO and Russian security forces.[206]

---

[195] S.C.O.R. (LIV), 3988th Meeting, 24 March 1999, at 11.

[196] S/1999/328, 26 March 1999.

[197] S.C.O.R. (LIV), 3989th Meeting, 26 March 1999, at 6. The 3 members in favor were China, Namibia, and Russia. The 12 members opposed were Argentina, Bahrain, Brazil, Canada, France, Gabon, Gambia, Malaysia, Netherlands, Slovenia, UK, and US.

[198] S/1999/649. This agreement also appears in S/RES/1244 of 10 June 1999, Annex 2.

[199] S/RES/1244 of 10 June 1999; S.C.O.R. (LIV), 4011th Meeting, 10 June 1999, at 9.

[200] S/RES/1244 of 10 June 1999, preamble.

[201] *Ibid.* The actual terms of this provision are somewhat ambiguous, covering with the authority of Chapter VII the "safety and security of international personnel and the implementation by all concerned of their responsibilities under the present resolution." *Ibid.*

[202] S/RES/1244 of 10 June 1999, para. 2.

[203] S/RES/1244 of 10 June 1999, para. 3.

[204] S/RES/1244 of 10 June 1999, para. 5.

[205] S/RES/1244 of 10 June 1999, paras. 6 and 10.

[206] S/RES/1244 of 10 June 1999, para. 7.

China abstained, because, its ambassador said, the resolution in effect ratified NATO's use of force. "In essence," he warned, "the 'human rights over sovereignty' theory" on which NATO had purported to act "serves to... promote hegemonism under the pretext of human rights."[207]

A more nuanced view was taken by the Kosovo Report of a Commission chaired by the eminent South African jurist Richard Goldstone, the former chief prosecutor of the International Criminal Tribunal for the Former Yugoslavia. It located the NATO action in a gray zone: technically illegal but morally legitimate[208] and emphasized that the crisis had been one in which "a vulnerable people" were "threatened with catastrophe." The Commission asked whether some new doctrine of humanitarian intervention would not have to emerge from the precedent "[i]f international law no longer provides acceptable guidelines in such a situation."[209]

Subsequent reactions have been mixed. A ministerial meeting of the Non-Aligned formally recorded its rejection of humanitarian intervention.[210] In addressing the 1999 General Assembly, President Clinton vaguely referred to NATO as having helped "to vindicate the principles and purposes of the Organization's Charter..."[211] It was left to the Netherlands ambassador to try to extract some normative implications from these events. He saw in Resolution 1244's easy passage and the earlier defeat of Russia's attempt to condemn NATO's action "a gradual shift occurring in international law...[to] the rule, now generally accepted..., that no sovereign State has the right to terrorize its own citizens."[212] However, for good and self-evident reasons, even he stopped short of enunciating the concomitant principle: that states, or groups of states, might now lawfully resort to force – on their own authority when the Council is stymied – to stop extreme instances of violations of humanitarian and human rights law. Such an ambitious proposition of law, he must have realized, while solving some problems, could create a host of others and is not, at least for now, widely acceptable.

---

[207] S.C.O.R. (LIV), 4011th Meeting, 10 June 1999, at 9.
[208] Independent International Commission on Kosovo, *The Kosovo Report: Conflict, International Response, Lessons Learned* 164 (2000).
[209] *Ibid.*
[210] UN Press Release GA/SPD/164, 18 September, 1999.
[211] Press Release GA/9599, 21 September 1999.
[212] S.C.O.R. (LIV), 4011th Meeting, 10 June 1999, at 19.

Conclusions

In expostulating his central thesis in international law and organization in 1933 – "there shall be no violence"[213] – Sir Hersch Lauterpacht imagined a world that, in its habitual peaceability, mirrored the highly civilized and socialized domestic community he took for granted in England. That world has not yet been realized and may even appear less imminent, today, than it did at the beginning of the 1930s. Arguably, the international order has become more, rather than less, chaotic and violent.

There are three rays of hope, however, cutting through this miasma. *First*, while there is more violence, states have partially succeeded in creating an institutional framework for addressing the mounting problems collectively. This would strike Judge Lauterpacht as important – although spotty – progress in the developing of a global institution-based peace-preserving regime. *Second*, while much of the regime based on the UN Charter has been made obsolete by a half-century of momentous technological and political developments, the system has also demonstrated extraordinary functional agility and resilience. It could be said, from the perspective of the new century, to have succeeded in reinventing itself, again and again, in the manner somewhat reminiscent of a durable national constitution. This resilience has been particularly useful in devising new operational ways for the UN system itself to deploy collective force and new parameters delimiting when such force should be deployed. *Third*, while the UN system aims to substitute its collective security for traditional state reliance on unilateral force, it has had some success in adjusting to a harsher reality. In particular, it has acquiesced, sometimes actively, at other times passively, in the measured expansion of the ambit for discretionary state action and has done so without altogether abandoning the effort evident in Article 2(4) to contain unilateral recourse to force. It has sought balance, rather than either absolute prohibition or license.

This balance is difficult to achieve. If the use of force by NATO in Kosovo is seen as a precedent for a reinterpretation of Article 2(4)'s absolute prohibition on the discretionary use of force by states, the substitution of a more "reasonable" principle, one that accommodates use of force by any government to stop what it believes to be an extreme violation of fundamental human rights in another state, could launch the

---

[213] H. Lauterpacht, *The Function of Law in the International Community* 64 (1933). For discussion see chapter 1 above (p. 1).

international system down the slippery slope into an abyss of anarchy. Lauterpacht expressed just this concern in the sentence quoted in chapter 1: "It is impossible, in the scheme of things devised to secure the reign of law, to provide machinery calculated to disregard the law in a manner binding on the party willing to abide by the law."[214]

The danger of treating NATO's use of force in the Kosovo crisis as simply a humane exception, an *in extremis* necessity, is that the law cannot hope to secure acquiescence in a norm that permits its violation at the sole discretion of a party to which it is addressed. Law is strengthened when it avoids absurdly rigid absolutes – for example, by requiring passivity in the face of destruction of entire populations – but only if exceptions intended to prevent such *reductio ad absurdum* are clearly understood and applied in a manner consonant with agreed notions of procedural and evidentiary fairness.[215]

Finally, the instances in which a state or group of states has intervened for humanitarian purposes without incurring significant opposition from the international system may indicate a certain willingness on the part of that community to brook some violation of the law in instances of clearly demonstrated necessity. It does not, however, indicate a fundamental change in the law to give wholesale permission to states to do that which is textually prohibited. Even less does it suggest that conduct which is textually prohibited has, through practice, become legally obligatory. It cannot, on the broadest interpretation of the legal significance of practice, be argued that the law now *requires* states to intervene with or without Security Council authorization, wherever and whenever there is evidence of a massive violation of humanitarian law or human rights. As a former British Foreign Secretary has recently pointed out:

---

[214] Lauterpacht, *The Function of Law in the International Community*, at 372–73.

[215] In testimony before the House of Commons' Foreign Affairs Committee, Oxford Professor Vaughn Lowe proposed such a set of standards for legitimating humanitarian intervention:

1. prior determination by the Security Council of a grave crisis, threatening international peace and security;
2. articulation by the Security Council of specific policies for the resolution of crises, the implementation of which can be secured or furthered by armed intervention;
3. an imminent human catastrophe which it is believed can be averted by the use of force and only by the use of force;
4. intervention by a multinational force.

Kosovo, Foreign Affairs Committee, n. 160 above, para. 140.

There is room for much argument about the nature of the cruelties which have been or are being inflicted in Chechnya, Tibet and the Occupied Territories of Palestine. But however great and unwarranted such cruelties, the international community will certainly prove unable or unwilling to intervene to stop them. The distribution of power in the world makes such intervention impossible... The fact that the international community cannot intervene everywhere to protect human rights need not be an argument against helping where we can... It is...a reason for not trying to confuse decisions of policy with obligations under international law.[216]

Or, put in lawyers' terms, it is important not to confuse what the law *in some limited circumstances may condone* or excuse with what is *required* by law in every circumstance. To help clarify that distinction, the final chapter 10 will examine the limited but potentially important role of a concept of mitigation or exculpation.

---

[216] "After all, who is my Neighbour?" Address by Rt. Hon. Douglas Hurd, circulated privately by UK Mission to UN, 7 March 2001.

10

What, eat the cabin boy? Uses of force that are illegal but justifiable

> The letter killeth, but the spirit giveth life.
>
> St. Paul, *2 Corinth. 3:6*

> Law that said what was necessary should not be done would seem an ass.
>
> A.W. Brian Simpson, *Cannibalism and the Common Law*, p. 216 (1984)

When does a state's recourse to force violate its legal obligations under the UN Charter? Does the answer lie exclusively with the black-letter text of Article 2(4), or is the practice of UN organs and of the constituent states also relevant?

In its judgment in the *Nicaragua* case, the World Court set out its view on the interaction between practice and the legal norm pertaining to armed intervention:[1]

> The significance for the Court of cases of State conduct prima facie inconsistent with the principle of non-intervention lies in the nature of the ground offered as justification. Reliance by a State on a novel right or an unprecedented exception to the principle might, if shared in principle by other States, tend towards modification of customary international law.

True, practice cannot by itself amend a treaty, but, as the Court has also pointed out, the practice of a UN organ may be seen to interpret the text and thereby to shape our understanding of it.[2] Persons other than lawyers may, however, be forgiven for thinking this a distinction without

---

[1] *Nicaragua* (Merits) [1986] I.C.J. Rep. 14, 109, para. 207.
[2] *See Namibia, Advisory Opinion* [1971] I.C.J. Rep. 16 at 22, para. 22, discussed in chapter 1 (p. 8).

much difference. Whether its effect is characterized as modification or interpretation of text, practice matters.

This is particularly so when strict construction of treaty text leads to a *reductio ad absurdum*.

Humanitarian intervention, the subject of chapter 9, poses just that dilemma: what might be called the paradox of a good law producing a very bad result. Charter Article 2(4), prohibiting use of force by states except in self-defense, if strictly obeyed and enforced, can lead in a specific instance to a disastrous result. Yet, as the legal maxim reminds us, hard cases may make bad law. If exceptions are allowed for situations in which adherence to the law might produce a bad result, what would be left of the law? To admit exceptions may undermine law's claim to legitimacy, which depends at least in part on its consistent application. On the other hand, the law's legitimacy is surely also undermined if, by its slavish implementation, it produces terrible consequences. The paradox arises from the seemingly irreconcilable choice, in such hard cases, between consistency and justice.

Some lawyers seek to escape from this paradox by strictly separating law from morality. Law, they say, does not need to produce good results to fulfill its role, which is to organize a peaceable kingdom. Indeed, the argument continues, Western civilization's progress towards freedom rests on the historic severance of morality from law because state-enforced morality is incompatible with the democratic underpinnings of the rule of law. What we call civil liberties derive from the emancipation of public notions of legality from private views of moral justification. Legal positivism, which defines law as normative texts deriving their legitimacy from the processes of duly constituted sovereignty – legislatures, executives, and judiciaries – leaves little room for moral absolutes because it rejects the autocratic processes by which moral absolutes are divined and implemented.[3] It does this by constructing a fire-break between law as it is and notions of law as it ought to be.[4]

For most of Western history, however, this separation of moral from legal norms was quite alien. In ancient Rome, despite there being one concept – the *jus civile* – for the laws proclaimed by the sovereign and another – the *jus gentium* – for rules generated by common intuition, or

---

[3] For a classical discussion *see* H.L.A. Hart, "Positivism and the Separation of Law and Morals," 71 Harv. L. Rev. 593 (1958).

[4] Lon L. Fuller has complained that many different concepts are exiled from real "law" with the stigma of "morality" or "ought-law." Lon L. Fuller, "Positivism and Fidelity to Law – a Reply to Professor Hart," 71 Harv. L. Rev. 630 at 635.

human nature, the two were supposed to be symbiotic parts of a single legal system. Although, in the thirteenth century, Thomas Aquinas claimed that the *jus civile*, reformulated as the *jus naturale*, proceeded from God and was thus entitled to priority over the law of the sovereign – a view still shared by Jean Bodin in *De Republica* (1576) and Blackstone in the introduction to his *Commentaries* (1765) – the two systems of rules were mostly seen as symbiotic.[5]

In due course, this uneasy mutual accommodation between positive and natural or divine law ceased. The Reformation undermined the credibility of the Church as legitimate expostulator of the moral aspect of legal systems. Instead, sovereigns bent on secular supremacy encouraged an historic shift to legal positivism. In keeping with this new secularism, natural law, from the time of Thomas Hobbes, began to be exiled from the law libraries. In *The Leviathan* (1651) Hobbes argued that might, the prerogative of sovereigns, was the only valid source of commands binding on the subject and that it was thus absolute and illimitable. Taken up by Vattel and transposed to international law in his *Law of Nations* (1758), this legal positivism laid the foundation for a universal system of norms in which such notions as "right reason" and "common moral sense" were banished to the theology schools.[6] International law, like national law, became exclusively defined by the will and expressed commands of sovereigns. In this view, there could only be law among states to the extent their sovereigns chose to make commitments to its strictures. International law, far from being the expression of a universal *jus gentium* or *jus naturale*, was now recognized as essentially a voluntarist system of positive law legitimized by sovereign consent and sovereign power, however much or little those sovereigns might agree to abide by common rules.

In modern times, this view of law as an emanation of secular power continued to inform the work of most jurisprudence, notably the work of John Austin, who, in *The Province of Jurisprudence Determined* (1832), defined law as nothing more or less than the enforced command of a sovereign to a subject. In this, Austin's view was not very different from that of Karl Marx and Friedrich Engels in *The German Ideology* (1859). In none of these power-based views of law (domestic or international) is there any role for norms autonomously validated by God, nature, or a common sense of right and justice.

---

[5] *Blackstone's Commentaries: With Notes of Reference*, St. George Tucker (ed.), vol. 5, p. 42 (1803).

[6] M. De Vattel, *The Law of Nations*, 7th Amer. edn. by Joseph Chitty (1849), p. lxvi.

By the end of the Second World War, however, the monopoly of the positivists was being challenged. At the Nuremberg Trials, it was apparent that some of the most heinous crimes committed by the Nazi defendants had been carried out in accordance with German law as defined positivistically. In the early 1940s, Harvard Professor Lon Fuller, seeking to narrow the gap between what was widely perceived as right or just and that which was mandated by positive law, reintroduced a rationalist version of natural law rooted in what he argued was a sociologically demonstrable universal sense of right and wrong.[7] At almost the same time, a certain skepticism began to gnaw at the roots of legal positivism. Words in legal texts, it was argued, had no fixed meaning. They needed always to be interpreted, and interpretation must inevitably introduce a degree of value subjectivity. Where does this subjectivity look for its inspiration, if not to a common intuition of natural justice? In Britain, Professor J.L. Brierly challenged strict positivism with the contention that law

is not a meaningless set of arbitrary principles to be mechanically applied by the courts, but... exists for certain ends, though those ends may have to be differently formulated in different times and places... This is so because the life with which any system of law has to deal is too complicated, and human foresight too limited, for law to be completely formulated in a set of rules, so that situations perpetually arise which fall outside all rules already formulated. Law cannot and does not refuse to solve a problem because it is new and unprovided for; it meets such situations by resorting to a principle, outside formulated law... appealing to reason as the justification for its decisions.

This "appeal to reason," Brierly explains, "is merely to appeal to a law of nature."[8]

While most modern lawyers may not be quite so willing to see the law of nature reinstated as consort to the majesty of positive law, there is no doubt that rulers, judges, and administrators, in international as in national legal systems, while nowadays still recognizing legality and morality as distinct social regulators, have also come to accept that the power of positive law is diminished if the gap between it and the common sense of values is allowed to become too wide. The capacity of the law to pull towards compliance those to whom it is addressed depends first and foremost on the public perception of its fairness, its reification of a widely shared notion of what is right. The law's self-interest,

[7] Lon L. Fuller, *The Law in Quest of Itself* 12ff. (1940).
[8] J.L. Brierly, *The Law of Nations* 24 (3rd edn., 1949).

therefore, demands that a way be found to bridge any gap between its own institutional commitment to consistent application of formal rules and the public sense that order should not be achieved at too high a cost in widely shared moral values.

When law permits or even requires behavior that is widely held to be unfair, immoral or unjust, it is not only persons but also the law that suffers. So, too, if law prohibits that which is widely believed to be just and moral. Consequently, it is in the law's self-interest to serve the bridging function.

A simple illustration may be helpful.

Tom and Jerry are chums. They are each ten years old, children of families living in adjacent houses. One day, Tom's and Jerry's fathers quarrel and Tom's father orders him "never to have anything to do with Jerry again."

The next morning, Tom, on his way to school, passes a small lake and sees that Jerry has fallen into it. Tom, unlike Jerry, knows how to swim and so rescues his friend.

On learning of this, Tom's father severely thrashes him for having disobeyed orders.

It must be all but impossible to find any reader of this scenario who would not agree to the following propositions:

1. Punishing Tom for rescuing Jerry is morally wrong.
2. Interpreting the paternal injunction "never to have anything to do with Jerry again" as requiring Tom to abandon his drowning friend Jerry profoundly undermines the father's parental authority, marking him as unfit to exercise it.

The reader might also agree that Tom's father should have understood that his authority would have been better preserved had he, given these circumstances, *not* enforced the injunction to his son "never to have anything to do with Jerry again." To his objection: "OK, but if I didn't enforce my orders, Tom would never respect me again," would we not reply that by enforcing his order in these circumstances he had seriously undermined, rather than reinforced, his authority?

Law – or, in this example, parental authority – does not thrive when its implementation produces *reductio ad absurdum*: when it grossly offends most persons' common moral sense of what is *right*.

This insight is relevant to all law, whether international or domestic. Which brings us to the title of this chapter, with its reference to cannibalism and the cabin-boy. In two famous cases, *Regina* v. *Dudley and*

Stephens[9] in Britain and *United States* v. *Holmes*[10] in America, the courts dealt with situations in which the strict letter of the law of murder collided with the common sense of justice and morality. In both cases, persons cast into a hopeless predicament at sea killed one of their number to save the rest. In the British case, persons starving and adrift in a lifeboat stayed alive by eating one of their shipmates. In the US case, crew on an overloaded lifeboat jettisoned passengers to prevent its sinking. These actions, of course, were strictly unlawful. Yet, in both instances the legal process, while it did not condone the killings, responded with utmost leniency.[11] In the English case, although the defendants were convicted and sentenced to death, Lord Coleridge for the unanimous court, commended them "most earnestly to the mercy of the Crown...," which, acting on the advice of the Home Secretary, commuted the sentences to six months' imprisonment, most of which had already been served.[12] In the American case, the penalty of six months' imprisonment was subsequently remitted.[13]

Put another way, in neither case was necessity treated as an exculpating defense to a charge of murder. The judges went out of their way to ensure that murder remained a crime, even in circumstances of extreme necessity. But these circumstances were not ignored: they effectively mitigated the penalties imposed on those whose acts were found to have been illegal but, in the extreme circumstances, justifiable. Necessity for action mitigated the consequences of illegal acts, although neither – on the one hand – fully exculpating the actors, nor – on the other – rendering the law nugatory.

It is integral to most national legal systems that an action may be regarded as illegal but that the degree of that illegality should be determined with due regard for extenuating or mitigating factors. Most criminal codes make some kind of distinction between *unlawfulness* – in the sense of an act violative of positive law – and *culpability*, with the latter connoting what Professor George Fletcher artfully describes as "the nature of crime as a moral or value-based category."[14] Similarly, Professor H.L.A. Hart states that in "the criminal law of every modern state

---

[9] 14 Q.B.D. 273 (1884).   [10] 26 Fed. Cas. 360, 1 Wall Jr. 1 (1842).

[11] For an excellent discussion of this distinction in the *Dudley and Stephens* litigation, see A.W. Brian Simpson, *Cannibalism and the Common Law* 225–70 (1984).

[12] Simpson, *Cannibalism and the Common Law* at 247.   [13] 26 Fed. Cas. 279 at 369.

[14] George Fletcher, "Introduction from a Common Lawyer's Point of View," in A. Eser and G.P. Fletcher, *Justification and Excuse: Comparative Perspectives* 9, 10 (1987). *See also* M.L. Corrado (ed.), *Justification and Excuse in Criminal Law* (1994).

responsibility for serious crimes is excluded or 'diminished' by some...
'excusing conditions.' "[15] To whatever extent law seeks to deter or to
punish acts it will often also create a category of justification or mitigation
that takes into account evidence that, in particular circumstances, the
act was less culpable. For example, section 3.02 of the 1985 US Model
Penal Code provides: "Conduct that the actor believes to be necessary
to himself or to another is justifiable, provided that... the harm or evil
sought to be avoided by such conduct is greater than that sought to be
prevented by the law defining the offense charged."[16] There may be
differences between national systems as to whether necessity excuses a
crime or mitigates its consequences, but all recognize the obligation of
the law to do one or the other.[17]

International law, like domestic law, also has begun gingerly to
develop ways to bridge the gap between what is requisite in strict
legality and what is generally regarded as just and moral. That it still
has difficulty in doing so is illustrated by the reaction of states and their
lawyers to NATO's action against Yugoslavia in 1999.

As we have seen, the positive law – that is, the UN Charter's
Articles 2(4), 42 and 51 – prohibits states using force "against the territorial integrity or political independence of any state" except in two
circumstances: *first*, "in self-defence if an armed attack occurs against
a Member of the United Nations" or, *second*, if the Security Council
approves the use of force "to maintain or restore international peace and
security." In the Kosovo instance, there was no armed attack against a
UN member and there was no decision by the Security Council to authorize the use of force. Indeed, some members, including at least two with
the power of veto, openly – although with diminishing vigor[18] – opposed

---

[15] H.L.A. Hart, "Legal Responsibility and Excuses," in Corrado (ed.), *Justification and Excuse: Comparative Perspectives* at 31.

[16] See Thomas Franck, *The Power of Legitimacy Among Nations* 73–75 (1990); Thomas Franck, "Break It, Don't Fake It," 78 *Foreign Affairs* 116 (1999).

[17] I am indebted to an excellent research essay by Devika Hovell, "Necessity: the Mother of In(ter)vention?" written to meet LL.M. requirements, Fall 2000, New York University.

[18] Russia "displays traces of a shifting attitude" to the intervention and to humanitarian intervention in general. Robert Legvold, "Foreword" in *Pugwash Study Group on Inter- vention, Sovereignty and International Security*, Pugwash Occasional Papers, vol. 2, no. 1, January 2001, p. 8. See also to the same effect, Vladimir Baranovsky, "Humanitarian Intervention: Russian Perspectives," Pugwash Occasional Papers, vol. 2, no.1, January 2001 at 12ff.; also, Chu Shulong, "China, Asia and Issues of Sovereignty and Intervention," Pugwash Occasional Papers, vol. 2, no.1, January 2001 at 39ff. Legvold points out, however, that Russian and Chinese consent to humanitarian

any rescue of the Kosovars that would involve military force. After the event, the Ministers of Foreign Affairs of the Group of 77 baldly "rejected the so-called right of humanitarian intervention" saying that it "had no basis in the UN Charter or in international law."[19]

Still, before NATO acted, the Council had already decided that events in Kosovo were creating a threat to peace, the very thing the UN system had been established to ameliorate.[20] The record of Serb forces' genocide in Bosnia, a few years earlier, made that threat palpable. Yet the UN's Charter-designated system of preventive response – Security Council action under Charter Chapter VII – was paralyzed by the threat of a veto. Thus, NATO decided to deploy force and, in so doing, violated strict Charter legality. It acted instead in reliance on mitigating circumstances and moral justification.

So: what is a lawyer to make of NATO's decision to use force?

In his seminal 1991 work, *International Law in Theory and Practice*, Oscar Schachter seems to have preconfigured a convincing answer to this issue. He prefers, of course, that a humanitarian rescue operation be endorsed by the Security Council, if possible, or the General Assembly. Failing that, however, "in the absence of such prior approval, a State or group of States using force to put an end to atrocities when the necessity is evident and the humanitarian intention is clear is likely to have its action pardoned."[21]

The report of the Independent (Goldstone) Commission on Kosovo concluded that NATO's action, while not strictly legal, was legitimate. It called for a revision of applicable international law to make it more

---

intervention "comes with a huge proviso. If coercion is to be used to preempt or end the egregious acts of government, it must occur under the auspices of the United Nations," Pugwash Occasional Papers, vol. 2, no.1, January 2001 at 9. Even this caveat may be overstated: the Soviet Union vigorously supported India's intervention in Pakistan to free Bangla Desh and, as Professor Alain Pellet has pointed out, the Soviets voted for Security Council Resolution 1244 (1999), making it "inconceivable" that they, or any of the other eleven supporters of the resolution, could have thought unlawful or criminal an action by NATO to which they thereby implicitly gave their blessing. Alain Pellet, "State Sovereignty and the Protection of Fundamental Human Rights: An International Law Perspective," in *Pugwash Study Group on Intervention, Sovereignty and International Security*, Pugwash Occasional Papers, vol. 1, no. 1, February 2000 at 42.

[19] Ministerial Declaration on the South Summit, adopted at the twenty-third annual meeting of the Ministers of Foreign Affairs of the Group of 77, September 24, 1999. Circulated by letter dated September 29, 1999 by Ambassador S.R. Insanally of Guyana, Chairman. A/54/432 at 18. UN Press Release GA/SPD/164, 18 September, 1999.

[20] S/RES/1199 (1998) and S/RES/1203 (1998).

[21] Oscar Schachter, *International Law in Theory and Practice* 126 (1991).

congruent with "an international moral consensus."[22] It may thus have taken a first step towards the enunciation of an internationally agreed concept bridging the gap – so starkly revealed by the Kosovo crisis – between legality and legitimacy, between strict legal positivism and a common sense of moral justice.

There is need for such creative rethinking of the rules. Kosovo was not, alas, an exotic happenstance. The paradox illuminated by the Goldstone Commission in the context of Kosovo is even more evident in the circumstances of the 1994 genocide in Rwanda. An Independent Inquiry by the Organization of African Unity concluded that a small number of major actors "could directly have prevented, halted or reduced the slaughter."[23] Secretary-General Kofi Annan in his address to the General Assembly on September 20, 1999, (quoted in chapter 1, p. 16) asked whether, had there been a regional coalition of the willing able to intervene in that country to prevent that genocide, states should have refrained from acting if one permanent member of the Security Council had withheld consent.[24] Surely the UN Charter, to paraphrase Supreme Court Justice Arthur Goldberg's comment about the US Constitution,[25] is not a genocide pact. The law must find some way to maintain respect for itself that does not require passivity in the face of such atrocities. What can the law gain by requiring strict adherence to a rule producing so awful an outcome? While consistency of application is an element in law's legitimacy, what benefit can a legal order derive from becoming an accomplice to moral depravity?

Not every government has welcomed the Goldstone Commission's tentative conclusion that an action – a humanitarian intervention by a coalition of states acting without Security Council authorization – may be technically illegal and yet legitimate, that there may be circumstances in which to act illegally is more just than to fail to act at all. In particular,

---

[22] See discussion in chapter 9 (pp. 163–70). Independent International Commission on Kosovo ("The Goldstone Commission"), *Kosovo Report: Conflict, International Response, Lessons Learned* 4, 163–98 (2000).

[23] OAU Report, "The Preventable Genocide," Executive Summary, p. 9, para. E.S. 44. 40 I.L.M. 141 (2001), 7 July, 2000. See also the Report of the Independent Inquiry into the actions of the United Nations during the 1994 genocide in Rwanda, S/1999/1257, 16 December 1999 ("The Carlsson Report").

[24] Report of the Secretary-General, G.A.O.R., 54th Sess., 4th Plenary Meeting, 20 September 1999, A/54/PV.4, p. 1 at 2.

[25] The US Constitution "is not a suicide pact." *Kennedy* v. *Mendoza-Martinez*, 372 U.S. 144, 159–60 (1963).

there is considerable unease among states and international lawyers[26] at the call of then British Foreign Minister Robin Cook in May 2000 for new principles defining the circumstances in which humanitarian intervention would be justified even in the absence of prior UN approval.[27]

Such a formulation of new norms may not as yet be possible. Sovereignty means much to governments: more, perhaps than to their citizenry. At the General Assembly neither Cook's proposal, nor the Secretary-General's admonition, was warmly received by representatives of governments. But would an assembly of the representatives of the world's people, arrayed behind what Harvard Professor John Rawls calls the "veil of ignorance" (i.e. not knowing whose ox is likely to be gored), agree to a law that insulates from external restraint regimes engaged in the systematic murder of large numbers of their own people?[28] A hint may be provided by the poll reported by *Noviye Izvestia* on March 31, just as the war over Kosovo began, in which "less than half of Russians condemn the United States and NATO."[29] Nevertheless, it is primarily governments, not people, who make international law; and those who govern – aligned or non-aligned, developed or not, weak or powerful – tend with unusual unanimity to resist infringements on their executory discretion.

But formal adjustment of the law may not be necessary. International law – like national law – is not so inflexible as to demand slavish adherence to a good rule when, exceptionally, compliance would bring about horrendous results. Governments reluctant to see any change in the law of Article 2(4) were willing enough to accommodate the ECOWAS/ECOMOG deployment of force in Liberia and Sierra Leone and to defeat the Russian attempt to censure NATO action in Kosovo.[30] This need not be seen as schizophrenia, any more than the actions of British and US courts in the lifeboat cases. Rather, case by

---

[26] See, for example, the closely reasoned essay by Bruno Simma, "NATO, the UN and the Use of Force: Legal Aspects," 10 Eur. J. Int'l L. 1, 5 (1999).

[27] The Foreign Affairs Committee of the House of Commons supported the Foreign Minister's "aim of establishing in the United Nations new principles governing humanitarian intervention." *Kosovo*, Foreign Affairs Committee, House of Commons (UK), Fourth Report, vol. 1, 23 May 2000, para. 144.

[28] See John Rawls, *The Law of Peoples* 30–58 (1999).

[29] "What the Papers Say: NATO's Balkans War: Is It for Love or Money?" *The Moscow Times* wire service, 3 April, 1999, sec. No. 1678, quoting *Noviye Izvestia* of March 31, 1999.

[30] The failed Russian resolution of censure received only 3 votes. S/1999/328 of 26 March 1999.

case, those with responsibility for interpreting and implementing the law employ a concept of mitigation to bridge the gap between the law and a common sense of moral justice.[31]

The preceding chapters have sought to demonstrate that international law is gradually emulating national legal systems in developing, around its codex of strict rules, a penumbra of reasonableness. This may be concluded from the Charter-based system's rigid responses in various norm-bending crises. The global political and judicial institutions, as they apply and interpret the system's normative framework, have let some technically illegal but morally justified actions pass with tacit approval, others without comment, and some with only minimal rebuke. They have, in effect, acted like the House of Lords and the Supreme Court in the *Dudley* and *Holmes* cases.

How international institutions perceive the role of mitigation is illustrated by the World Court's opinion in the *Corfu Channel* case. In 1949, the Royal Navy swept Albanian waters after a stray mine had hit a British vessel. The International Court recognized that the Royal Navy thereby had violated Albanian sovereignty; but it concluded that "the Albanian Government's complete failure to carry out its duties after the explosion, and the dilatory nature of its diplomatic notes, are extenuating circumstances for the action of the United Kingdom Government."[32] Again, in the 1980 *Teheran Hostages* case,[33] the Court noted the technically illegal and ill-fated US military attempt to rescue

---

[31] Chesterman, however, argues that the plea that uses of force for humanitarian reasons should be judged less harshly than the aggressive use of force to advance national self-interest amounts to a claim "that certain acts are against the law, but that the decision whether to condemn them is outside the law." Simon Chesterman, *Just War or Just Peace* 227–28 (2001). This surely misconceives the role of law in justification and mitigation. When such pleas are raised in domestic courts, they are considered as part of the case although, in some circumstances, they may also enter into considerations of executive clemency. In the international setting, the law may be applied by political bodies, but still with concern for the law and its relation to the common good. The Security Council, for example, is a political body, but one that is conscious of its law-making role. There is little doubt that decisions by the Council to react, or not to react, to a "humanitarian intervention" are made in awareness that each precedent affects the contours of normative text. Chesterman is perhaps too pessimistic when he concludes that "the circumstances in which the law may be violated are not themselves susceptible of legal regulation," Chesterman, *Just War or Just Peace* at 230. His view does coincide, however, with that of Judge Lauterpacht quoted in the second paragraph of chapter 1 (p. 1).

[32] *Corfu Channel Case, Judgment of 9th April, 1949*, I.C.J. Reports, 1949, 4 at 35.

[33] *Case concerning United States Diplomatic and Consular Staff in Teheran (United States of America v. Iran), Judgment of 24 May 1980*, I.C.J. Reports, 1980, 3 at 17–18, para. 32, 43 at para. 93.

its hostages, but its majority also understood that this had occurred after months of fruitless diplomatic efforts to secure the release of diplomats held prisoner in violation of Security Council resolutions and the Court's own interim judicial order. Professor Rosalyn Higgins has observed that the "Court carefully did not pronounce upon the lawfulness or not of the United States action, but in some carefully chosen phrases indicated that it thought it inappropriate for the action to have been mounted while the matter was before the Court."[34] This mild reprimand, however, in no way affected the Court's decision in favor of the Americans.

Thus do international, like national, legal institutions seek to narrow the gap between what, on the one hand, is required by the letter of the law and what, on the other, is a generally perceived requisite of fairness. In this bridging effort, the legal concept of mitigation plays an essential role.

A plea in mitigation is not merely a summons to temper the law with considerations of moral legitimacy, but is also a reminder to consider the specific facts of a case before applying general normative principles. Such an approach is particularly appropriate when a technically illegal action has occurred in unforeseeable and extraordinarily grave circumstances threatening the very public order law seeks to uphold. A plea in mitigation calls upon those charged with implementing the law to consider not only the text of the applicable rule but also the contextual specifics of a situation that may not have been within the contemplation of the rule's drafters. The essence of mitigation is that the law recognizes the continuing force of the rule in general, while also accepting that, in extraordinary circumstances, condoning a carefully calibrated and justifiable violation may do more to rescue the law's legitimacy than would its rigorous implementation.

Those opposed to such accommodation advance a "slippery slope" argument: that any legal recognition of a right of humanitarian intervention is open to abuse. In reply, Judge Higgins has drawn on an analogy to the principle of self-defense. She points out that "there have been countless abusive claims of the right to self-defence. That does not lead us to say that there should be no right of self-defence today . . . We delude ourselves if we think that the role of norms is to remove the possibility of abusive claims ever being made." In the international system, despite the absence of an all-powerful judiciary to settle disputed cases, there "are a variety of important decision-makers, other than courts, who can

---

[34] Rosalyn Higgins, *International Law and the Avoidance, Containment and Resolution of Disputes, General Course on Public International Law*, Recueil des cours, 230 (1991-V), 315.

pronounce on the validity of claims advanced; and claims which may in very restricted exceptional circumstances be regarded as lawful should not *a priori* be disallowed because on occasion they may be unjustly invoked."[35]

Pronouncing on the validity of claims advanced in mitigation of an unlawful but justifiable recourse to force is the task of these decision-makers. Some of this fact-and-context-specific calibration goes on in international tribunals, but most of it occurs in the political organs of the UN system, which constitutes something approximating a global jury: assessing the facts of a crisis, the motives of those reacting to the crisis, and the *bona fides* of the pleas of extreme necessity. This jurying goes on not only in instances of humanitarian intervention but whenever there is a confrontation between the strict, literal text of the Charter and a plea of justice and extenuating moral necessity. As this study has sought to demonstrate, the practice of the Security Council and General Assembly reveals a fairly coherent continuum of responses to such pleas in mitigation. At one end of that continuum are the clear cases: the Security Council's *post hoc* approval of ECOMOG military action in Liberia and, implicitly, of NATO's humanitarian intervention in Kosovo. Towards the middle of the spectrum is the Council's and Assembly's silent acquiescence in France's use of force to remove Emperor Bokassa from the Central African Empire and Tanzania's ouster of Uganda's Idi Amin. Slightly further along is the system's mild disapprobation of India's intervention in Bangladesh, Vietnam's ouster of Cambodia's Khmer Rouge, and Israel's 1976 incursion at Entebbe airport in Uganda. These unlawful exercises of force were generally deemed to have produced a salutary result but to have set a potentially dangerous precedent. Towards the far end of the approval/disapproval scale is the Assembly's severe rejection of justifications advanced by the Soviets for their use of force in Hungary and by the US for its invasions of Grenada and Panama. And, finally, there is the Security Council's emphatic negation of North Korea's and Iraq's excuses for recourse to force and the system's authorization of collective resistance by coalitions of the willing. The political organs have demonstrated their ability and readiness, when faced with states' recourse to force, to calibrate their responses by sophisticated judgment, taking into account the full panoply of specific circumstances.

[35] Higgins, *International Law and the Avoidance, Containment and Resolution of Disputes* at 316.

The results of the process may not always be to one's liking or accord with everyone's sense of justice and morality. But there is now in place a process able to weigh considerations of legality against the common public sense of legitimacy. While men and women in international (as in national) institutions are not angels, it may be more remarkable that international institutions now routinely and sensibly do weigh what is legal against what is just.

Should this be celebrated? In a political institution made up of the representatives of almost 200 governments – most with foreign policies based on national interests, alliances, animosities, and sympathies – would one really expect to find the stuff of a credible jury? Surprisingly, the answer is "yes." There are several reasons for this. First, most conflicts that come before the United Nations. do not directly engage the national interest of any but a few states, leaving the judgment of the others relatively unencumbered by commitments to one side or the other. This was not true at the height of the Cold War, and, even now, a few issues still elicit conditioned reflexes from many states rather than their rigorous assessments. Kosovo, Sierra Leone, Liberia, and the fight against terrorism, however, are recent instances where UN members have acted more as responsible jurors than committed partisans. A second reason is that most governments are conscious of the importance of practice as precedent. They know that how they (individually and collectively) respond to an issue before the Assembly or Council affects the systemic rules of conduct in which they have a greater stake than in the outcome of one particular controversy. They therefore tend to speak and vote as members of a jury who are not without feelings and biases, but whose first concern is to do the right thing by the norms under which all must live. Finally, the response of many (especially smaller) states to issues put before them is significantly influenced by a preference for being seen as good institutional citizens who are highly regarded by those other states who look to them for leadership and prefer them for election to the system's important organs and subsidiary bodies. Governments' need for the high regard of their peers is not very different from that of persons. Peer-group approval should not be underestimated as a counterweight to baser instincts and interests.

Observing this incipient, creative jurying process at work is no cause for pessimism. In some of the instances considered in preceding chapters – such as ECOMOG's interventions in Liberia and Sierra Leone, or India's in Goa and Bangla Desh – it was the norms that were bent to accommodate special facts. Such accommodation is not necessarily harmful to the law, providing the law is upheld in general practice.

Conversely, in extraordinary circumstances it may be the facts that are bent to simulate compliance with a rule rather than admit an exception to it. This, too – used sparingly – may serve to bridge the gap between legality and moral intuition. In our domestic legal system such fact-dissimulations are called "legal fictions," and these, too, have sometimes saved good law from being made to seem absurd or vicious in unexpected circumstances. Similarly, legal fictions have their redemptive uses in international law. For example, when the Security council authorized the use of force by a "coalition of the willing" to oust the Haitian military junta, it contrived the fiction that, by causing a flow of refugees, the junta was causing a threat to international peace and security such as to justify international collective action under Chapter VII of the Charter. Everyone understood, of course, that the military regime's intolerable treatment of its own citizens, and not the refugee problem as such, was uppermost in the world's mind. But some states still had trouble admitting that gross oppression by a government of its own citizenry could justify such intervention and felt more comfortable authorizing military action to stop behavior that had some semblance of transnational effects. So, too, the very notions of "indirect attack" and "anticipatory self-defense" employ legal fictions. (They are discussed in chapters 4 and 8.) Resorting to a bit of legal fiction may sometimes be the easiest way to help precedent-conscious members of legal systems adjust quickly to moral requisites in a new situation of great urgency.

In respect of humanitarian intervention, however, the reconciling of law and justice is better pursued by having at law's disposal a concept of mitigation to which recourse may be had when warranted by well-demonstrated circumstances, rather than by torturing the facts of a crisis or the text of a law.

Which brings us back once more to the unfortunate cabin boy.

To consider a plea in mitigation of an otherwise unlawful act, it is necessary to compare potential outcomes of action and inaction in precise circumstances. The taking of the cabin boy's life appears in a different light if, demonstrably, it was the only way to save the lives of many. From time to time, similar calls have to be made in the international arena. Would Yugoslavia – and in particular, Kosovo – have been better off had NATO strictly followed the path to passivity demarcated by the Charter? Would the Bengali people have been better off if India had let Pakistan extinguish the Bangla Desh insurgency? Would Uganda have been better off if Tanzania had left Idi Amin in place? Would Cambodia have been better off had Vietnam left Pol Pot to finish his genocide? Would Grenada have been alright under General Hudson Austin?[36] Would the world be better off with Eichmann forgotten in Argentina? If the answer to any of these questions is "no," must the law insist on "yes"? Or must it find a way to adapt what law requires of us to the common intuition of the moral conscience?

History teaches us that all claims to use force righteously should always be viewed skeptically. But experience also shows that there *are* genuine catastrophes for which preventive or remedial action is justifiable, especially when supported by a widely shared moral consensus and implemented by a broadly based "coalition of the willing."[37] Against this, critics argue that, in practice, states are likely to use force only in self-interest, rather than from truly humanitarian motives and that states will use force only selectively, against the weakest offenders. Both points, even if true, are also irrelevant.

That India in Bangla Desh, Tanzania in Uganda, Vietnam in Cambodia, the US in Grenada, or ECOWAS in Liberia may have acted out of mixed motives and that these might have included the pursuit of their national interest should not, in itself, discount credible evidence of impending humanitarian catastrophes which only timely intervention could have prevented. Actions taken in assertion of humanitarian purpose should be judged primarily by whether there really was a humanitarian crisis, whether other remedies had been exhausted, and whether the crisis was averted or assuaged by the intervenor, with the least possible collateral damage.

But it is no argument that states willing to intervene in Kosovo may not be equally willing to intervene in Chechnya or Tibet. Such inconstancy demonstrates little but states' sensible tactical realism. The ultimate test of a humanitarian intervention's legitimacy is whether it results in significantly more good than harm, not whether there has been a consistent pattern of such interventions whenever and wherever humanitarian crises have arisen. That humanitarian interventions may occur selectively is entirely inevitable and beside the point. Not everyone

---

[36] General Austin, in his brief moment in power, had opened fire on a protesting crowd, killed Prime Minister Maurice Bishop and several of his cabinet and his forces had beaten to death Education Minister Jacqueline Craft. Department of State Bull., No. 2081, December 1983.

[37] See Danesh Sarooshi, *The United Nations and the Development of Collective Security* 167–246 (1999).

who cheats on taxes or speeds on the highway is apprehended and prosecuted because invariable enforcement would be exorbitantly costly and impossible in practice. Instead, selective action is taken against some, in part to affect the conduct of the many by "making an example" of the few.

It is true that law derives part of its legitimacy from its consistent and equal application: the treating alike of like cases. But the element of "alikeness" of humanitarian crises is not demonstrable solely by superficial (and possibly inaccurate) claims that Government A is acting "just like" Government B. There are many variables to be taken into account in such comparisons: one of which is the likelihood of success were an intervention to be undertaken on behalf of human rights.

The problem of equality before the law, however, further exemplifies the advantage of treating humanitarian intervention not as a new legal right (to which requirement of equal application of the law may be said to apply) but as a mitigating circumstance that does not create law and which is recognized as purely circumstantial and discretionary relief, rather like the early uses of equity. Unanticipated factors and extreme necessity may exceptionally mitigate the consequences of acting "off the Charter," while still leaving the Charter's norms intact. Indeed, a law with an eye to mitigating circumstances is likely to be seen as more legitimate than one that brooks no exceptions.

That, however, leaves the onus of proof squarely with those seeking a dispensation from the general rule. Those advancing a plea in extenuating circumstances must be able to demonstrate those circumstances, as well as their good faith in the choice of proportional and humane means (as set out, for example, in the 1949 Geneva Conventions.[38]) Even the court in *United States* v. *Holmes*, while granting that extreme necessity might excuse the jettisoning of passengers in an overcrowded lifeboat, pointed out the importance of just means in justifying ends: that the selection should have been made by drawing lots, since "[i]n no other than this or some like way are those having equal rights put upon an equal footing..."[39]

---

[38] 75 U.N.T.S. Nos. 970–973 of 12 August 1949.

[39] *United States* v. *Holmes*, n. 10 above, at 367. In *Holmes*, some reliance was placed by the defendant and the court on the fact that lots had been drawn, whereas in *Dudley and Stephens* the cabin boy had been selected, it was argued by counsel for the defendants, on the ground that he was ill and thus the most likely to die anyway, as well as on the fact that the others had families who had to be supported whereas the victim did not. See, further, Simpson, n. 11 above, at 233–36.

So, what is the international lawyer to say about a future Kosovo? Asked to advise as to the law in a situation falling within what the Goldstone Commission has called the "gray area" between legality and legitimacy, the lawyer has a professional obligation to tell government not only about the legal text but also about systemic practice. If a genocide is about to occur but the Security Council is incapacitated by a veto, the lawyer should advise that the law will not hold a government hard to account for doing what is palpably necessary to stop the commission of an imminent and greater wrong.

In giving this advice, it is not necessary to insist that humanitarian intervention has become legal: in the sense, for example, that the rescue of one's endangered civilians abroad, or "anticipatory self-defence" may have become legal through state practice and *opinio juris*.[40] In the practice of the UN political organs, the distinction between what is justified (exculpated) and what is excusable (mitigated) is so fine as to be of pure (yet also considerable) theoretical interest. What the lawyer can say with some certitude is that if the imminence of a genocide can be demonstrated, few if any governments will seek to impose a significant penalty on those who act sensitively to prevent it.[41] Indeed, the problem for the system is not so much how to accommodate such interventions in its framework of legality but how to find states willing to undertake the necessary rescue.

---

[40] While *opinio juris* is an important and necessary adjunct to state practice in defining customary law and the law of bilateral treaties (*Nicaragua, Merits*, I.C.J. Rep. [1986] 14, 108, para. 206 and 109, para. 207), it is less so when interpreting the law as implemented in a forum of almost 200 member states whose reasons for acting are likely to be very diverse. What matters most is what they do. Thus the Court has given effect to general practices that profoundly affect the Charter's rules without requiring evidence of *opinio juris*. (*Namibia Advisory Opinion*, I.C.J. Rep. 16 at 22, para. 22 [1971], referring to the effect of a permanent member's abstention in a Security Council vote.)

[41] *See* Francis Kofi Abiew, The Evolution of the Doctrine and Practice of Humanitarian Intervention 223–58 (199) in *Enforcing Restraint: Collective Intervention in Domestic Conflict*, Lori Fisler Damrosch (ed.) (1993). *See also* Ian Brownlie, "Thoughts on Kind-Hearted Gunmen," in R.B. Lillich (ed.), *Humanitarian Intervention and the United Nations* 139, 146 (1973).

Index

gun-boat diplomacy. *See* attacks against
citizens abroad, self-defense against

Hijacking Convention (1970), 83
Hobbes (*The Leviathan*), 176
human rights and freedoms
  collective security arrangements, impact on,
    21
  repression as threat to the peace, 4, 41, 136
  UN Charter, 4, 21, 136
    San Francisco acknowledgment of role, 17
    UK/USSR refusal to include in Art. 1(3),
      18
  UN practice, 18, 41
humanitarian intervention. *See also* attacks
    against citizens abroad, self-defense
    against; Bangla Desh (Indian
    intervention in East Pakistan) (1971);
    ECOMOG intervention in Liberia
    (1989–98) *and* Sierra Leone
    (1991–2000); French interventions;
    Kosovo (NATO intervention) (1999);
    Tanzania–Uganda (1971); Vietnam
    intervention in Kampuchea (1978–79)
  absence of provision in Charter, 136
  adaptation of Charter and, 171
  autonomous State action, 9
    assessment of developments/risks, 171
    SC authorization, 136
    without SC authorization, 137
  burden of proof, 151, 190
  coalitions of the willing, 137
  equality of application of the law and, 190
  in case of wrong
    erga omnes, 135
    in violation of customary international
      law, 135
    prohibited by international agreement,
      135
  justice/peace equation, 138
  justification by reference to additional
    factors, 137
    avoidance by defenders of NATO action
      in Kosovo, 166
    motivation in doubt, 150, 189
    self-defense, 145, 160
    support of spontaneous uprising, 147
    threat to the peace, 137, 152
  legitimacy/legality balance, 142, 143, 169,
    175
    Goldstone Commission, 170, 181
    Schachter (*International Law in Theory and
      Practice*), 181
    "mitigating circumstances" doctrine as key
      to, 188, 190
  objections to, 138
  practice of UN organs and

  ambiguity, 138
  tolerance, 145, 151, 153, 158
  requirements
    authorization by SC, 162. *See also*
      ECOMOG intervention in Liberia
      (1989–97) *and* Sierra Leone
      (1991–2000)
    exhaustion of alternative remedies, 135,
      166, 167
    in absence of SC authorization, 142
      absence of alternative, 155
      necessity, 155
      inability of other state to deal with
        distress, 155
    proportionality, 144, 150
  Russian attitude, 180
  scholarly opinion, 138
  selective participation, relevance, 189
  state practice, ambiguity, 138
  willingness to act without SC support
    UK, 182
    US, 154

ICJ advisory opinions
  Certain Expenses of the UN (1962), 38
  Legality of the Threat or Use of Nuclear Weapons,
    91
  Namibia (1971), 8
    Court's call for economic measures to
      implement, 111
    GA resolution 36/121A calling for
      military support, 111
    state practice, 191
  optional nature of resort to, 112
  Western Sahara, 121
ICJ judgments
  Corfu Channel, 133
    mitigating circumstances, 184
    enforcement (Art. 94(2)), 110
  Nicaragua, 61
    state practice, effect, 174, 191
    threshold considerations, 62
    September 11 attacks distinguished
    US veto on implementation, 111
  Teheran Hostages, mitigating circumstances,
    184
ideological subversion from abroad
  as armed attack, 75
  definition, 69
  practice of UN principal organs and, 75
  self-defense and, 75
    proportionality, need for, 75
    rejection, 69, 70, 73
  USA-Dominican Republic (1965), 72
  USSR-Czechoslovakia (1968), 73
  Warsaw Pact–Hungary (1956), 70. *See also*
    Warsaw Pact–Hungary (1956)

THE RSPB is the largest nature conservation charity in the UK. Formed over 120 years ago, the RSPB works to provide a home for nature and protect species from decline. It has more than a million members.

First published 2021 by Walker Books Ltd, 87 Vauxhall Walk, London SE11 5HJ

2 4 6 8 10 9 7 5 3 1

Compilation © Walker Books Ltd 2021
Illustrations © Harry Tennant 2021
The right of Harry Tennant to be identified as illustrator of this work has been asserted by him in accordance with the Copyright, Designs and Patents Act 1988

This book has been typeset in Sabon, Rig Shaded and Pauline

Printed in China

British Library Cataloguing in Publication Data: a catalogue record for this book is available from the British Library
The RSPB logo is a registered trade mark of the Royal Society for the Protection of Birds.
ISBN 978-1-4063-9778-9
www.walker.co.uk

Published under licence from RSPB Sales Limited to raise awareness of the RSPB (charity registration in England and Wales no 207076 and Scotland no SC037654).

Walker Books Limited will donate a minimum of 6% of its receipts from sales of this book to RSPB Sales Ltd, which gives all its distributable profits through Gift Aid to the RSPB.

WATCHING THE
SWALLOWS
A BOOK OF BIRD POEMS

ILLUSTRATED BY
HARRY TENNANT

WALKER
BOOKS

CONTENTS

A NOTE TO THE READER

Wherever you live, whether deep in the city or far out in the countryside, there are birds nearby. And the poems in this book are arranged according to where you might find these birds, from ducks "a-dabbling" in your local pond to an owl perched in a church belfry, skylarks hovering over a field of corn, or wild geese soaring overhead on their winter journey south.

It's worth taking a little time to consider when each poem was written. Many of these poets lived at a time before there were photographs to study for tiny details, or videos to play, pause and pore over; some were even writing before the existence of binoculars.

Yet their poems contain such vivid and precise pictures: to read about Dorothy Wordsworth's swallows is to see their "glancing", "twinkling" shadows; read on through the book and you'll meet Tennyson's eagle, clasping a rock face with "crooked hands" before falling "like a thunderbolt".

This collection was chosen with young readers and their families in mind, and alongside classic and well-known poems you'll find some gems written for children by superb modern poets. Grace Nichols describes nose-diving hummingbirds and Charles Waters the "splashes of color on a toucan's bill", while Shazea Quraishi captures "a day and night of birds" in her hauntingly beautiful poem.

Wherever they are in the world, these precious creatures need protecting. But in living memory, here in the UK, much-loved and familiar birds like the house sparrow, starling and skylark have gradually and seriously declined in numbers. The RSPB, with whom this book is published in partnership, is working to protect these birds – and their habitats across our towns, coast and countryside.

We hope there's a poem in this book that will strike a chord with you. And we also hope that, in the bustle of your day, there is time to share in the thrill, charm and wonder of the birds on your doorstep.

OUTSIDE
YOUR
WINDOW

A BIRD CAME DOWN THE WALK

Emily Dickinson

A bird came down the walk:
He did not know I saw;
He bit an angle-worm in halves
And ate the fellow, raw.

And then he drank a dew
From a convenient grass,
And then hopped sidewise to the wall
To let a beetle pass.

He glanced with rapid eyes
That hurried all abroad –
They looked like frightened beads, I thought;
He stirred his velvet head

Like one in danger; cautious,
I offered him a crumb,
And he unrolled his feathers
And rowed him softer home

Than oars divide the ocean,
Too silver for a seam,
Or butterflies, off banks of noon,
Leap, splashless, as they swim.

BE LIKE THE BIRD
Victor Hugo

Be like the bird, who
Resting in his flight
On a twig too slight
Feels it bend beneath him,
Yet sings
Knowing he has wings.

WOODPECKER
Elizabeth Madox Roberts

The woodpecker pecked out a little round hole
And made him a house in the telephone pole.
One day when I watched he poked out his head,
And he had on a hood and a collar of red.

When the streams of rain pour out of the sky,
And the sparkles of lightning go flashing by,
And the big, big wheels of thunder roll,
He can snuggle back in the telephone pole.

LITTLE TROTTY WAGTAIL
John Clare

Little trotty wagtail he went in the rain
And tittering tottering sideways he near got straight again
He stooped to get a worm and looked up to catch a fly
And then he flew away, ere his feathers they were dry

Little trotty wagtail he waddled in the mud
And left his little footmarks' trample where he would.
He waddled in the water pudge and waggle went his tail
And chirruped up his wings to dry upon the garden rail.

Little trotty wagtail you nimble all about
And in the dimpling water pudge you waddle in and out
Your home is nigh at hand, and in the warm pigsty –
So little Master Wagtail I'll bid you a "Goodbye".

A LINNET IN A GILDED CAGE

Christina Rossetti

A linnet in a gilded cage,
A linnet on a bough,
In frosty winter one might doubt
Which bird is luckier now.
But let the trees burst out in leaf,
And nests be on the bough,
Which linnet is the luckier bird,
Oh who could doubt it now?

FROM THE OLD APPLE TREE

Paul Laurence Dunbar

I would hide within its shelter,
Settlin' in some cosy nook,
Where no calls nor threats could stir me
From the pages of my book.

Oh, that quiet, sweet seclusion
In its fullness passes words!
It was deeper than the deepest
That my sanctum now affords.

Why, the jaybirds an' the robins,
They was hand in glove with me,
As they winked at me an' warbled
In that old apple tree.

CROW: A HAIKU
Matsuo Bashō

On a withered branch
A crow is sitting
This autumn eve.

NIGHT HERON: A HAIKU
Matsuo Bashō

A flash of lightning:
The screech of a night heron
Flying in the darkness.

THE OWL
Alfred, Lord Tennyson

When cats run home and light is come,
And dew is cold upon the ground,
And the far-off stream is dumb,
And the whirring sail goes round,
And the whirring sail goes round;
Alone and warming his five wits,
The white owl in the belfry sits.

WATCHING THE SWALLOWS
Dorothy Wordsworth

Watching the swallows
That flew about restlessly,
And flung their shadows
Upon the sunbright walls of the old building;
The shadows glanced and twinkled,
Interchanged and crossed each other,
Expanded and shrunk up,
Appeared and disappeared, every instant;
As I observed to William and Coleridge,
Seeming more like living things
Than the birds themselves.

BIRDS AT WINTER NIGHTFALL

Thomas Hardy

Around the house the flakes fly faster,
And all the berries now are gone
From holly and cotoneaster
Around the house. The flakes fly! – faster
Shutting indoors that crumb-outcaster
We used to see upon the lawn just
Around the house. The flakes fly faster,
And all the berries now are gone!

A BLACKBIRD SINGING

R.S. Thomas

It seems wrong that out of this bird,
Black, bold, a suggestion of dark
Places about it, there yet should come
Such rich music, as though the notes'
Ore were changed to a rare metal
At one touch of that bright bill.

You have heard it often, alone at your desk
In a green April, your mind drawn
Away from its work by sweet disturbance
Of the mild evening outside your room.

A slow singer, but loading each phrase
With history's overtones, love, joy
And grief learned by his dark tribe
In other orchards and passed on
Instinctively as they are now,
But fresh always with new tears.

BY THE
WATER

THE SANDPIPER

Celia Thaxter

Across the lonely beach we flit,
One little sandpiper and I,
And fast I gather, but by bit,
The scattered drift-wood, bleached and dry.

The wild waves reach their hands for it,
The wild wind raves, the tide runs high,
As up and down the beach we flit,
One little sandpiper and I.

GULLS ALOFT
Ted Hughes

Gulls are glanced from the lift
Of cliffing air
And left
Loitering in the descending drift,
Or tilt gradient and go
Down steep invisible clefts in the grain
Of air, blading against the blow,

Back-flip, wisp
Over the foam-galled green
Building seas, and they scissor
Tossed spray, shave sheen,
Wing-waltzing their shadows
Over the green hollows,

Or rise again in the wind's landward rush
And, hurdling the thundering bush,
With the stone wall flung in their faces,
Repeat their graces.

DUCKS' DITTY
Kenneth Grahame

All along the backwater,
Through the rushes tall,
Ducks are a-dabbling,
Up tails all!

Ducks' tails, drakes' tails,
Yellow feet a-quiver,
Yellow bills all out of sight
Busy in the river!

Slushy green undergrowth
Where the roach swim –
Here we keep our larder,
Cool and full and dim.

Everyone for what he likes!
We like to be
Heads down, tails up,
Dabbling free!

High in the blue above
Swifts whirl and call –
We are down a-dabbling
Up tails all!

The Prayer of the Little Ducks

Carmen Bernos de Gasztold
translated by Rumer Godden

Dear God,
give us a flood of water.
Let it rain tomorrow and always.
Give us plenty of little slugs
and other luscious things to eat.
Protect all folk who quack
and everyone who knows how to swim.
Amen.

SWANS

Sara Teasdale

Night is over the park, and a few brave stars
Look on the lights that link it with chains of gold,
The lake bears up their reflection in broken bars
That seem too heavy for tremulous water to hold.

We watch the swans that sleep in a shadowy place,
And now and again one wakes and uplifts its head;
How still you are – your gaze is on my face –
We watch the swans and never a word is said.

FROM THE COOT
Mary Howitt

Oh Coot! Oh bold, adventurous Coot,
I pray thee tell to me,
The perils of that stormy lime
That bore thee to the sea!

I saw thee on the river fair,
Within thy sedgy screen;
Around thee grew the bulrush tall.
And reeds so strong and green.

The kingfisher came back again
To view thy fairy place;
The stately swan sailed statelier by,
As if thy home to grace.

FROM RIGHT AND LEFT
Yone Noguchi

The mountain green at my right:
The sunlight yellow at my left:
The laughing winds pass between.

The river white at my left:
The flowers red at my right:
The laughing girls go between.

The clouds sail away at my right:
The birds flap down at my left:
The laughing moon appears between.

EGRETS

Po Chü-i

Snowy coats and snowy crests and beaks of blue jade
Flock above the fish in the brook and dart at their
   own shadows,
In startled flight show up far back against the green hills,
The blossoms of a whole pear tree shed by the evening wind.

CRANES
Du Mu

The western wind has blown but a few days;
Yet the first leaf already flies from my bough.
On the drying paths I walk in my thin shoes;
In the first cold I have donned my quilted coat.
Through shallow ditches the floods are clearing away;
Through sparse bamboos trickles a slanting light.
In the early dusk, down an alley of green moss,
The garden-boy is leading the cranes home.

GHAZAL WITH RAIN AND BIRDS
Shazea Quraishi

Day opens its eyes: sky's pillowed with cloud.
Each morning's a gift, a melody bright with birds.

Rain is beginning, and rain is ending,
longed-for and sudden, as heavy, as light as birds.

A tree is a village, a garden, a town,
a thunder of wingbeats, a day and night of birds.

Streets freshly watered, a telephone line
is strung as if pearled, with white after white after white bird.

The breeze brings a kite painted with flowers –
it's caught in the arms of the tree, alight with birds.

Come to the river, to its bed full of stones,
Come rest on the green of its bank, a delight for birds.

IN AMONG
THE TREES

THE TREE IN THE WOOD

Anonymous

All in the wood there grew a fine tree,
The finest tree that ever you might see,
And the green leaves flourished around.
All on this tree there grew a fine bough,
And all on this bough there grew a fine twig.
On this twig there was a fine nest,
In this nest there was a fine bird,
The finest bird that ever you did see;
And on this bird there grew a fine feather,
And out of the feather was made a fine bed,
And on this fine bed was laid a fine babe,
And out of the babe there grew a fine man,
And the man put an acorn into the earth,
And out of the acorn there grew a fine tree,
And the tree was of the acorn,
And the acorn of the man,
And the man was from the babe,
And the babe was on the bed,
And the bed was of the feather,
And the feather of the bird,
And the bird was in the nest,
And the nest was on the twig,
And the twig was on the bough,
And the bough was on the tree,
And the tree was in the wood.
And the green leaves flourished
Around, around, around,
And the green leaves flourished around.

THE BIRD'S NEST
John Drinkwater

I know a place, in the ivy on a tree,
Where a bird's nest is, and the eggs are three,
And the bird is brown, and the eggs are blue,
And the twigs are old, but the moss is new,
And I go quite near, though I think I should have heard
The sound of me watching, if I had been a bird.

THE SECRET
Anonymous

We have a secret, just we three,
The robin, and I, and the sweet cherry tree;
The bird told the tree, and the tree told me,
And nobody knows it but just us three.

But of course the robin knows it best,
Because she built the – I shan't tell the rest;
And laid the four little – something in it –
I'm afraid I shall tell it every minute.

But if the tree and the robin don't peep,
I'll try my best the secret to keep;
Though I know when the little birds fly about
Then the whole secret will be out.

THE CUCKOO
Gerard Manley Hopkins

Repeat that, repeat
Cuckoo, bird, and open ear wells, heart-springs,
  delightfully sweet,
With a ballad, with a ballad, a rebound
Off trundled timber and scoops of the hillside ground,
  hollow hollow hollow ground:
The whole landscape flushes on a sudden at a sound.

FROM A LITTLE BIRD SINGS
Alice Dunbar Nelson

Way out in the grove a little bird sings,
Out in the young, green trees,
Lilting and trilling with fluttering wings,
Out in the young, green trees.
He lilts and he tilts and he sways in the leaves,
For the sun is a-shine, and a gold fabric weaves,
And his throat bursts with song, and the blue air it cleaves,
Out in the young, green trees.

FROM SPRING
Gerard Manley Hopkins

Nothing is so beautiful as Spring –
When weeds, in wheels, shoot long and lovely and lush;
Thrush's eggs look little low heavens, and thrush
Through the echoing timber does so rinse and wring
The ear, it strikes like lightnings to hear him sing:

The glassy pear tree leaves and blooms, they brush
The descending blue; that blue is all in a rush
With richness; the racing lambs too have fair their fling.

MOTHER PARROT'S ADVICE TO HER CHILDREN

Ganda, Africa
translated by A.K. Nyabongo

Never get up till the sun gets up,
Or the mists will give you a cold,
And a parrot whose lungs have once been touched
Will never live to be old.
Never eat plums that are not quite ripe,
For perhaps they will give you a pain:
And never dispute what the hornbill says,
Or you'll never dispute again.
Never despise the power of speech:
Learn every word as it comes,
For this is the pride of the parrot race,
That it speaks in a thousand tongues.
Never stay up when the sun goes down,
But sleep in your own home bed,
And if you've been good, as a parrot should,
You will dream that your tail is red.

VISITING AN OLD FRIEND
Charles Waters

Ebony,
Cobalt,
Frosted
Gold,
Gazing at this
Never gets old,
Ruby,
Chestnut
And
Daffodil
Splashes of color
On a toucan's bill.

REDBIRDS

Sara Teasdale

Redbirds, redbirds,
Long and long ago,
What a honey-call you had
In hills I used to know;

Redbud, buckberry,
Wild plum tree
And proud river sweeping
Southward to the sea,

Brown and gold in the sun
Sparkling far below,
Trailing stately round her bluffs
Where the poplars grow –

Redbirds, redbirds,
Are you singing still
As you sang one May day
On Saxton's Hill?

THAW
Edward Thomas

Over the land freckled with snow half-thawed
The speculating rooks at their nests cawed
And saw from elm-tops, delicate as flower of grass,
What we below could not see – Winter pass.

ON THE
WING

THE FLIGHT

Sara Teasdale

We are two eagles
Flying together
Under the heavens
Over the mountains,
Stretched on the wind.
Sunlight heartens us,
Blind snow baffles us,
Clouds wheel after us,
Ravelled and thinned.

THE EAGLE
Alfred, Lord Tennyson

He clasps the crag with crooked hands;
Close to the sun in lonely lands,
Ringed with the azure world, he stands.

The wrinkled sea beneath him crawls;
He watches from his mountain walls,
And like a thunderbolt he falls.

azure bright blue

HUMMINGBIRD

Grace Nichols

Hovering in mid air
Like no other
Forward
Backward
Upward
The nosediving downward
Iridescent bomber
Bringing no harm to the heart of a flower
The flower that gives up her nectar
But expects you, Hummingbird, to carry the golden dust
    of her desire
No wonder the ancient Aztecs named you:
Pollinating child of the sun

FROM I STOOD TIP-TOE UPON A LITTLE HILL
John Keats

Sometimes goldfinches one by one will drop
From low hung branches; little space they stop;
But sip, and twitter, and their feathers sleek;
Then off at once, as in a wanton freak:
Or perhaps, to show their black and golden wings,
Pausing upon their yellow flutterings.

THIS BIG SKY
Pat Mora

This sky is big enough
for all my dreams.

Two ravens burst black
from a pinon tree
into the blare
of blazing sun.

I follow their wide ebony flight
over copper hills,
down canyons shimmering gold
autumn leaves.

Two ravens spread their wings, rise
into whispers
of giant pines, over mountains blue
with memories.

This sky is big enough
for all my dreams.

PIGEONS
Vikram Seth

The pigeons swing across the square,
Suddenly voiceless in mid air,
Flaunting, against their civic coats,
The glossy oils that scarf their throats.

STARLINGS
Grace Nichols

How they startle the air
With the wings of their flair

FROM AUTUMN BIRDS

John Clare

The wild duck startles like a sudden thought,
And heron slow as if it might be caught.
The flopping crows on weary wings go by
And grey beard jackdaws noising as they fly.
The crowds of starnels whizz and hurry by,
And darken like a clod the evening sky.

starnels starlings

SOMETHING TOLD THE WILD GEESE
Rachel Field

Something told the wild geese
It was time to go.
Though the fields lay golden
Something whispered, – "Snow."
Leaves were green and stirring,
Berries, luster-glossed,
But beneath warm feathers
Something cautioned, – "Frost."
All the sagging orchards
Steamed with amber spice,
But each wild breast stiffened
At remembered ice.
Something told the wild geese
It was time to fly, –
Summer sun was on their wings,
Winter in their cry.

FROM WINTER SLEEP

Elinor Wylie

Little birds like bubbles of glass
Fly to other Americas,
Birds as bright as sparkles of wine
Fly in the nite to the Argentine,
Birds of azure and flame-birds go
To the tropical Gulf of Mexico:
They chase the sun, they follow the heat,
It is sweet in their bones, O sweet, sweet, sweet!
It's not with them that I'd love to be,
But under the roots of the balsam tree.

Just as the spiniest chestnut-burr
Is lined within with the finest fur,
So the stoney-walled, snow-roofed house
Of every squirrel and mole and mouse
Is lined with thistledown, sea-gull's feather,
Velvet mullein-leaf, heaped together
With balsam and juniper, dry and curled,
Sweeter than anything else in the world.

O what a warm and darksome nest
Where the wildest things are hidden to rest!
It's there that I'd love to lie and sleep,
Soft, soft, soft, and deep, deep, deep!

THESE ARE THE DAYS WHEN BIRDS COME BACK
Emily Dickinson

These are the days when Birds come back –
A very few – a Bird or two –
To take a backward look.

These are the days when skies resume
The old – old sophistries of June –
A blue and gold mistake.

IN AND BEYOND
THE FIELDS

A BOY'S SONG

James Hogg

Where the pools are bright and deep
Where the grey trout lies asleep
Up the river and over the lea
That's the way for Billy and me

Where the blackbird sings the latest
Where the hawthorn blooms the sweetest
Where the nestlings plentiest be
That's the way for Billy and me

Where the mowers mow the cleanest
Where the hay lies thick and greenest
There to trace the homeward bee
That's the way for Billy and me

Where the poplar grows the smallest
Where old pine waves the tallest
Pies and rooks know who we are
That's the way for Billy and me

PHEASANT: A HAIKU
Yosa Buson

Treading on the tail
Of the copper pheasant,
The setting sun of spring.

SKYLARK: A HAIKU
Matsuo Bashō

Singing, singing,
All the long day,
But not long enough for the skylark.

SPRING

Sarojini Naidu

Young leaves grow green on the banyan twigs,
And red on the peepul tree,
The honey-birds pipe to the budding figs,
And honey-blooms call to the bee.

Poppies squander their fragile gold
In the silvery aloe-brake;
Coral and ivory lilies unfold
Their delicate lives on the lake.

Kingfishers ruffle the feathery sedge,
And all the vivid air thrills
With butterfly-wings in the wild-rose hedge,
And the luminous blue of the hills.

MEADOWLARKS

Sara Teasdale

In the silver light after a storm,
Under dripping boughs of bright new green,
I take the low path to hear the meadowlarks
Alone and high-hearted as if I were a queen.

What have I to fear in life or death
Who have known three things: the kiss in the night,
The white flying joy when a song is born,
And meadowlarks whistling in silver light.

MAGPIE RHYME
Anonymous

One for sorrow,
Two for joy,
Three for a girl,
Four for a boy,
Five for silver,
Six for gold,
Seven for a secret,
Never to be told.

A VARIATION ON THE MAGPIE RHYME
Anonymous

One for sorrow,
Two for joy,
Three for a present,
Four for a letter,
Five for something better.

FROM A GREEN CORNFIELD

Christina Rossetti

The earth was green, the sky was blue:
I saw and heard one sunny morn
A skylark hang between the two,
A singing speck above the corn;

A stage below, in gay accord,
White butterflies danced on the wing,
And still the singing skylark soared,
And silent sank and soared to sing.

ANSWER TO A CHILD'S QUESTION

Samuel Taylor Coleridge

Do you ask what the birds say? The Sparrow, the Dove,
The Linnet and Thrush say, "I love and I love!"
In the winter they're silent – the wind is so strong;
What it says, I don't know, but it sings a loud song.
But green leaves, and blossoms, and sunny warm weather,
And singing, and loving – all come back together.

But the Lark is so brimful of gladness and love,
The green fields below him, the blue sky above,
That he sings, and he sings; and for ever sings he –
"I love my Love, and my Love loves me!"

Pleasant Sounds
John Clare

The rustling of leaves under the feet in woods
   and under hedges;
The crumpling of cat-ice and snow down wood-rides,
   narrow lanes, and every street causeway;
Rustling through a wood or rather rushing, while the
   wind halloos in the oak-toop like thunder;
The rustle of birds' wings startled from their nests or
   flying unseen into the bushes;
The whizzing of larger birds overhead in a wood,
   such as crows, puddocks, buzzards;
The trample of robins and woodlarks on the brown
   leaves, and the patter of squirrels on the green moss;
The fall of an acorn on the ground, the pattering of
   nuts on the hazel branches as they fall from ripeness;
The flirt of the groundlark's wing from the stubbles –
   how sweet such pictures on dewy mornings,
   when the dew flashes from its brown feathers.

puddocks red kites

EVERYONE SANG
Siegfried Sassoon

Everyone suddenly burst out singing;
And I was filled with such delight
As prisoned birds must find in freedom,
Winging wildly across the white
Orchards and dark-green fields; on – on – and out of sight.

Everyone's voice was suddenly lifted;
And beauty came like the setting sun:
My heart was shaken with tears; and horror
Drifted away ... O, but Everyone
Was a bird; and the song was wordless; the singing
   will never be done.

ADLESTROP
Edward Thomas

Yes. I remember Adlestrop –
The name, because one afternoon
Of heat the express-train drew up there
Unwontedly. It was late June.

The steam hissed. Someone cleared his throat.
No one left and no one came
On the bare platform. What I saw
Was Adlestrop – only the name

And willows, willow-herb, and grass,
And meadowsweet, and haycocks dry,
No whit less still and lonely fair
Than the high cloudlets in the sky.

And for that minute a blackbird sang
Close by, and round him, mistier,
Farther and farther, all the birds
Of Oxfordshire and Gloucestershire.

BIOGRAPHIES

Matsuo Bashō (1644–94)
The great haiku master Matsuo Bashō was born near Kyoto in Japan; as a young man he moved to Edo (now Tokyo), where he joined a literary community. He went on to study Zen Buddhism, and many of his haikus explore contrasts of stillness and movement within the natural world.

Carmen Bernos de Gasztold (1919–45)
Carmen Bernos de Gasztold was born in France and spent her childhood in Bordeaux. Her most famous work, *Prayers from the Ark*, published in 1947. It was later translated from French into English by Rumer Godden, who spent time with the poet at her home – a Benedictine abbey – while she created her translation.

Yosa Buson (1716–84)
The Japanese poet Yosa Buson studied painting and haiku in Edo. Like his literary hero Matsuo Bashō, Buson travelled widely through Japan and published notes from his journeys. Today, Buson is remembered as one of the "Great Four" haiku poets – alongside Bashō, Kobayashi Issa and Masaoka Shiki.

John Clare (1793–1864)
Born in Northamptonshire, John Clare worked as a farm labourer alongside writing poetry. Much of his work focused on the nature around him, capturing the changing seasons. Though he was successful in his lifetime, the tag "peasant poet" stayed with Clare, as he didn't have the background expected of poets at the time.

Samuel Taylor Coleridge (1772–1834)
Born the youngest of ten children, Samuel Taylor Coleridge

went on to become one of England's foremost poets and critics. Alongside his friend William Wordsworth, he published *Lyrical Ballads* in 1798 – a volume of poems that marked the start of the Romantic period of English literature.

Emily Dickinson (1830–86)

Emily Dickinson is remembered as one of the most important American poets. While she wrote many poems during her life, and shared them with friends, her first volume of poetry was not published until after she died – after her sister discovered her compiled collections.

John Drinkwater (1882–1937)

John Drinkwater was an English poet and playwright. Born in London, he left school at the age of fifteen to work as an insurance clerk, before publishing his first volume of poetry at the age of 21. His poetry often explores the imagery of personal growth, war and natural beauty.

Paul Laurence Dunbar (1872–1906)

Paul Laurence Dunbar was one of the first African American poets to gain national recognition. He was the son of two freed slaves from Kentucky and his writing often drew on their stories of plantation life. He went on to travel the world and penned around 400 poems during his thirteen-year career.

Rachel Field (1894–1942)

An American author and poet, Rachel Field was born in New York. She studied at Radcliffe College in Massachusetts, and went on to write the children's book *Hitty*, which was awarded the Newbery Medal for children's literature. Sadly Field's career was cut short as she died of pneumonia at just 47 years old.

Kenneth Grahame (1859–1932)

Kenneth Grahame's mother died when he was five and he was raised by his grandmother in Berkshire. The children's classic *The Wind in the Willows* is his best-known work, the setting of which is thought to be inspired by the area in which Grahame was raised, including Quarry Wood and the River Thames.

Thomas Hardy (1840–1928)

Poet and novelist Thomas Hardy lived most of his life in a region of woodland, heath and moor in Dorset, where most of his novels are set – the best-known being *Far from the Madding Crowd* and *Tess of the D'Urbervilles*. He viewed nature as a tremendous force, which had a profound effect on the lives of his characters.

James Hogg (1770–1835)

The Scottish poet, novelist and essayist James Hogg lived and worked most of his life in the Scottish Borders. He became interested in literature in his early twenties, writing in both Scots and English, and his work soon started to be published – leading him to become one of Scotland's most renowned novelists.

Gerard Manley Hopkins (1844–89)

Born into a prosperous and artistic family, Gerard Manley Hopkins was one of the Victorian era's greatest poets. In his twenties, he became a priest and burnt all of his former poetic works; he started to write again after a German ship, the *Deutschland*, was wrecked during a storm at the mouth of the Thames.

Mary Howitt (1799–1888)

Mary Howitt was an English poet who began writing poems and short stories at a very early age. Often working with her husband, the couple were friends with many literary figures. During the

1840's, Mary became interested in Scandinavian literature and translated many of Hans Christian Andersen's fairy tales.

Ted Hughes (1930–98)

Ted Hughes was born in Yorkshire and studied at the University of Cambridge, where he met and married the US poet Sylvia Plath. He was Poet Laureate from 1984 until his death in 1998, and also wrote for children – *The Iron Man* is still regarded as one of the finest children's books ever written.

Victor Hugo (1802–85)

While regarded as one of France's greatest poets, Victor Hugo is better known abroad for novels such as *The Hunchback of Notre-Dame* and *Les Misérables*. After a period of extreme poverty in his teens, Hugo established himself as a major literary figure; after his death, he was buried at the Panthéon in Paris.

John Keats (1795–1821)

John Keats was a Romantic poet who died of tuberculosis at the young age of 25. Born in London, Keats worked as a surgeon, though was devoted to the arts and literature. Keats' reputation grew after his death, and he is today considered one of the greatest English poets of all time.

Pat Mora

Born on the Mexico-US border in El Paso, Texas, Pat Mora is an award-winning author of poetry, non-fiction and children's books. Mora is a strong advocate of bilingual literacy, with her writing often incorporating code-switching between English and Spanish words.

Du Mu (803–852)

Du Mu was a leading Chinese poet of the late T'ang dynasty. He was skilled in shi, fu and ancient Chinese prose, as well as quatrains; one of his best-known poems is "Qingming Festival", named for a day of remembrance when people visit the graves of their ancestors to pay respect.

Sarojini Naidu (1879–1949)

Sarojini Naidu earned the nickname "The Nightingale of India" for her contribution to poetry. Alongside her writing, Naidu was an Indian political activist and an important figure in India's struggle for independence from British colonial rule – and went on to become India's first female governor.

Alice Dunbar Nelson (1875–1935)

Alice Dunbar Nelson was among the first generation of African Americans born free in New Orleans after the American Civil War. Her African American, Anglo, Native American and Creole heritage contributed to her complex understandings of gender, race and ethnicity, subjects which she often addressed in her work.

Grace Nichols

Grace Nichols was born in Guyana and has lived in Britain since 1977. She has written many books for both adults and children, and won the 1983 Commonwealth Poetry Prize for her first collection *I Is a Long-Memoried Woman*. Her collections for children include *Paint Me a Poem* and *Cosmic Disco*.

Yone Noguchi (1875–1947)

Poet and literary critic Yone Noguchi was the first Japanese-born writer to publish poetry in English. Noguchi studied at Keio Gijuku University in Tokyo before living in San Francisco. He later returned to Japan, where his writing career flourished.

Po Chü-i (772–846)

Po Chü-i was a renowned Chinese poet and T'ang dynasty official, best known for his ballads and satirical poems. He was one of the most productive T'ang writers, composing over 3,500 poems, and believed that poetry should be accessible to everyone – and his poems were often concerned with social and political issues.

Shazea Quraishi

Shazea Quraishi was born in Pakistan and lived in Canada and Spain before moving to London, where she works as a writer, translator, and teacher. She is a trustee on the Board of English PEN, an organisation that defends writers and readers around the world whose human right to freedom of expression is at risk.

Elizabeth Madox Roberts (1881–1941)

Elizabeth Madox Roberts was an American novelist and poet. She was born in Kentucky and spent most of her life there, and was known for her stories about the Kentucky mountain people, as well as her distinct rhythmic prose.

Christina Rossetti (1830–94)

Christina Rossetti was born into a London family of artists, scholars and writers; her brothers were founding members of the Pre-Raphaelite Brotherhood. She had her first book of poetry privately printed by her grandfather when she was just twelve years old.

Siegfried Sassoon (1886–1967)

Siegfried Sassoon seemed to live three different lives: before, during and after the First World War. He grew up in Kent and Sussex before becoming a soldier – and his writing changed from quiet pastorals to brutal depictions of life in the trenches. When the war was over, he returned to his former style.

Vikram Seth

Vikram Seth is an Indian novelist, poet and travel writer. Born in Calcutta, he has also lived in China, Britain and California – and is best known for his acclaimed novel *A Suitable Boy*. In 2006, Seth became a leader of the campaign against Section 377 of the Indian Penal Code, a law against homosexuality.

Sara Teasdale (1884–1933)

Sara Teasdale was born in St. Louis, Missouri. In her twenties she became friends with Harriet Monroe who published several of her poems in her *Poetry* magazine. Later, Teasdale moved to New York with her husband and won the Columbia Poetry Prize in 1918.

Alfred, Lord Tennyson (1802–92)

In the latter half of the nineteenth century, Tennyson was considered England's greatest poet. He was born in Lincolnshire, the fourth of twelve children. His best-known poems include "The Charge of the Light Brigade" and "The Lady of Shallot". He is buried in the Poets' Corner of Westminster Abbey.

Celia Thaxter (1835–94)

Celia Thaxter grew up on the Isles of Shoals, where her father was the lighthouse keeper, and later on Appledore Island. In later life, she took over her father's hotel, Appledore House, and welcomed many writers and artists to the island, publishing her most famous book, *An Island Garden*, in the last year of her life.

Edward Thomas (1878–1917)

Edward Thomas is commonly considered a war poet, although few of his poems deal directly with the war. He was great friends with the poet Robert Frost, whose poem "The Road Not Taken" is thought to be inspired by Thomas' indecisiveness on their walks together.

R.S. Thomas (1913–2000)

Ronald Stuart Thomas wrote about his ideal of Wales and the role of the English in stripping it of its wild essence. Thomas always believed that he learned to speak Welsh too late to be able to write poetry effectively in it, but he did produce some works in the language.

Charles Waters

Born in Philadelphia, Charles Waters is an American poet and actor. His books include *Can I Touch Your Hair? Poems of Race, Mistakes and Friendship*, co-written with Irene Latham, a collection of poems that explores racial difference in the context of school, family and the local community.

Dorothy Wordsworth (1771–1855)

Spending most of her life in the Lake District, Dorothy Wordsworth wrote a very early account of an ascent of Scafell Pike, the highest mountain in England. She was close to her brother, William Wordsworth, and he is thought to have drawn on her journals to write some of his best-known poems – including "Daffodils".

Elinor Wylie (1885–1928)

American poet and novelist Elinor Wylie, who was popular in the '20s and '30s, was labelled "the reigning queen of American poetry". Her first poetry collection was called *Nets to Catch the Wind* and all her works of fiction were allegories; they dealt with the supernatural, the strange and the unusual.

HARRY TENNANT is London-born, but escaped to the coves of Cornwall to study Illustration at University College Falmouth, before returning to the capital once more. He now works as an illustrator, using a mixture of hand-drawn and digital techniques to create his striking artwork. He lives in East London.

ACKNOWLEDGMENTS

"A Blackbird Singing" © R.S. Thomas 1993, from *Collected Poems: 1945–1990* by R.S. Thomas. Reproduced by permission of The Orion Publishing Group, London, and first published in Great Britain by J.M. Dent in 1993. Paperback edition published in 2000 by Phoenix, an imprint of Orion Books Ltd; fifth impression, 2004. Extract taken from "Gulls Aloft", Copyright the Estate of Ted Hughes, first appeared in *Ted Hughes' Collected Poems for Children*. Reproduced by permission of Faber & Faber Ltd. "The Prayer of the Little Ducks" by Carmen Bernos de Gasztold, from *Prayers from the Ark* (Macmillan), translated by Rumer Godden; translation © Rumer Godden 1992, and reprinted here by kind permission of Rumer Godden. "Ghazal with Rain and Birds" © Shazea Quraishi 2019, from *Poems from a Green and Blue Planet* (Hachette) and reprinted here by kind permission of the poet. "Visiting an Old Friend" © Charles Waters 2012, from *National Geographic Book of Animal Poetry: 200 Poems with Photographs That Squeak, Soar, and Roar* (National Geographic Children's Books) and reprinted here by kind permission of the poet. "Hummingbird" and "Starlings" © Grace Nichols 2013, from *Cosmic Disco* (Frances Lincoln Children's Books) and reprinted here by kind permission of the poet. "This Big Sky" © Pat Mora 1998, from *This Big Sky* (Hachette), 2002 reprint edition, and reprinted here by kind permission of the poet. "Pigeons" © Vikram Seth 1987, 1990, from *All You Who Sleep Tonight* (Alfred A. Knopf, a division of Random House, Inc.) and reprinted here by kind permission of the poet.